Clark
GABLE

Other Books by Jane Ellen Wayne

Robert Taylor: The Man with the Perfect Face
Kings of Tragedy
Stanwyck
Gable's Women
Crawford's Men
Cooper's Women
Ava's Men
The Life and Loves of Grace Kelly
Marilyn's Men

Clark Gable

Portrait of a Misfit

Jane Ellen Wayne

St. Martin's Press
New York

CLARK GABLE: PORTRAIT OF A MISFIT.
Copyright © 1993 by Jane Ellen Wayne.
All rights reserved. Printed in the United
States of America. No part of this book
may be used or reproduced in any
manner whatsoever without written
permission except in the case of brief
quotations embodied in critical articles
or reviews. For information, address
St. Martin's Press, 175 Fifth Avenue,
New York, N.Y. 10010.

Photograph insert credits: first
photograph courtesy Bettmann Archive;
all others courtesy the Kobal Collection.

**Library of Congress Cataloging-in-
Publication Data**
Wayne, Jane Ellen.
    Clark Gable : portrait of a misfit /
Jane Ellen Wayne.
        p.   cm.
    ISBN 0-312-09259-8
        1. Gable, Clark, 1901-1960.
    2. Motion picture actors and
actresses—United States—Biography.
    I. Title.
PN2287.G3W385   1993
791.43′028′092—dc20
    [B]   93-678
                                          CIP

First published in Great Britain by
Robson Books Ltd.

First U.S. Edition: July 1993
10   9   8   7   6   5   4   3   2   1

For everyone from the wrong side of the tracks

CONTENTS

FOREWORD

I am fortunate that my career as an author began in the late sixties, when so many of the great Golden Era movie stars and moguls were still alive. At the time, I had no idea that eight film-actor biographies would follow the one I was then writing about MGM's longest contract player Robert Taylor. He was so well liked in Hollywood that no one refused to be interviewed. Still, though Taylor had had his share of love affairs and a nasty divorce from actress Barbara Stanwyck, he had lived a relatively clean life; consequently, my interviews often ended with lengthy discussions about *other* MGM personalities—Clark Gable, in particular.

MGM press agent George Nichols and I often met at the Cock 'n' Bull restaurant on Sunset Boulevard. Movie extras, stand-ins, technicians, and stuntmen also gathered at our table late afternoons. The word had got around that I was doing a book about Robert Taylor, so old-timers had a good excuse to get together for some reminiscing and, I admit, inside gossip. Nichols said there were two prime interests in Hollywood: movies and gossip. Everybody knew everybody else's business, and the stories related to me were amusing, raunchy, revealing, and very rewarding. John Wayne, Andy Devine, and John Huston, to name a few, saw George and sat down with us for a chat.

I was also privileged to spend a good deal of time with Howard Strickling, MGM's West Coast publicity chief and one of Clark Gable's best friends. Howard protected his galaxy of stars and ultimately took many of Hollywood's deepest secrets to his grave. But he wanted to cooperate with me, he said, because he cared especially for Taylor. "Bob was an innocent kid, but he and Clark were alike in many ways. The three of us were very close friends."

Howard arranged for me to meet writer Adela Rogers St. Johns, directors William Wellman and Tay Garnett, and a slew of others who worked at MGM during the twenties, thirties, forties, and fifties. They loved Bob Taylor but relished talking off the cuff about the unpredictable Clark Gable. I sensed they were comparing the two men, who hunted and fished together *and* romanced the same women.

Then there was Joan Crawford, who said she'd *love* to talk about Robert Taylor. On my first visit to her New York apartment, though, she talked entirely about Clark Gable, whom she described as the love of her life. "Come back another time," she told me. "Then we'll talk about Bob." When my second interview was an echo of the first, I gave up on her. But Joan called to apologize, and we tried again. After my third visit, I could have written a book called *Crawford's Hollywood*. Vodka in hand, she did not mince words about her costars, lovers, or husbands. Certainly, Crawford knew Gable as well as or better than anyone else. Had she married him, as she nearly did in 1932, their life together might have been one long Fourth of July. Instead, their romance inspired fireworks in the front office.

Though my association with Joan Crawford was exasperating, she did give me sound advice about researching my book. "If you want a list of impressive names in your acknowledgements," Joan said, "go ahead. But remember, the bigger they are, the less they tell. Talk to the writers, technicians, security guards—the 'little people,' who are bigger than life. I leaned on them. They knew more about me than I did."

Joan waited until the last minute to discuss Taylor, but when she did, she was as original with her information about him as she had been telling me about the Crawford image. Through her, I entered into the glittering world of MGM, a world she had helped to mold. If the glamour of stars like Joan Crawford and her Hollywood colleagues had endured longer, perhaps the chiffon and tinsel might still exist today.

Director George Cukor told me that I would struggle with my conscience over revealing unflattering stories in my biography of Robert Taylor. But "it takes the bad and the good for an honest portrayal," he stressed. "One cannot paint a true picture of a rose without the thorns."

The ancient Egyptians had their temples and gods. Great Britain has its kings and queens. America's royalty reigns in Hollywood. Our stars made us laugh during Prohibition and the Depression and marched beside us during World War II. And as we approach the twenty-first century, the stars of the Golden Era will play a more significant role in American history and tradition.

Clark Gable is a memorable chapter. . . .

INTRODUCTION

*H*e was an alcoholic, a bland lover, a scoundrel, an egotist, and an opportunist who hit the casting couch for a homosexual encounter with a well-known leading man to get into films. He used women and married them to further his acting career. He removed his false teeth in public and washed down amphetamines with bourbon. And he was the most enduring actor in the history of motion pictures.

There were movie idols, and then there was Clark Gable. He was crowned "King of Hollywood" in 1937, and he has never been dethroned. Perhaps Gable's undimmed popularity rests with the ongoing success of the much-revived *Gone With the Wind*. Ironically, he hadn't wanted to appear in the film and refused to speak with a southern accent, hoping MGM would replace him. Forced nonetheless into playing Rhett Butler, he sought revenge from day one of filming. Eventually, Vivien Leigh's portrayal of Scarlett O'Hara won her an Oscar. But Gable, who was nominated for best actor, lost—perhaps because few performers earn the award for playing themselves—and he was stunned and angry that his Hollywood peers had not voted for him.

Gable may have lost the battle, but he surely won the war, because casting Rhett Butler in the forthcoming sequel to *Gone With the Wind* means casting an actor who can portray Clark Gable. Rhett contender Tom Selleck confirms this theory: "No one is a bigger fan of Clark Gable than I am, but I'm not Gable." (Interestingly, there's been little mention lately of Vivien Leigh, who followed author Margaret Mitchell's concept of Scarlett to a T.) Except for his name, Rhett's entire identity has vanished into the body and soul of Clark Gable. In his later years, Gable admitted that *Gone With the Wind* was responsible for his durability as an actor. And without the film's periodical theatrical releases and, more recently, television broadcasts, Gable might have become just a "very familiar" face.

But Gable has a vast following of young fans who react in much the same way their elders did in the thirties and forties. Women still want to be roughed up and kissed by Gable, and men still admire his brazen technique with the opposite sex. And even as they watch Gable marry the long-frustrated heroine at the end of a picture, husbands still tell their wives, "No woman can ever tame or possess Gable."

The King of Hollywood had enemies, but they liked him. He was cunning, shrewd and cocky, at least, that is, until the woman he loved was killed in a plane crash while returning to Hollywood from a war-bond rally. The sudden death of his third wife, Carole Lombard, was a devastating blow to Gable, and for reasons in addition to the more obvious ones. It was Gable who had convinced Lombard to travel without him, and she had hurried back to abort her husband's (possibly nonexistent) affair with his blonde leading lady. Gable was having his one last fling at the very moment that Lombard's plane crashed; he struggled with this guilt for the rest of his life.

Joan Crawford told me that Gable came to see her when he heard about Lombard's death. "A stranger walked [out] my door that night and never returned," Crawford said. "He was in another world and never came back to us."

Crawford and Gable were lovers and friends from 1931 until his death in 1960. But during the dark period following Lombard's death, Gable turned away from most of his other Hollywood intimates because they reminded him of his happy third marriage. He joined the air force and volunteered for numerous dangerous missions over Germany; in doing so, he risked the lives of other pilots, who were told to prevent German fighters from shooting at Gable's plane (there was a price on Gable's head). Gable was not a fearless hero; in fact, he was drunk on these missions. When he was sent home, his commanding officer was *very* relieved.

Gable was a shell of a man when he returned to Hollywood in 1945. He accepted few social invitations, went on fishing trips alone, and raced the wind on his motorcycle until the MGM brass put an end to his recklessness. They could not control Gable's heavy drinking, however. In those days, it was not unusual for him to finish a bottle of liquor before dinner.

Single for the first time in almost twenty years, Gable dated blonde women with class, money and breeding. He proposed marriage more often than one might expect, and was turned down more often than one can believe. How could any woman in her right mind say no to Clark Gable? She could when she saw that he was a lonely guy who drank too much. However, Gable did not propose to women who were eager and ready to be his wife. Despite his desperate state of mind, he knew the difference between needing and wanting.

Gable's air-force buddies were amazed that he chose to be with ugly women. He explained that such women appreciated "it" more and didn't bother him afterward. Perhaps Gable was punishing himself for his indiscretions during his marriage to Lombard. He liked prostitutes, too, because they did not discuss his ineptitude as a lover. But Gable was still the one and only King of Hollywood, and his magnetism was as potent offscreen as on.

Hollywood did not manufacture Clark Gable, as it had most of its legendary stars. But his signature on a contract gave MGM complete possession of him, personally and professionally. Like a wild mustang, however, he could not be controlled. Most of Gable's bosses at MGM were Jewish, and his snide remarks about studio head Louis B. Mayer may have been misconstrued as bigotry. In fact, the two men did not get along from the start; theirs was more likely a clash of personalities than an ethnic battle. Gable referred to Mayer as "that Jew" on more than one occasion, but as Joan Crawford explained, "Clark ran out of names. He wasn't anti-Semitic. Every nationality had a label like 'wop' or 'limey.' L.B. just happened to be Jewish."

Gable was just as blunt with director George Cukor, calling him a "fairy" to his face during the filming of *Gone With the Wind*. Cukor *was* discreetly gay, but it was not his sexual preference that prompted his eventual dismissal from *GWTW*; rather, it was Gable's certainty that Cukor knew about his leading man's onetime liaison with actor William Haines (not to mention Gable's rage when Cukor called him "dear" on the set).

Carole Lombard adored Billy Haines, who had become an interior decorator after MGM fired him for flaunting his homosexuality. Lombard was one of the first to give Haines a design job; he decorated her new house (before she became involved with Gable). Lombard remained loyal to Haines, referring to him as her "best girlfriend."

Lombard kept Gable in line, offsetting his ego with her deprecatory remarks. She told friends she loved him dearly even though he was the "worst lay in town" (she blamed this on his marriages to older, easily satisfied women).

When Gable was crowned King of Hollywood, Lombard remarked to a friend, "If Clark had an inch less, he'd be

Queen of the Movies." Lombard's comment got back to Gable, who, to his credit, laughed louder than anyone. Later, when they decided to marry, Lombard heard a rumor that Gable was seeing another woman and promptly called him. "Our engagement is off, you son of a bitch!" she shouted. "Here's one dame who isn't chasing you."

Lombard had her own opinion as to why Gable did not want to do *Gone With the Wind*: "He doesn't like the idea that Scarlett isn't head over heels in love with him at first sight. Clark isn't used to that."

The banter and laughter ended when Carole Lombard was killed, burned beyond recognition in that plane crash. All that was left of the vibrant screwball was a lock of hair and a charred diamond brooch.

For the next thirteen years Gable lived on the edge. He married again, during a drunken binge; he left MGM before they could fire him; he partied at Errol Flynn's orgies and drank so heavily that he resembled a bloated Buddha rather than a king.

But Gable usually managed to get himself into shape for the camera, and his volcanic charm came through vividly even up to his last film, *The Misfits*. Method actor Montgomery Clift bowed to him, Marilyn Monroe was in awe of him, and professional stuntmen watched in silence as the "old man" performed dangerous feats in the Nevada desert, where temperatures reached 115 degrees. Gable paid with his life three months later.

Maybe Clark Gable wasn't the lover fans thought he was, but his image as the royal cocksman never diminished. He was a sexual challenge: a guy who could love one woman with all his heart and yet not be faithful to her.

Gable's talent was playing himself, and to see *him* was why fans lined up at the box office. He played a gangster, a cowboy, a test pilot, a wildcatter, a minister, a newspaper reporter, and the rogue who pestered Scarlett O'Hara. But always, and in any manner of costumes, he was Clark Gable.

He was tough, often crude, arrogantly debonair. He had an

earthy, dimpled grin, daring eyes set into a rugged face, hands like baseball mitts—and, notoriously, huge ears: someone once compared his head to a sugar bowl. At the beginning of his film career, makeup artists taped back his ears, but Gable would have none of this and removed the tape. In his early Hollywood days, one columnist described him as "ugly–good-looking" acknowledging that Gable's brand of masculinity contrasted with that of his romantic predecessors John Gilbert, Rudolph Valentino, and Ramon Novarro, whose faces bordered on beautiful.

Gable's first wife, who described him as a "gorgeous skeleton," groomed him for the stage. When he got his first break, though, Gable left her and married a rich woman, who supported him. She, in turn, was of no further use after he achieved stardom.

Gable lived a full and fascinating life from the day he was born. Lacking education and social graces, he might have become a truck driver or a lumberjack, but the motherless boy found the attention he craved from the stage. When his father called him a "sissy," Clark hopped a freight train, embarking on an adventurous and reckless career.

In 1932, Gable said, "When you get to Hollywood, you find yourself in lots of chains of accidents. If it turns out all right, you're a star. If you're a gambler move to Hollywood. Maybe you'll like it and maybe not. It's my business to work, not to think."

1.

Reflections

*M*etro-Goldwyn-Mayer created
star personalities, gave them new names, and polished their
backgrounds. If there was anything objectionable in the truth,
the greatest studio publicity department in the world simply
rewrote it.

MGM's leading men were said to be six feet tall, regardless
of their real height. Clark Gable exceeded this all-American
ideal male image by an inch. Entering a room, he filled the
doorway with his broad shoulders and large head, hands and
feet. Gable was a giant in all respects.

When Howard Strickling met Gable for the first time, he
worried that "the big guy" might kill someone in a brawl. In
the mid-thirties, director Bill Wellman, angry with Gable for
holding up production during *Call of the Wild*, chewed out his
star in front of the cast and crew. "He took it," Wellman

said, "and he could have wiped me out with one punch. But I had one thing in my favor. His face was his livelihood, and he couldn't afford to tangle even with a little guy like me."

Gable was hard-boiled but gentle. In contrast to the way he played his tough-guy roles, he approached life with a simplicity that was almost boring to the Hollywood press. It's been said he never read a book—including *Gone With the Wind*—but Grace Kelly said he enjoyed reading poetry to her. She was courting him at the time—and making progress, apparently, if he took to verse.

Gable enjoyed hunting and fishing in remote places far away from the glare of Hollywood. Adela Rogers St. Johns said, "Clark's priorities were outdoor sports, gambling, drinking, working, and women. In that order. He had a sleeping bag that was big enough to make his camping trips cozier. There wasn't a girl who was happy with that uncomfortable arrangement! However, Clark took his hunting and fishing quite seriously."

Adela Rogers St. Johns met Gable shortly before he signed his first MGM contract in 1930. They were intimate for ten years, though she admitted their affair only to her closest friends. Rumors persisted long after Gable's death that St. Johns had borne him a child.

St. Johns was a respected screenwriter and Hearst journalist who knew everyone in Hollywood and Washington, D.C., by their first name. I recall her as a plain-looking woman wearing casual clothes and very little makeup. Her hair was always a mess and she had a habit of running her hands through the thick tresses that nearly covered her eyes. A brilliant woman with a heart of gold, she helped Gable through hard times, and he was always there when she needed him.

Gable was a man's man, and too proud to confide in his buddies about his shortcomings and fears. He turned to women with his tribulations and spoke bluntly of his distaste for his bad film roles and of his battles with Louis B. Mayer.

Gable had a mother complex, which first manifested itself in his young adulthood. He preferred the company of older women and sought them out for advice, solace, and security. Otherwise, he had very little respect for women. In separate conversations with me, Howard Strickling hinted at this, and Joan Crawford confirmed it. "Clark thought it was a man's world," she explained. "He was yesterday's version of a male chauvinist."

Comparing Gable to Robert Taylor, Strickling said, "Bob was close to his mother and father. He went to college and dated nice girls. Clark never had a real home. There was no high-school proms or fraternities, and his women were not exactly candidates for Queen of the May."

Gable's second wife, a Houston socialite, and Metro-Goldwyn-Mayer were responsible for Gable's introduction to the finer things in life: a distinguished wardrobe, including longer shirt cuffs to camouflage his big hands; a proper set of false teeth; an expensive gun collection; and big cars.

Howard Strickling explained to me that MGM wanted Gable and Robert Taylor to appear as rugged offscreen as on. "We'd send a photographer along, and he'd have to wade up to his waist in the streams to take publicity pictures. But Clark and Bob were naturals at hunting and fishing. There was nothing phony about it. They couldn't wait to finish a film and take off for the wilds."

Louis B. Mayer considered MGM's roster of stars his family, and he wanted each of them to consider him their father. "If you have a problem," he would say, "come to me. My door is always open." This worked for Taylor, but Gable disliked Mayer from the start. The feeling was mutual. "If it hadn't been for Howard Strickling," Gable said, "I'd be driving a truck." Strickling was responsible not only for getting the names of MGM players into gossip columns and fan magazines but for keeping their names *out* of the press when they misbehaved.

Gable attributed his good fortune in Hollywood to a series of lucky breaks, and meeting Howard Strickling was surely one of them, but the future King of Hollywood was an unlikely candidate for stardom when he left home as a young man. Gable wasn't initially headed for California, and he hated it when he got there. What happened along the way was a chain of events that defies probability and challenges the imagination.

Clark Gable was born in Cadiz, Ohio, at 5:30 A.M. on February 1, 1901, weighing in at almost eleven pounds. The doctor's fee was ten dollars.

MGM claimed that the name on Gable's birth certificate was William Clark Gable and that the "William" was dropped when the actor began his film career. Of course, Metro liked to take credit for changing the names of *all* their contract players. Ava Gardner, for instance, was born Ava Gardner, but MGM made up a phony name and took credit for the one on her birth certificate. But in most cases, the studio really did create the names that matched the faces of their discoveries.

Lucille LeSueur became Joan Crawford, Harlean Carpentier was known as Jean Harlow, Hedy Lamarr was more glamorous than Hedwig Kiesler, and Spangler Arlington Brugh became Robert Taylor. Frederick Austerlitz danced as Fred Astaire, and Joe Yule, Jr., turned into Mickey Rooney.

Both Clark and his father, William, were nicknamed "Bill," which has fed the mistaken speculation that William Clark Gable was the boy's name. But if Gable's birth certificate settles the controversy over his name, it does contain serious errors: it declares Meadville, Pennsylvania, as the town where he was born, 2nd "female" as his gender.

The name Gable was derived from Goebel, a fact that MGM preferred not to mention. Clark's ancestors emigrated from Germany; here, they joined fellow Germans in Pennsylvania, where they were known as Pennsylvania Dutchmen. The majority of the Gables were farmers, but when oil was discovered in Harrison County, Ohio, at the turn of the century, William abandoned agriculture, moved west, got his own drilling rig, and became a hard-bitten, hard-drinking, hardheaded wildcatter. Indeed, Will was an unlikely candidate to become the husband of the frail Adeline Hershelman. He was a Protestant; she was a Catholic. He was a truculent laborer; she dabbled in painting and had the sensitivity of an artist.

Precisely where and when Addie and Will were married isn't known, but they were both in their late twenties at the time, and they settled in Cadiz to be near the oil fields where Will worked six days a week. They lived on the top floor of a two-story white house on Charleston Street. Addie relied on their downstairs neighbors, the Reeses, for companionship and for help with everyday chores that were a hardship for her. Addie's physician, Dr. John Campbell, advised her not to have children, but true to her religious faith and deeply in love with her husband, Addie became pregnant. Though she was thrilled with the prospect of having a child, it's unlikely that Will realized the seriousness of his wife's condition. When he was sober, it's possible that Will rewarded Addie with some degree of comfort, but he was not one to show much warmth or affection. He made no attempt, however, to conceal his pride when Addie gave birth to a robust boy who was all ears, hands, and feet, which made the baby appear heavier than its nearly eleven pounds. It was Addie who wanted her son called Clark, the family name of one of her grandmothers.

Carrying and delivering such a big baby drained Addie of whatever strength she had left. Her last days were spent in bed, holding and cuddling Clark. Whether Will gave his approval or not we do not know, but Addie had her son baptized by a Catholic priest when the baby was three months old. Possibly she had had a premonition that this was her last chance to save her son's soul; soon after the baptism, Addie's health declined rapidly. Will took her back to Headville, where she died at her parents' home on November 15, 1901, at the age of thirty-one. Epilepsy was recorded as the cause of death. Apparently, her seizures began after Clark's birth.

Will Gable wasted no time mourning his wife or worrying about "the kid," who was left in the care of Addie's parents, on their farm. Will took off to find oil—and a new wife. He needed a woman to make a home for him and his son.

The Hershelmans were devoted to Clark and did all they could for him. Though only ten months old when his mother died, he instinctively suffered from her absence. There was a new emptiness that had not been there when she'd cuddled and rocked him. He withdrew, not understanding why she was gone. Addie's brother Tom and his wife took Clark in for a while. The couple had no children of their own, and within a few short months, the three became a close family.

In the meantime, Will was living in nearby Hopedale, Ohio, where he met seamstress Jennie Dunlap. She was a plainlooking thirty-year-old, but her lively personality appealed to the wildcatter, and they were married in April 1903.

When Will came to retrieve his son, Tom Hershelman and his wife were devastated. They begged to be allowed to keep Clark, but Will said that he was building a house in Hopedale, and that that's where his son belonged. His father's taking him was traumatic for Clark; the boy barely knew Will, who had not been a frequent visitor. In later years, Clark said that he had been shuttled from home to home, never knowing what it was to have a devoted family.

Jennie would be the most positive influence on her young stepson. Childless herself, she accepted "Clarkie" as her own and looked after him like a true mother. Indeed, people who did not know the truth thought Jennie *was* Clark's mother, such was her devotion. Meanwhile, Will worked in the Scio oil fields and came home on weekends. His gusher had yet to come in, but he was making a decent living. As for "the kid," Will was adamant that Clark attend the local Methodist church and that he grow up to be a farmer or a wildcatter. He would criticize Jennie for pampering Clark and dressing him up like a "sissy." She, in turn, cringed when Will roughhoused with his son in the dirt. Jennie, too, had plans for Clark. Above all else, she wanted him to be a gentleman.

Under her tutelage, Clark played the French horn in the school band, sang in the chorus, and participated in sports. At thirteen, Clark was six feet tall, lanky and shy. When he applied himself in school, his marks were good. But more often, he was inattentive and satisfied with Cs. His teachers remembered him as an average boy who played hooky once in a while. He attended church picnics and hung out with other boys on the sidelines at school dances. (Gable was never fond of dancing, other than a slow fox-trot.)

Every year, Clark was given a festive, lavish birthday party. He and his friends looked forward to this annual event, but no one was more excited than Jennie, who made sure that no one else in town had a finer birthday party, or finer birthday presents: Clark was one of the first boys in Hopedale to have a bicycle.

In retrospect, one may wonder why the adult Gable spoke bitterly about his adolescence and referred to his step-mother as "Jennie Dunlap," giving the impression that she was his father's mistress. No doubt, his unhappy recollections were colored by his memories of Will, who often made fun of Clark's acting in school plays and of his penchant for talking his way out of fights rather than defending himself with his fists. According to Howard Strickling, Gable got more satisfaction using his charm than his huge knuckles: "Clark told me he was never involved in a brawl. But he was such a big guy that, I suppose, it would have been the easy way out."

Will was a scrapper and expected his son to defend himself like he thought a man should. But what Will Gable did not understand was Clark's fear of hurting someone, of drawing blood—or worse. According to Will's conception of masculinity, real men did not read books or paint landscapes. They regarded women as subservient. They used their hands, not their brains. And they fought.

Clark was more inclined to emulate Jennie's good manners and her respect for others. She encouraged him to take part in school plays and musicals, urged him to read good books and to study hard, to make something of himself. Most likely,

Clark was torn between appreciating his father's ability to support the family in fine fashion, even if Will's fingernails *were* permanently stained from the grime of the oil fields, and desiring a more dignified profession for himself. Clark must have learned at an early age that money was of paramount importance, for at the age of thirteen, and of his own volition, he started working at odd jobs during the summer.

Clark was not a particularly good-looking teenager, so most girls were not interested in him. His ears were too big, and his teeth were too small. But he was a likable fellow and a good sport, and he did acquire a girlfriend: Thelma Lewis, the sister of a close friend.

When Clark was nearly sixteen, Will sold his house and oil rig and bought a farm near Ravenna, Ohio. Gable biographers differ as to why. Some say the oil fields were drying up in Harrison County; others claim that Jennie had made clear she was tired of having only a part-time husband. Will said simply, "I was offered a good price for my rig and house, so I decided to sell."

This was a drastic uprooting for Clark. Leaving behind familiar surroundings and his only friends was traumatic. Jennie had misgivings, too, because Clark had been talking seriously about becoming a doctor, and on a farm, she knew, he would be obligated to share all the work with his father and would have little time for studies.

Many years later, Gable described this new life: "Working on the farm meant getting up at four in the morning every day of the year, spring, summer, fall, and winter, and the winters were cold in Ohio. I fed the hogs, the rest of the stock, plowed in the morning until every muscle ached, and forked hay in the hot sun until I was sweating crops of calluses. I did what I was expected to do on the farm, but I didn't have what it takes."

He missed Hopedale, too—acting in the high-school plays, romping on second base when he wasn't hitting well, and playing on the basketball team. "Nothing was the same," he said. "I towered over the other kids on the school bus, hated doing homework, and dreaded coming back to that farm. When I was sixteen, I made up my mind to go back to Hopedale and work for a while. For five dollars a day hauling water for miners, I might be able to afford a Model T. A buddy of mine, Andy Means, said he was going to Akron because there were good-paying jobs in the rubber industry, so instead, I went along with him."

Gable would remember well how Jennie sided with him during his bitter fights with Will, who made it clear he would not support his son on this foolish venture. "I respected my father and wanted his blessing," Gable said. "It was Jennie who convinced him to let me go in peace. If it hadn't been for her, I'd probably still be pitching hay in Ohio. She told me not to be proud. If things didn't work out, I should come back home."

Jennie regretted her stepson's quitting school. Clark did, too, but said he had no choice. To console her (and maybe himself, too), he told Jennie that if he went to Akron, there was a chance that he could work, finish school, and then go to college. Certainly, there was little chance of completing his education if he stayed on the farm. Jennie agreed. Losing "Clarkie" broke Jennie's heart, but she vowed to help if he needed anything. What kept Jennie going was a strong religious belief, because hard work on the farm was taking its toll on her.

Clark rented a room in Akron and got a job as a timekeeper at the Miller Rubber Company for twenty-five dollars a week. Jennie sent him boxes of homemade treats and was relieved and happy when Clark reported that he was doing well. Whether he was or not is another story. Clark was scared in Akron; he found the city overwhelming, the people so much different than the farmers and small-town friends he was used to. But he never let on to Jennie that he feared a thing.

In Akron, Clark discovered acting. "I'd never been to a movie," he would recall. "We didn't have theaters where I came from. I loved westerns, but it never entered my mind about becoming a movie star. It was the stage that thrilled me.

The Music Hall on Exchange Street was featuring a play called *Bird of Paradise*, about the South Sea islands. I'd never seen anything so exciting in my life—but then, one has to realize where I came from."

All other dreams and ambitions were forgotten—medicine, money, and cars. Clark later claimed that he worked at the Music Hall as a callboy for nothing but tips although others who were there at the time remembered only that he hung around constantly. Gable described his first contact with the theater: "getting the actors on cue and even sewing buttons on costumes. I slept in the theater and showered at the YMCA." Eventually, he got a walk-on part that required three words: "Good evening, sir."

At the Music Hall, Clark Gable fell in love with the theater and decided to become an actor. Though fame and money would be his eventually, he never forgot the exhilaration of walking onto a stage for the first time. But a telegram from his father interrupted his new career. Jennie was seriously ill. Clark returned to the farm and was with Jennie when she died. "I lost my best friend," he later said.

Will needed help on the farm and assumed his son would return home permanently. But there was nothing left there for Clark now that Jennie was gone. He returned to Akron, hoping the stock company would use him on stage again. In the meantime, he ran errands for the troupe and lived on meager tips, sleeping in the theater and grubbing food from anyone who had an extra bite.

Will decided to sell the farm and go back to wildcatting. He stopped off to see Clark in Akron on his way to Oklahoma. Father and son managed to get along well for a few days, even though Clark expressed no interest in the oil business. They parted amicably and promised to keep in touch. Then, suddenly, Clark found himself alone again. The stock company left town and he was not asked to join them. A new group of players ignored him completely.

In September 1920, Clark reluctantly joined his father at an oil field near Bigheart, Oklahoma, where he worked as an apprentice. For twelve dollars a day he chopped wood to fuel the boiler fires, handled a jackhammer, and cleaned the stills in the oil refineries. He slept in a hot tent during the summer and in a shack during the cold winter. Only one thing kept him going—the thought of collecting the three hundred dollars willed him by his grandfather Hershelman, payable on his twenty-first birthday.

On February 1, 1922, Clark collected his inheritance at the courthouse in Meadville, Pennsylvania. Will expected him to return to Oklahoma, but Clark went to Kansas City, where a new repertory company was being organized. He had heard that some of his friends from the Akron Music Hall might be in Kansas City.

"I was shocked," Will later reported. "I told the stubborn mule if he left me this time, he need never come back. I was through with him!" He also called Clark a "sissy" for wanting to be an actor.

Young Clark had no emotional bonds after Jennie's death and felt no familial obligation whatsoever to his father. Had William ever understood him? Tried to? Had he ever had any feelings for anyone other than himself? Perhaps unaware of it at the time, Clark was developing a mistrust of other men. In Akron, his friend Andy Means had run home when he lost his job, but Jennie had labored over a stove when she could barely stand to make sure that "Clarkie" didn't go hungry. Besides food, she sent him money, secretly, for fear Will would find out. Clark knew the depth of her sacrifices and developed a hatred of his father that lasted forever. William had no respect for Clark, even when his son's name appeared on movie-theater marquees. "Actors are sissies," he maintained to the last.

In his formative years, Clark had no heroes, only maternal heroines like Addie and Jennie. It seems that he did not have close relationships with women his own age. In Oklahoma, prostitutes came from town to "service" the men. As dirty as the wildcatters, these women were young in years, but worn-out and old long before their time. To prove himself a man,

Clark could hardly turn away these hags of the night with his father around. It must have been an ugly experience for a guy who had a fetish for cleanliness. He later said that he preferred blonde women because brunettes looked dirty to him. And yet, his first two wives had dark hair, as did many of his girlfriends. One possibly apocryphal story is that he once chose a blonde prostitute in Oklahoma and was disgusted to find out she was really a brunette.

When Will became known as "Clark Gable's father," his version of Clark's sojourn in Oklahoma was different than his son's, and may be more believable than Clark's story that Will promised to find him an acting job, reneged, and put his son to work in the oil fields. Though Clark would later admit that these strenuous months developed his muscles and kept him in good shape, he would never concede that he had actually volunteered to work with his father in Oklahoma. Eventually, the two parted once again; both hoped it was for the last time.

Clark now referred to himself as Billy Gable. Perhaps he thought the name Clark was too formal; perhaps the wildcatters, assuming his real name was William, had given him the nickname.

Clark did not find his theatrical friends in Kansas City, and the only job he could land was with a traveling tent show. He assumed at first that he'd been hired to act, but what the owners saw was a husky brute ideal for hoisting tents. "I did a little bit of everything for ten dollars a week," he said. "I played the French horn in the orchestra, hawked plays dressed as a clown on street corners, and only occasionally had a chance to act. That's what they said it was, anyway."

Gable later mentioned having had an affair with an older woman who was a member of the tent show; he said she had only one eye. Maybe he was joking, for he added that there was nothing else to do when the tent show arrived in Butte, Montana, and was snowed in. If true, this story is another example of Gable's penchant for older women and his ability to take advantage of whatever was available to him.

Without a doubt, Clark had grown up significantly in a short time. When the tent show folded, he hopped a freight train and rode to Bend, Oregon. "The first thing I saw was a lumber company near the tracks," Gable woud relate, "so I went inside to get warm. They were hiring, and I stayed for three months. My hands were raw because I couldn't afford gloves. I toughened them with vinegar and lard. Never needed the gloves after that."

When he accumulated some money, Clark headed for Portland, the nearest city. "I figured I might find a theater there," Gable said. He got a job selling neckties at Meir and Frank's department store, where he became friendly with his co-worker Earle Larimore, an actor and director with the Red Lantern Players, a local theater group. Earle invited Clark to hang around backstage and observe the troupe. When Earle decided to join a stock company in nearby Astoria, Gable quit his job at the department store and tagged along—"to try my luck," he would recall.

2.

Luck and Love

On stage in Astoria, Clark played the part of Eliza, a black cook, in *When Women Rule*, on July 23, 1922, the one and only time he corked his face for a role. In *The Villain Still Pursued Her*, he was dressed as a baby and was seen in a huge crib. He never minded that the audience laughed, as long as they reacted. Clark liked the players, the scenery, the makeup, and the costumes, and his heart beat a little faster as the audience filed into their seats. Surely he was dedicated, for only dedication could have persuaded him to put on baby clothes and be wheeled around in a baby carriage. He never felt humiliated, he never complained, and he was never discouraged. Anything, he thought, was better than working with his hands—chopping wood, digging for oil, or plowing on the farm.

Maybe falling in love had something to do with his optimism.

Franz Dorfler was twenty-two years old. Five feet two inches tall, she had light brown hair and soft, dreamy eyes. She had given up schoolteaching to become an actress. Spunky and bright, Franz was serious about the theater and cared little for dating until she met Clark Gable at an audition for the Astoria Stock Company.

"I wasn't impressed with him at first," Franz later said. "He was big, but not healthy-looking. His complexion was yellow and sallow. He was clumsy, too, and stumbled over his words with a high-pitched voice. However, he *was* well dressed, because he got his clothes at a discount where he was working."

At the audition, Clark was flirting with another girl, who was also trying out, but he offered Franz a sip of his soda when her name was called. She would remember her resentment at being distracted. Still, she got the job, and she was leaving the theater when Clark offered to walk her home.

"No, thank you," she said firmly, and continued on her way with him not far behind. Franz thought he came on too strong: "I had no idea where he came from or what he wanted, and I wasn't interested in finding out." But Clark refused to give up, and complimented her all the way home. He told her it was love at first sight; "I can't help myself," he said. By the time they arrived at Franz's home, he had almost convinced her he couldn't live without her.

Clark was not to be discouraged easily, not by Franz or the stock company. He hadn't been chosen yet for any important roles, but he showed up for tryouts every night they were held. "I found it difficult to ignore him," Franz said. "He wasn't good-looking or very mature, and he was lonely and undernourished. He had no one except Earle, who was with his girlfriend all the time."

Within a few days Clark had told everyone at the theater how much he loved Franz, and showed his jealousy if another man spoke to her. He knew his lines for auditions, but he had a better line where Franz was concerned. "It was impossible not to like him," she said. "But I felt sorry for him, too."

Rex Jewell, director of the Astoria Stock Company, rejected Clark. "He had nothing, absolutely nothing, to offer the stage. He tried so hard, and I tried to find something in his readings or how he carried himself, but he was, in my opinion, hopeless. He barely got on and off stage without a great deal of difficulty."

Clark wasn't able to convince Rex Jewell to take a chance on him, but Franz, meanwhile, was melting. She was getting used to having him around, but how long, she thought, does a drifter stay in one place? Still, she grew to understand his frustration and restlessness, and she admired his determination, despite the odds against him, and began to take an interest in his future. Clark wanted to be on the stage as much as she did, and their common goal brought them closer together.

But was it too late? The stock company, including Franz, was preparing to go on tour. Clark asked Franz not to go. He had a steady job selling ties, he told her; they'd find another theater group and work on the stage together. Franz had no intention of giving up the Astoria tour, but she worried that she might never see Clark again. She and Earle Larimore entreated Rex Jewell. Could Clark fill in for the other actors? After all, he knew all the parts. And he could help with the scenery and the trunks. Jewell went along with the plan, if only because Clark was willing to work for nothing.

It was a glorious day when the little theater group boarded the paddle wheeler that would take them up the Columbia River. Franz and Clark became very close in this romantic setting, telling each other their life stories and deepest secrets. Pathetically, he blurted out his loneliness. He'd never had anyone to lean on, he said. He had never been loved or cared for, only ignored. "That's why I'm so happy with you," he said. Love had overcome the obstacles and suffering, and filled the emptiness in his life.

Gable had developed a way with women, a knack for getting

their attention and gaining their sympathy. On this excursion, he poured it on and grabbed his first kiss from Franz. "I was shocked," she said. "But I liked what he did so impulsively. It was wonderful, because we could share each other. He was my first beau, and I was his first girlfriend. We had been looking for each other."

Franz was two years older than Clark. Her father, a prosperous farmer in Silverton, Oregon, had only reluctantly allowed her to give up schoolteaching for acting, but she pursued her newly chosen profession diligently. Marriage had not been one of her goals, not until Clark came along; still, she had no intention of giving up acting for any man.

Clark didn't seem to mind that he wasn't as talented as Franz, or as organized. He appreciated that she knew what she wanted and had the patience to wait for it, proving her ability while she waited. One of her plans was to share her career with a man she loved. Knowing this would be difficult, even impossible, she had never dated much or gone to parties. But on those beautiful nights sailing up the Columbia, Franz knew she had found the right man. Of course, she would have to wait until he mastered acting and got enough experience to earn a decent living. Meanwhile, her gallant Romeo stood in the wings while she graced the stage every night. When he became depressed, she encouraged him. It was apparent to everyone in the company that Clark leaned on Franz completely. It was rather cute, they agreed. He was so big and she was so tiny.

Clark chose not to let Franz know of his tender relationship with Jennie. Instead, he told her that his stepmother had never loved him. No one ever had. Ignoring the truth to gain sympathy worked in his favor on the riverboat with Franz, and it would be effective with every woman Clark ever knew, except Carole Lombard, who didn't believe his pathetic childhood tales.

Clark told Franz that she was fortunate to have a loving family and to have grown up on a beautiful farm. He asked her to tell him everything about her family and about how they got along with one another. What was Clark fishing for? she wondered. An invitation, no doubt: a warm bed, free food, a hammock for an afternoon nap, and the chance to sit down to dinner with a prosperous farmer instead of a drunken bum like Will Gable. In many ways, Gable was similar to the Hal Carter character in *Picnic*: a hitchhiker with a questionable background who gets by on masculine charm, a bare chest, and sweet talk.

Franz would recall emphatically Clark's outstanding trait: "What I liked most about him was his ability to always look immaculate. He had that scrubbed look. I never saw him unkempt."

Did he flirt with other girls? No, Franz said. She satisfied him completely. For now, anyway.

Gable's big break came when one of the actors in the company quit. Rex Jewell recalled, "He fell down the first night, but managed to stay on his feet after that. But he staggered, stumbled, and stammered all over the stage. It was a disaster, but I was stuck with him."

Circumstances forced Jewell to shut down the Astoria Stock Company for a while. He told the group, "I plan to reorganize, so if you're in the area, I'll let you know." Franz had no second thoughts about staying in Astoria. Clark stayed too; he was sure Jewell would give him another chance. "I wasn't making ten dollars a week," he would remember, "and sometimes not even that. All we were really guaranteed was a place to sleep, but it was a challenge. You're always scared the first time you find yourself broke. Later, you just feel interested in what's going to lift you out of it this time."

Clark, Franz, and other members of the company passed the time at a borrowed cottage in Seaside, Oregon, taking turns sleeping on the beach. These were happy times—breezy, romantic, and free. The actors built fires on the beach, sang songs, and discussed their dreams. Clark proposed marriage to Franz, and she accepted. They would tour with Jewell, they decided, save their money, and pursue the theater together.

In September 1922, Clark, Franz, and the rest of the Astoria troupe boarded a milk boat and began another tour. Living conditions were dreadful, but Clark acted every night. Because of his high-pitched voice and his clumsiness, he was deemed a natural for comedy; in drama, the audience laughed, but for the wrong reasons. Still, Clark was content, snuggling up to Franz on deck after shows as they read to each other under the stars. Only youth and love could withstand a wooden floor for a bed—or having to sleep out-of-doors in the rain.

After Jewell closed down the company once again, Franz and Clark went to her parents' farm in the Willamette Valley, near Portland. He earned money picking hops and spent his spare time trying to impress the Dorflers. At the end of the hop season, Clark got a job with a lumber company for three dollars a day and lived in a boardinghouse. He spent every weekend on the farm with Franz. To his way of thinking, her family was his family.

The Dorflers, however, began to question their daughter's relationship with this drifter. When Franz hinted at marriage, they tried to discourage her. It was all right for a girl to be an actress, they conceded, but marrying an actor was asking for trouble. They liked Clark but made it clear they could not accept him as a son-in-law.

Without explanation or warning, Franz announced she was going to live in Portland, with her brother. It's possible the Dorflers were responsible for this sudden decision. Clark was stunned. Why hadn't Franz discussed this with him? One day they were happy together, and the next she announced, "I want to be near the theater." Clark was forced to stay behind to earn some money. The Dorflers made him welcome on the farm and tried to cheer him up over a lonely Christmas. A month later, he quit his job at the lumber company and headed for Portland to be with Franz—who, he discovered, had left for Seattle. He found out later that heavy snowstorms had delayed her letter to him explaining that she had been offered a part in a good play.

Putting his own ambitions aside, Clark got a job as a telephone lineman in order to earn enough money to marry Franz as soon as possible. Meanwhile, they exchanged letters. Hers were full of encouragement. "You have such a fine singing voice," she wrote. "Why don't you take vocal lessons?"

Clark thought about it. Maybe she was right. If it made her happy, he'd be a singer. Franz attended a recital of his in June 1923. "He wasn't bad," she would recall. "Before I returned to Seattle, I promised to marry him by the end of the year."

Optimistic once again and looking forward to a Christmas wedding, Clark worked hard at the telephone company, and paid for his music lessons with extra money he earned as a garage mechanic. The Dorflers had changed their minds about their would-be son-in-law now that he was a respectable, hardworking young man with a steady job. He spent weekends with them, and he would never forget how they welcomed him when he knocked on their screen door.

Although Franz expressed her approval of Clark's singing debut, she privately gave him more credit for going through with it than for any ability he had displayed. Franz knew that Clark's talent, what there was of it, was for acting. And after all, their goal *was* the Broadway stage.

Clark wrote to Franz every day, saying that he missed her terribly, and he clung to her with his every written word. He seemed to be obsessed with pleasing Franz and getting married, and he hoped that her ambition and talent would eventually rub off on him.

Clark was so smitten with Franz that he didn't care that she had chosen him to be her husband primarily because he, too, wanted a stage career. She had no intention of settling down in Portland with any ordinary man, and she wasn't interested in money, either. What she had in mind was a life patterned after Lunt and Fontanne's.

When Clark made his singing debut, Franz had actually come home for her sister's wedding. Possibly, he had worked it out so that she could attend both. If so, he was the one making all the sacrifices. Franz expressed her concern about Clark's part-time garage job; she felt that he was spending too much time working with his hands and not enough time studying acting. She wrote to him about a drama coach who had recently moved to Portland. Franz urged Clark to begin training with this woman, who had once appeared on the Broadway stage; and she added an incentive: "I'll enroll, too, when I come home in December."

Clark had not yet saved enough money to get married. Summer was almost over, and he had only a few short months more to accumulate a respectable sum of money. But Franz was so enthusiastic about the new drama coach that Clark felt obligated to pursue his studies again. He still wanted to be an actor, but his stage appearances, he knew, had been disastrous; when Rex Jewell had organized another acting group in Seattle, Clark was overlooked. Franz had been hired, but Clark hadn't even been offered a bit part or a walk-on. More lonely for Franz than disappointed, Clark kept going, thinking about marriage. To marry, he knew, he needed money, not acting lessons. Besides, he hated studying, hated auditioning, hated hearing titters from the wings. How the devil could he read for a drama coach who had appeared on Broadway? She'd most likely laugh loud enough for Will to hear in Oklahoma.

But Clark would do anything for Franz. . . .

3.

Josephine

osephine Dillon was born in 1888 in Denver, Colorado. She graduated from Stanford University in 1908 and completed her education in New York and Paris before joining her family in Long Beach, California. Her father was a judge, and her mother, when she wasn't busy caring for her six children and their eighteen-room house, busied herself with the arts. Josephine's only brother became a lawyer, and the Dillon sisters studied opera, painting, and music composition.

Josephine chose the theater for her profession, and though she did appear on Broadway, she felt that she lacked the personality for the stage. She preferred teaching aspiring actors how to present themselves before an audience. After appearing in a play with Edward Everett Horton in

Portland, Oregon, Josephine decided it was the perfect city in which to open a drama school. Hers was an immediate success. -

When Clark signed up for Josephine's evening classes, he was accompanied, she would later recall, by a young lady who sat restlessly in a corner, reading a magazine. Obviously, Josephine thought, this girl was interested in Clark, not in acting. Josephine once remarked that she didn't think she ever saw this particular girl again—but she wasn't absolutely sure, because "he had so many." Even at this stage in his life, when he wasn't thought especially handsome or charming, it seems that Clark's inborn charisma had manifested itself.

It takes a particular breed to be a street hawker or a carnival con artist. If, like the Pied Piper, Clark could lure a crowd to a tent show, he had the power to entice women, despite his physical drawbacks.

Josephine would recall that Clark was young, sad, and expressionless—but deep, she felt, and thoughtful. Though he appeared tired and undernourished, he had a winning smile and the eagerness that Josephine believed necessary for the theater. "Desire often compensates for talent," she said. "I could tell he was absorbing my every word."

Josephine claimed she made up her mind from the start to concentrate on Clark's growth as an actor, though one might wonder whether her motivation was the professional challenge or a personal fascination. A worldly and learned woman, Josephine never hinted at a physical attraction. She was too sophisticated for that. Instead, she emphasized her keen insight.

When the first session was over, Clark approached Josephine. Could he have a few words with her in private? Citing the late hour, she asked him to stop by the following day instead.

To Josephine's dismay, she was unable to get Clark out of her mind when she tried to sleep that night. In the morning, she wondered what time he would arrive at the studio. Though she knew nothing about the young man—how old he was, where he came from, where he worked—she found herself looking out the window for him.

If Josephine was expecting a shy knock on the door, she must have been greatly surprised when Clark dashed into the studio, offering only a brief, enthusiastic greeting before bursting forth with a litany of his fondest desires and ambitions. Josephine sat and listened.

"It was a great reading last night," he began. "I want to act. I have to act, but not the kind I've been doing. I know I can be a good actor if someone will give me a chance. My goal is Hollywood. I'm not sure you want to hear that, but it's what I want. The stage is fun, but if you goof, well . . . that's it, you know? In Hollywood, if I make a mistake, I can do it again and get it right. I like westerns . . . Tom Mix, mostly. I could fit in, don't you think so? *I* do. If I learn the techniques . . . that is, if you'll teach me, I'm willing to study. But I want to know all the tricks, too. I think I could do it. How does a guy break into the movies? How do I go about it? Where do I start?"

Josephine watched Clark pace the floor and listened until he ran out of words. He was talking so fast that there was no way she could get a word in. She knew he had to get it out—everything that was locked up inside him. He had to tell her his ambitions. It was a showdown of sorts, she felt: she could take him or leave him. "He was very, very determined," she would recall. "I saw an abundance of strength in his eyes and heard it in his voice. He was going to do whatever it was he wanted, with or without me, but there was a plea for my guidance that came through."

Josephine had little regard for Hollywood. She knew that the majority of enthusiastic hopefuls who arrived there by the thousands left broke and defeated. Hollywood was a dream-world for few and a nightmare for most, she told Clark. But still, she did not try to talk him out of his Hollywood ambitions. Instead, she told him he would have to make sacrifices. Building a film career would take a long time, and there were no guarantees.

"What do I do first?" he asked.

"Learn," she replied. "And then the key—practice."

"What else?"

"More practice."

Clark told her that no one had ever taken an interest in him before. People pretended to, he said, and then they laughed behind his back. He made audiences laugh when they were supposed to cry, he bumped into props when he should have been picking them up, and he stepped on the other actors' cues. Once, he confessed, he had even fallen, literally, on his face.

"That's nervousness," she explained. "Maybe you were too anxious. The true essence of acting is being in control, and that takes timing. Practice and timing . . ."

Clark was ready to get started then and there; he wanted to read or recite or talk about himself. Instead, Josephine showed him out. He stood in the doorway for a moment, looked in her eyes, and exclaimed. "You're a fine-looking girl!" Josephine, who knew she wasn't the least bit pretty, was taken aback; she couldn't remember any man's having said that to her. Clark's compliment overwhelmed the thirty-six-year-old spinster; she soon realized that it was the giver, not the praise, that had touched her.

During another restless night, Josephine thought of little else than her ardent new pupil. The other students were better performers, but suddenly they were unimportant to her. Yes, she admitted to herself, the cocky young man with space between his front teeth and sallow skin was a terrible actor. But what audiences hadn't yet recognized, she had. What the other players complained about, she would correct.

As the weeks passed, Clark became Josephine's sole obsession; her acting classes, she would later assert, got smaller and smaller. Perhaps Clark's later fame led her to exaggerate her early efforts on his behalf. It seems unlikely that this otherwise astute woman would have allowed a fresh kid to interfere with her business.

It is also unlikely, despite Josephine's later memories of this time, that Clark was running around with a slew of girls. After all, he worked all day for the telephone company, and he studied every night. Josephine insisted, however, that her pet student attracted women of all ages. Billed as William C. Gable, Clark gave a poetry reading for Portland's Women's Club; it was well received, but the audience was more entranced with the man than with his verse, Josephine insisted. "Some of these ladies came to my studio looking for him," she said.

Though Clark's many letters to Franz Dorfler were glowing ones about Josephine Dillon's belief in him and his renewed faith in himself as an actor, Franz suspected that something was amiss when Clark wrote that he was taking a vacation in the country because Miss Dillon thought he needed fresh air, exercise, and a healthy diet. Knowing that Clark was perpetually short of money, Franz surmised that Josephine was paying his expenses. Clark's letters to Franz dwindled from several a day to one or two a week, if that. And though her fiancé did not hint at any change in their wedding plans, Franz read between the lines. She knew that Clark had never met a woman like Josephine Dillon—a Broadway actress, an artist. Clark wondered, he wrote Franz, how Josephine could ever have left the stage to devote time to others so that they might experience the magic of assuredly facing an audience. How could she have turned her back on Broadway, given it all up for a drama school in Portland? Clark's admiration overflowed.

Josephine Dillon had short, dark hair, a low forehead, a broad nose with oversized nostrils, and thin lips. Her piercing eyes were narrow but sympathetic, and her face was square and well-defined, which made it look, at first glance, hard. She was a small woman with fine posture. Some who had seen Josephine on the stage described her as prematurely mature-looking, resembling someone's mother. She was said to have had a pleasant, quiet personality and an ability to discuss any subject intelligently. Josephine was not a woman who warranted a second glance.

Clark was attracted to Josephine's knowledge. He was impressed that she had devoted her entire life to the theater. So after five years of pitching tents, whistling in freight cars, and stumbling across the stage like a newborn colt, he was proud to be seated next to her on a piano bench, searching for his vocal range. This was an amazing technique, he said, as she plied the keyboard. Routine, she said, smiling. Vocal exercise is a mystery to the novice actor, she told him, but it is more important than anything else. She told Clark to forget everything he had learned in the past. She would teach him how to walk, talk, and breathe all over again.

Josephine later described the Clark she first met as a "gorgeous skeleton" with a straight-lipped, set mouth of the do-or-die type—he was the sort of man, she said, who fought alone and tells nothing. Initially, she was concerned about his health, viewing with dismay his yellowish complexion and bad teeth, his muscles melting away to the bone. Once she noticed him making progress with his speech and breathing, though, she insisted that he quit his job at the telephone company, and she arranged for him to work on a farm, where he could regain his health. Then she got him a singing job at the Portland Hotel, where local society gathered for dinner on Saturday nights.

Josephine played the role of Clark's mother. She took telephone messages from other women, watched impassively as he disappeared with wealthy matrons in expensive cars, never asked where he had been or with whom, and patiently prepared his acting lessons day after day. Though it was she who had turned his life around in just a few months, she also recognized that he was young and needed time with girls who were interested in long romantic drives to nowhere, laughter, dancing, and petting in the moonlight. Josephine did not want a sexually frustrated Clark to turn his back on her. If she was concerned about other women, she never said so, and Clark was too energetic and driven to be engaged in any serious discussions of a personal nature.

What personal interest Josephine expressed was in Clark's preparedness. Had he read the book she'd given him? Yes—they discussed it at length. Was he taking his singing lessons regularly? Yes—the music teacher said he was always prompt. Was he practicing his breathing exercises? Yes—she could see the positive results.

As Christmas approached, Franz wrote Clark that she had been offered a play in Portland and that they could be married as planned. If she had had any doubts about her fiancé's future as an actor, they were banished when she laid eyes on Josephine Dillon's creation. Clark had become all that she had hoped for and never thought possible. His eyes were radiant, his formerly pale, yellow skin was bronze from the sun, and his six-foot-one-inch frame had filled out impressively. "I have so much to tell you!" he exclaimed.

Franz was told about the dowdy goddess who had worked miracles with Clark's health, his career, and his mental well-being. He said that Josephine had given him the courage to earn a living with a talent he hadn't known he had—singing. He wasn't afraid anymore, and above all, he believed in himself. "But," he said, "I have a lot more to learn."

Clark showed Franz his work sheets, books, and scripts; with the zeal of a convert, he encouraged her to breathe properly and to walk with her knees slightly bent. But not *once* did he mention their getting married. Finally she came out with it: "Mother would like to begin making plans for the wedding."

"I think we should wait," he said.

"But you were so anxious a few months ago."

"One thing at a time."

"I don't understand."

"I've made up my mind to study for a few years."

"A few years?" she gasped.

"At least."

"But we planned to do that together!"

"Things have changed," Clark said. "We thought it would be easy. Fun. But it isn't like that."

"We both want the same thing," Franz insisted. "We can help each other."

"I don't love you anymore," he said. "The most important thing to me is working with Miss Dillon."

Franz was stunned, brokenhearted. It was bad enough to hear Clark say those words, but his lack of emotion devastated her. Was he in love with Josephine Dillon? Close to tears, Franz couldn't bear to ask. Suddenly, they were strangers. His boyishness had disappeared. He was no longer the puppy who had followed her around, begging for attention and affection.

Christmas 1923 was depressing for Franz; she could neither eat nor sleep. On New Year's Eve, Clark phoned her. "I didn't mean those awful things I said the other night," he apologized. "Can I see you?"

Their meeting was strained, their embrace less than passionate. Clark insisted that he hadn't really stopped loving her, but Franz remained uncomfortable. Did he feel sorry for her? Was he trying to soothe his guilty conscience? Bewildered, she told him it might be best to call off their engagement. He agreed, adding, "A doctor told me once I should never get married." Franz was floored.

"Why?" she asked.

"I'd rather not discuss it, but that's what he said."

Franz continued to date Clark occasionally, holding on to a glimmer of hope. He was, after all, very fond of her parents, and he enjoyed visiting their farm.

Meanwhile, Franz was very anxious to meet the phenomenal Miss Dillon. Clark proudly invited Franz to a rehearsal at the drama school. Whether Josephine realized that Franz was not just another one of Clark's girlfriends isn't certain, but she was probably too observant not to notice a difference in his behavior. Josephine took charge of her protégé, and the rehearsals began. According to Franz, Clark skillfully (and rudely) upstaged the other actors. These were the tricks of the trade, he said afterwards, and there was nothing rude or unprofessional about it.

"I felt upstaged that night, too," Franz would recall. "I was given the impression that I was not a part of Clark's life any longer . . . that I wasn't wanted."

Clark was still jealous of other men who paid attention to Franz, and he acted possessive if she showed interest in them. When there was competition, he was in love with her. When she warmed up to him, he felt crowded. He wanted Franz, it seemed, on his terms—when and if he needed her.

Clark let Franz know that she had made her choice many months before: she had left him alone in Portland when he had wanted so desperately to marry her. In turn, she asked him whether there was another woman. "No," he replied. "I don't think I'll ever get married."

Though Franz was the wounded one, she had to take partial blame for the breakup: she had, after all, run off to Seattle alone and then recommended Josephine Dillon to Clark. She suffered for her selfishness the rest of her life. Franz never married. Clark Gable was her one and only love. But perhaps she might have had a chance at happiness if he had stayed away from her over the years. . . .

As for Josephine, she was Jennie's replacement—another mother figure to replace the one Clark had never known. Jennie had always said her stepson deserved the very best; so did Josephine. Both women were eager to guide, counsel, and serve him.

And so it was that Josephine proved who came first in Clark's life. Under the pretext of borrowing some scenery, she asked him to accompany her to the theater where Franz was performing. Once there, Josephine snubbed her rival. It was embarrassing to Franz, but this meeting proved to her that Clark's drama teacher was very much in love with him.

Josephine considered Franz—and, in particular, Clark's visits to her parents' farm—a threat. He spoke of the Dorflers' hospitality and warmth. Theirs was a close family attachment, he said, that could never be severed. Though he had hated farming as a boy, he felt now that it would always be a part of his life. It was clean, relaxing, and a refreshing break from the city. As long as Clark continued to look forward to his visits with the Dorflers, Josephine felt, there was a chance that Franz could worm her way back into his heart.

Josephine decided to close her school in Portland. "I was concentrating on Clark totally," she later admitted. "Gradually, the other students dropped out, and I wasn't recruiting new ones." With more than a hundred thousand actors registered in Hollywood, she figured, what better place to open up a new drama school?

She told Clark a different story: "It's time for you to break away, to begin getting some valuable experience on the stage and to meet people in the theater. When I'm settled, I'll send for you. In the meantime, I've made arrangements for you to work for a stock company here in Portland this summer."

Franz was also a member of this company, but Josephine knew precisely what she was doing. This would be the supreme test for Clark—and a chance that Josephine had to take. She needed proof that Clark was not carrying a torch for his on-again, off-again girlfriend. Franz, meanwhile, regretted having broken her engagement to Clark and hoped for a reconciliation now that Josephine had moved away. But not only did Clark keep his distance from Franz, he dated other women. There were no more visits to the Dorfler farm, either.

Franz felt that she was being punished, and that when Clark was satisfied, he would return to her. A few weeks later, he did, but just for long enough to announce: "I'm going to Hollywood."

Once again, Franz was shattered. "I threw his love letters into the fireplace," she would recall, "and cried every night for a long time."

4.

Hollywood

*I*n August 1924, Josephine sent Clark fifty dollars to cover his traveling expenses from Portland to Los Angeles. He arrived with spirit and enthusiasm, babbling like a kid at the circus. The excitement of Hollywood was everywhere, even in the dingy hotel where Josephine had arranged for him to stay.

The evening of his arrival, Clark and Josephine talked all through dinner at an eatery and long into the night in his tiny room. It was an exhilarating reunion. Until she could establish her drama school, Josephine was reading and typing scripts for Paramount Pictures. Her twenty-dollar-a-month bungalow was being painted when Clark arrived. "I won't show it to you until it's finished," she teased.

Clark said he would get work as a garage mechanic. "You know how much I love tinkering with cars." He grinned.

"But only temporarily," she said. "Conscientious studying and practice come first. You won't have time to work."

But Clark was no longer interested in the movies. He had got over his fear of the stage and had come to believe that filmmaking had no merit.

At the time, scandal was rampant in Hollywood, a constant reminder that the movie industry attracted greed and evil, not talent.

In 1920, actress Olive Thomas, who was married to Mary Pickford's brother, Jack, and known as "The Most Beautiful Woman in the World," had committed suicide by ingesting an overdose of bichloride-of-mercury granules. Why had this gorgeous twenty-two-year-old *Ziegfeld Follies* queen, star of Selznick Pictures productions and sister-in-law of "America's Sweetheart," killed herself? Apparently because Jack had infected her with syphilis. The cover-up story was that Olive's overdose was accidental, but rumors persisted that Olive had been hopelessly addicted to cocaine and heroin.

In 1921, comedy king Roscoe "Fatty" Arbuckle was accused of raping and killing starlet Virginia Rappe during a wild party in San Francisco. Arbuckle was tried three times; Hollywood was on trial, too, as testimony exposed stories of bootleg booze, orgies, bigamy, and dope. Arbuckle was eventually acquitted, but his career was ruined.

While Fatty Arbuckle sat in a courtroom sweating for his life, the press was racing to keep up with Hollywood scandal. In 1922, Clark Gable's birthday, February 1, director William Desmond Taylor was shot to death in his bungalow apartment. Among Taylor's effects, police found mono-grammed lingerie belonging to Paramount's virginal beauty Mary Miles Minter and letters written by Mack Sennett's star and mistress, Mabel Normand. Both actresses were eventually forced to retire. Taylor's killer was never found.

In 1922, popular leading man Wallace Reid, "the All-American Boy," was admitted to a private sanitarium—for exhaustion, supposedly. But poor Wally had been relying for years on injections of morphine to keep him going. A human robot, he had been abused by Hollywood—rushed from film to film without a break. Happily married, handsome, and humble, Wally nevertheless died in a padded cell, from morphine.

Dead at thirty-two, Wally Reid—the wholesome chap every girl would be proud to bring home to Mother, a guy one would expect to meet at a church picnic—was a pawn of the camera that focused on him seven days a week, as the studios ground out moneymaking films that benefited everyone but him, an innocent who is remembered, pathetically, only for his drug addiction.

The twenties roared with Hollywood scandal, but this was not the reason that Gable had opted for the stage. To be in a Broadway play, he felt, was still the ultimate achievement for an actor. In 1924 the Barrymores, William Boyd, Irene Dunne, Basil Rathbone, Walter Huston and Fred Astaire, to name just a few, were appearing on Broadway but would succumb to Hollywood. The majority were lured by money and never returned to the stage.

Nineteen twenty-four, the year of Clark Gable's arrival in Hollywood, was also the year in which what would become the most powerful and prestigious studio in the world—Metro-Goldwyn-Mayer—was born. The MGM trademark was the now-famous roaring lion embraced by the words "Ars Gratia Artis"—"Art for Art's Sake."

Josephine thrived on her hectic schedule, working days at Paramount and then hurrying home to make dinner and to tutor Clark. He had, by now, won her heart, but she would never admit to being intimate with him. They were a team, she said, not lovers. She admitted to falling in love, never to making love. Josephine always insisted that going to bed with Clark would have cost her his respect. Her goal, she said, was gaining recognition through his success.

The relationship between Josephine Dillon and Clark Gable has continued to puzzle, fascinate, and defy belief. Those who knew him well in later years found it hard to accept that he had not given himself bodily to Josephine as payment for her efforts. If a woman was available, they said, that was reason enough for Gable to dim the lights. "One woman is just like another" was the theory not only of the characters he would play but of the man himself.

Josephine described their time together as work, work, work: exercises in breathing, walking, sitting, standing, smiling, dancing, climbing stairs, descending stairs, making an entrance, and making an exit. Not to mention the eternal diaphragmatic breathing exercises.

She taught him social graces, the language of the upper class—and how to hold his tongue under any circumstances. Clark displayed an instinct for good grooming and choosing a wardrobe. "He knew all about fine clothes," Franz Dorfler would recall. "He always wore French cuffs to detract from his big hands. When he had only one suit, somehow it was always clean and pressed."

In November 1924, Josephine bought Clark an old car for sixty dollars. "It's time for you to make the rounds of theatrical producers," she said. "I'll do some inquiring, too." There was as yet no talk of motion pictures; Josephine wanted Clark to learn acting on the stage and to get the feel of a live audience. But their efforts were fruitless. It took Clark less than a month to miss his weekly income as a mechanic and to feel the sting of rejection once again.

Josephine had little money herself, but she was not nearly as discouraged as Clark was. "I've been thinking about your getting work as an extra in pictures," she said. "It isn't what I wanted, but we need the money and you might meet someone who's connected with a theater group."

Clark would never forget the sight of the thousands of people waiting outside the studios for bit parts. The few times he got to the front of the line, he was either too late or too tall. Some days, when he couldn't afford gas for his car, Josephine would stay home to work with him on his diction, reading Shakespeare with him and reviewing the basics over and over again. The combined responsibilities of working, teaching, cleaning, washing and ironing, cooking, and trying to organize a drama school must have been burdensome, but through it all, she never complained or lost faith in the young man she had once called "a gorgeous skeleton."

But Clark was discouraged and moody. With Josephine handling what little money they had, he felt like a caged gigolo, a frustrated philanderer, a lost child clinging to his mother for survival.

Strange as it may seem, Clark decided that marriage to Josephine was the only way for him to gain his freedom. "I've been thinking," he said to Josephine, out of the blue. "If I didn't have to live in a hotel, that would save us some money, wouldn't it?"

"Yes," she said, "but I haven't room for you in my bungalow, and besides, it wouldn't look right."

"Why don't we get married?" he asked.

"Because you're not in love with me."

"We can't go on like this for much longer," he concluded.

Josephine must have been thrilled beyond words. The proposal was hardly romantic, but at least Clark was the one who had brought up the subject. If nothing else, it meant that Clark did not want to go back to Franz Dorfler or to go off on his own. He wanted to marry *her*: Josephine Dillon, spinster, teacher, and thirteen years his senior. "Maybe it would work," she managed to say.

"You'll do it?" he yelped.

She nodded.

He hugged her and said, "You're a very special woman. I'll never forget you."

"Our marriage was in name only," Josephine would always maintain.

Josephine Dillon and Clark Gable were married by a minister named Meadows on December 18, 1924. Clark gave his age as twenty-four; he was twenty-three. Josephine admitted to thirty-four; she was thirty-six. There was no honeymoon and, according to the bride, no wedding night per se.

But where did the groom sleep if the bride's bungalow had only *one* bedroom?

Clark was as devoted to Josephine after the wedding as he'd been before. But though he never questioned her advice, he was depressed at having to drive to the film studios every morning knowing he would then wait in line—if he could find the end of it—for a mere three-dollars-a-day walk-on part. He made the rounds of the studios faithfully each day before dawn until he realized that hundreds of players slept near the gates each night. Josephine refused to let him do that. "Our evenings are devoted to your lessons," she insisted, "and it's vital you look well rested in the morning."

After weeks of waiting, standing, and hoping, Clark decided he was wasting valuable time. The more he saw of the movie business, the more he hated it. He told Josephine she'd been right about Hollywood. "It's depressing, dull, and humiliating," he growled. "I've been observing what's going on. The same damn people get work. It's who you know around here, and it makes me sick! Hollywood doesn't interest me anymore."

"You had to get it out of your system," Josephine said, smiling. "I knew that."

"You're right. You're always right. It's the Broadway stage that matters. Now that I found out for myself what I really want, it won't bother me to stand in those long lines, because it's just for the money. It's different when you don't care, isn't it?"

Yes, Josephine said to herself, it is. When I didn't love him, I was better off. He's become my life, my whole world, my reason for working eighteen hours a day. He makes me laugh, he makes me young, he makes my heart sing in the morning and dance when I sleep. If he only knew the wonderment of it and how much joy came into my life when he walked into my studio. But he mustn't know. I might frighten him away, though I find he needs me and will for a long time.

Josephine chose their friends carefully. She surrounded

Clark with struggling artists, painters, and composers, people with talent and culture. Sometimes the upper crust could slum at the Gables' parties, and Clark, who was attracted to wealth, would scan a roomful of people looking for women wearing expensive jewelry. Within the hour he'd be dancing cheek to cheek with one of them. These ladies found him shy, sincere, flattering, and very persistent. The first time Josephine saw Clark whispering into a diamond-studded ear, she was crushed. If the hope of money was the sole reason for their marriage, she knew, a younger and wealthy woman could easily take him away from her. Losing Clark was Josephine's greatest fear. How long, she wondered, could he hold out in a city of lavish mansions and rich movie stars who flaunted themselves in polished McFarlans, Rolls-Royces, Packards, and Lancias?

Josephine and Clark's relationship deteriorated quickly after they took their marriage vows. Their cramped living arrangement afforded him no privacy or freedom, and "that piece of paper," as he called it, had proved to be a tight collar attached to a short leash.

Some of Gable's latter-day friends said that he married Josephine to further his ambitions, and they asserted that he would have repaid his obligations to her in bed, payment due. Gable always refused to discuss this period of his life, but a close acquaintance said, "I don't think the Clark Gable in 1925 was any different from the one who signed a contract with MGM. It meant nothing for him to hop in bed, get it over with, turn his back and go to sleep. I've seen him with women who made Josephine look like Miss America. She was a means to an end, and he was the kind of a guy who paid. In my opinion, Josephine stuck to her story to protect him."

Gable's stick-to-itiveness finally paid off when he got a fifteen-dollar-a-day bit part in the film *White Man*. It's doubtful, though, that Josephine saw any of this money: Clark came home one evening with a set of secondhand golf clubs. Though she must have been put out at his spending time on the links while she worked up to eighteen hours a day,

she said nothing. That was the deal. She also kept quiet about
the times he didn't come home at all. Even when they were
together, she knew, he had a roving eye. The only way
Josephine could keep him at home was to work him
unmercifully. Often he grew exasperated going over the same
recitations and exercises again and again. Clark listened to
her criticism, then ran out into the night, slamming the door
behind him.

Years later, each would complain about the other's
obsession with the theater. "I don't know what he thought
about other than acting," Josephine once said. "He never
discussed anything else with me. I haven't any idea what went
on in his head." Gable, in turn, grumbled, "I'd come home
and she'd start teaching. I wasn't walking right, I wasn't
breathing deeply, or I entered the room all wrong. My voice
was too high. She never did anything but teach, teach, teach!"

Ten days' work in *White Man* earned Clark $150; he kept
all of it, explaining, "I like to have money in my pocket."
Josephine later said that Clark gave her only two gifts during
their five-year marriage: a pair of shoes and an alarm clock.
"He wanted to make sure I was able to walk to the studio on
time," she explained.

Clark was paid five dollars to be an extra in *Forbidden
Paradise*, which featured Pola Negri, Rod La Rocque, and
Adolphe Menjou. He waltzed on a crowded dance floor
alongside stars John Gilbert and Mae Murray in *The Merry
Widow*. He would dethrone Gilbert within ten years, but in
1925, Clark Gable's appearance in this film earned him a
mere seven dollars and fifty cents, while Gilbert was paid
thousands. As an extra, Clark felt lost amid the huge cast and
elaborate production of *The Merry Widow*. Being one of the
crowd made the big man feel very small. "I'm tired of being
shoved around," he told Josephine. "Those big shots make me
feel like dirt."

"The West Coast Players are auditioning for *Romeo and
Juliet* with Jane Cowl. Be patient, honey."

"Who's Jane Cowl?" he asked.

"She is one of the most talented and respected actresses in the theater. It's hard for me to believe you don't know who she is."

"*Romeo and Juliet*, huh?"

"Yes, and the West Coast Players are taking it on tour for about three months."

"Swell!" Clark said with a grin, secretly looking forward to getting away from Josephine. She warned him not to get his hopes up about the tryout.

But Clark was fairly confident he would get something. *Anything.* By now he was thoroughly fed up with Josephine's preaching and penny-pinching. And he hated working in movies—waiting around for hours while the leading man argued with the director and the leading lady complained about her costume and makeup.

Though Clark was bored with Josephine, he never tired of her stories about life on the stage in New York, about the thrill of performing with great artists and hearing applause from audiences that appreciated fine acting.

On the day the West Coast Players held auditions for *Romeo and Juliet*, Clark was one of the first to arrive at the theater. Jane Cowl, starring as the teenage Juliet, was then forty-one years old, but she had the talent, the youthful face, and the figure to carry off the role. She watched the auditions intently, pointed to Clark, and exclaimed, "I want him!" He stepped forward, virtually drooling with appreciation, his ambition outweighed only by his shy sincerity. He was going to be on the professional stage at last. Nothing else mattered. For thirty dollars a week, Clark Gable would play the part of—a spear carrier!

During rehearsals, Clark was Miss Cowl's obedient servant, picking up after her, fetching her a glass of water, fawning over her when she was upset and massaging her shoulders when she was weary. Cowl was so impressed by his gallantry that she offered to give him, privately, her professional opinion as to how he might most effectively hold his spear onstage. These lessons were conducted in her dressing room over dinner. Clark was such a good student, he later reported, that Cowl promoted him to "leader of the extras." Carrying a spear does not take much practice, but handling a leading lady does. Clark must have learned quickly, for in less than a week, Cowl asked him to continue on with the group to Vancouver, Seattle, and Portland. And she raised his salary to forty dollars a week.

Josephine was overjoyed that her student-cum-husband was touring in Shakespeare. Clark traveled the Northwest feeling every bit a hero where, not too long ago, he had suffered from starvation, depression, and rejection. Beside him was the famous Jane Cowl, whom, he was sure, his onetime fiancée, Franz, idolized. Once again, Clark Gable had used his magic charm and gained ground without displaying much, if any, talent.

The producer–director of the West Coast Players, Lillian Albertson MacLoon, offered Clark a minor part in *What Price Glory?*, Maxwell Anderson and Laurence Stallings' play about World War I. Shortly after production began, one of the leading men left the play, and Clark was chosen to replace him. During rehearsals in Los Angeles, Josephine decided to take over. She went with Clark to the theater every day, coaching him into a nervous frenzy. Her invasion disrupted the entire cast's timing, so MacLoon, deciding that one director was enough, banned Josephine from the theater. This would not be the last time Clark was embarrassed by his wife's overbearing interference.

A play called *The Lullaby* took Clark to San Francisco, where he ran into Franz, who was working as a dance instructor in a studio near the playhouse. She had kept track of his stage career, but it was a shock for her to meet him again face-to-face. Though he made every effort to see her while he was in San Francisco, he seemed to take their reunion in his stride. Franz tried to do the same, but it was difficult for her. She might have felt more indifferent had Clark told her he was married, but it apparently slipped his mind to do so, even when Franz said, "Miss Dillon has improved your acting immensely."

Gable returned to San Francisco in other plays and always made sure to see Franz. She later said that he'd become very sure of himself but was not conceited. He had updated and polished his charm, reined in his gift of gab, and perfected his lines. Privately, there was a special something about him that one did not yet see when he was onstage, she recalled.

Franz finally gave in to her hope of happiness with Clark and prayed that his apparent desire to make the most of their reconciliation was genuine. His kisses were long and passionate, but he did not pursue their intimacy much further. He was, however, still jealous of other men in her life, and still displayed a possessive and often obnoxious attitude. So it was no wonder that Franz was hurt and confused when Clark casually remarked that his marriage to Josephine was one of convenience, and that they were no longer living together. Why hadn't he told her before? she demanded. Was he afraid of losing her now that they had found each other again? Or was his timing carefully planned? Obviously the latter, because Franz was now more in love with Clark than she'd ever been.

While on tour with the West Coast Players' road company, Clark never sent money home to Josephine. His letters were filled instead with backstage gossip and reports of how many curtain calls he got. She always knew when he was coming home because his laundry would arrive first, with a note: "Will need clean shirts. Have them ready when I get home."

As she waited for Clark's return, Josephine's old fears reasserted themselves. Clinging to the hope that she and Clark could make a real marriage of their treaty, Josephine did what she could to make herself more attractive for his homecoming. Without money for new clothes, this couldn't have been easy. So instead, she concentrated on laundering his expensive silk shirts and underwear, and cooking him lavish dinners.

Clark was usually in a good mood until Josephine began her assessment of his stage appearances promptly after dinner. He was awkward and clumsy, she said, and he had yet to master the art of lowering his voice. They would have to work very hard before he was ready for New York.

Clark would grab his clean clothes and walk out.

Over time, his letters changed from theater talk to sarcastic remarks about how other women enjoyed his performances without finding fault. Maybe it was time she treated him more like a man and less like a little boy, he suggested. How about some encouragement once in a while? What about his accomplishments?

Josephine didn't think he had any. He was too impressed by his leading ladies and by praise from people who knew nothing about acting, she told him. She wanted to know whether he was practicing his diction and doing his breathing exercises regularly. Was he conscious of how he made his entrances, and of how he walked onstage? Was he reading the books she gave him? Did he take time to get into character? Was he becoming that other being instead of Clark Gable, "because," she wrote, "you seem to enjoy being yourself and that is not acting. Nor is it what the audience paid to see. If you are taken with the admiration of a few flighty girls who are stagestruck, I fear for your future as an actor."

Because she did not take advantage of his brief visits by giving him the encouragement he wanted from her, his teacher, Clark avoided being with Josephine for any length of time. Adamantly insisting that he showed no improvement whatsoever, Josephine tried to cram his lessons into their infrequent and short encounters. Clark warned Josephine that if she could not be more comforting, there were other women waiting at the stage door to cheer him up. If she had been sympathetic to and proud of his achievements, insignificant as she might have deemed them, she might have seen him more often. But what she saw coming through the front door was an actor, not a husband. A touch of compassion on Josephine's part might have made a difference to the Gables' marriage.

Josephine forged ahead nevertheless and began a campaign

to improve Clark's appearance. She convinced Clark that his teeth were a liability. "The front ones should be capped," she said.

"Yeah?" he said, scowling. "Well, I can't afford it."

"I can't, either," she replied, "but we'll make a deal with the dentist and pay him off." Josephine accepted this financial burden alone and was still in debt long after Clark was out of her life for good.

In between plays, Clark continued to look for work as an extra in movies. He'd made a few friends in the industry, including good-looking Billy Haines, who was one of MGM's most popular leading men in the late twenties and a discreet homosexual. Precisely when they met and under what circumstances isn't known, but Clark was apparently desperate enough for a job to go along with whatever favors Haines wanted in exchange for star-powered influence.

In 1925, Clark was an extra in Haines's picture *The Pacemakers*; then Haines got him a job with Joseph P. Kennedy's Preferred Pictures in *The Plastic Age*, which starred Clara Bow.

Joan Crawford, who costarred with Billy Haines and became a very close friend of his, laughed about his brief friendship with Clark Gable. "Jobs were hard to get," she said. "If you didn't know somebody, forget it. There was a lot of that sort of thing going on in dark corners."

In 1926, Clark was an extra for the last time, in *North Star*, for Associated Exhibitors. He would not require the assistance of Billy Haines again.

5.

Broadway

*C*lark's extramarital affairs during these lean years, conducted only to further his career, were numerous. He took advantage of older women and one man, but they used him for their own gratification, too. Franz was an innocent victim of Clark's game because she wasn't familiar with the rules. And Josephine sacrificed her own ambitions, which were far more promising than anything Clark had to offer her. It's worth noting that everyone went along with these liaisons, and because Clark was not a guy to make promises, the success of his technique is that much more intriguing.

In 1926, Clark played a minor part in the play *Madame X*, again for the West Coast Players. The leading lady was stage and screen actress Pauline Frederick, forty-four years old, famous, rich, and a three-time divorcée. She was a femme fatale, on and off the stage. Just as Jane Cowl had looked Clark over carefully and announced that she liked what she saw, Pauline, too, made her approval of Clark obvious. An irresistible, full-figured, dark-haired, energetic, multitalented lady, she had already left behind her a string of broken-hearted lovers. One young man committed suicide when she discarded him, leaving behind a note lamenting his unrequited love. Pauline was the "other woman" in a number of divorce cases, and she did not deny her overwhelming appetite for sex. She was exquisite, witty, dramatic, and lived life to the hilt. Clark was moving up in class when he had an affair with this elegant actress.

Whatever unfavorable publicity Pauline received during her career, audiences continued to adore her, packing theaters wherever she performed. By the time she met Clark, she had also made some forty films. Critics praised her unique ability to project emotion with her eyes and hands. She was one of the first actresses to use her shoulders effectively—one up and the other down, or one thrown back and the other thrust forward. She knew more about lighting and camera angles than the technicians, but she had a gentle, professional approach with fellow cast members and crew. Those who knew her well commented that she never aged. "Pauline went from one phase of youth to another" was one assessment.

On the opening night of *Madame X*, Pauline received more than thirty curtain calls. No one in the cast kept precise count, because they were too busy crying with joy—all but Clark, who watched carefully as this fascinating star took her bows, each different from the others. It wasn't the applause that he noticed, but how she received the honor. Pauline knew a hundred ways to show her appreciation—each more glamorous than the last.

While Josephine struggled with the opening of her drama school, and typed scripts to pay her husband's dental bills, Pauline insisted that Clark have his teeth capped properly, at her expense—a small gesture of thanks for his nightly company at her fabulous mansion on Sunset Boulevard.

Gable later described Pauline as "a woman who acts as if she's never going to go to bed with another man." He complained at the time of stomach trouble, though, "because Pauline insists I eat lots of oysters to get me through the exhausting nights." This electrifying affair gave Clark the courage to move out of Josephine's humble little bungalow and into his own apartment, with his new wardrobe, his dazzling capped teeth, and gifts of gold from Pauline. If he had been so inclined, convincing the influential star to help get him into more films would have been a cinch, but Clark wanted the Broadway stage above all else.

When *Madame X* closed, Pauline went abroad and conquered Europe while Clark stayed on with the West Coast Players; the lovers parted with no great pain on either side. Clark accepted a small part in *The Copperhead*, starring Lionel Barrymore, who was amused and flattered when the young actor followed him around the theater. "Barrymore was my idol," Gable later said, "and I wanted to impress him. But on opening night, I stumbled over something and my hat dropped into a well. To make things worse, I tried to dig out my hat! Barrymore chopped my head off. I was sure he was going to fire me, but after he cooled off, we got along well and he helped me over the rough spots."

Clark's stage faux pas could not have happened at a worse time. Appearing in a play with Lionel Barrymore meant so much to him that the horror of stumbling over himself was not easily forgotten.

"I think you'd do better in motion pictures," Barrymore said.

Clark thanked him for the advice, but stayed on with the West Coast Players to appear in *Chicago*, starring Nancy Carroll, who had just signed a five-thousand-dollar-a-week contract with Paramount. The only notable aspect of his performance as Jake, a loudmouthed newspaperman, was the way in which he adapted the character into the persona of Clark Gable: hat tilted back on his head, coat collar turned up, cocky grin, lumberman's stride. This was also his first chance to use the upstaging techniques Josephine had taught him. When he wasn't stage center, he still managed to get attention, standing with a smirk on his face and the devil in his eyes. *Chicago* got good reviews, and Clark got special mention. He enjoyed the role of Jake, no doubt because he got to play himself. "Reporters don't have to stand up straight, walk like a gigolo, and talk like royalty," he said.

Gable would eventually play the part of a newspaperman in nine films, but in 1927, he showed no interest in MGM's offer of a screen test. Unfortunately, despite his good showing in *Chicago*, there were no more stage offers. His love life came to a standstill, too. Suddenly, the passionate nights, the traveling, and the exhilarating applause came to a halt. Disappointed, confused, and broke, he turned to Josephine.

"Maybe I should make the damn screen test," he muttered.

"No."

"What the hell am I going to do?"

"Give me time. We'll work it out," she said, a touch of softness in her voice.

Now that Clark needed her again, it was difficult for Josephine to nag him about his faults. She decided that he needed expert training with a good stock company. If he gave in to films now, she knew, he'd never make it to Broadway. She had seen it happen too often.

"How much do you want that dream that brought us together in Portland?" she asked.

"Very much," he replied.

Within a few weeks, she had accepted an offer on his behalf for work with a Houston stock company. "The Gene Lewis Players put on a different play every week," Josephine said with great enthusiasm.

"But I don't learn that fast," he argued. "It'll never work out."

Josephine convinced Clark to go to Houston, he'd been promised lead roles, she pointed out. "The experience will be invaluable," she said. "The money is good, too."

"How much?"

"What's the difference? You've only earned two thousand dollars in the past two years."

Gable couldn't argue with that, but he was unhappy about going to Texas.

Once again, Josephine did not attempt to hold on to her husband, who had willingly returned to her bed. She knew about Pauline Frederick and his other paramours, but she did not blame Clark. "Women chased *him*," she said later.

Clark went to Texas reluctantly, but within one month he had landed the lead role of Mat Burke in Eugene O'Neill's *Anna Christie*, earning two hundred dollars a week. When he called Josephine with the good news, she rushed to Houston and tried to take over once again, interrupting rehearsals with her incessant suggestions. Clark was furious, as was the director, who told Josephine to go home. Josephine stayed in Texas long enough to see the crowds of teenage fans waiting for Clark at the stage door. Gifts from admirers arrived at his dressing room every day, and young girls begged for his autograph. Society matrons were subtler; they sent him engraved invitations to elite Houston parties. Clark was flattered, and never failed to give the dowagers a sheepish grin when they rubbed their plump bodies against his. At the age of twenty-six, the legendary Clark Gable was taking form. The sallow complexion had disappeared permanently; his crooked teeth had been straightened. His huge hands were partially concealed with French cuffs held together with solid gold links. His ears were still prominent, but the smiling face between them was sensuously handsome. His dimples were more prominent, and his lips curved dangerously, perfectly.

In Texas, Josephine and Clark had a showdown before she went home to Los Angeles. He resented her going around Houston introducing herself as Mrs. Gable, he told her. Their marriage meant nothing, he said. And he didn't want her coaching anymore. Their partnership was over.

"I'll consent to a divorce," she said, "but we made a deal, and I'm going to see it through to the end. I won't give you up until you appear on the Broadway stage. That's the way it's going to be."

Clark wanted her to go home before she ruined his social life in Houston. Josephine suspected that he was yet again involved with another woman, but she blamed herself for insisting that he go to Texas. There was further conflict: "Clark didn't know I had turned down an offer made to him by actress Dorothy Davenport, widow of Wallace Reid," Josephine later said. "I told her that Clark was committed, but he wasn't at the time. He never forgave me for that."

It's not clear whether Clark was truly upset that his wife had lied to him or whether he used this as a convenient excuse for divorce. But his blaming Josephine for putting him on the path to New York doesn't make sense. What does make sense, however, is Josephine's never forgiving *herself* for throwing him into the arms of another woman.

Just as Franz Dorfler had been responsible for Clark's meeting Josephine Dillon, so Josephine was responsible for making her own worst fear a reality.

As the story of Clark Gable unfolds into a series of romances, no one will deny that Franz and Josephine had the greatest impact on his life. One of them would be mentioned in his will. The other would come to the rescue when his Hollywood career was almost ruined by scandal. Franz never married, and Josephine wished to be called "Mrs. Gable" for the rest of her life. Both women outlived him. And forgave him.

Clark wanted to forget the past. His success in Houston was a boost to his ego, and he liked the taste of recognition. He nurtured his social connections and took advantage of every opportunity. In the meantime, Josephine was in New York, making the rounds for him. Though Gable's name was not recognized on Broadway in 1928, his recommendation letters from Houston were an impressive introduction.

Producer Arthur Hopkins was casting for *Machinal*, a new play by Sophie Treadwell about the inhumanity of city life.

Clark read for the lead opposite Zita Johann, who wanted a well-known actor in the part. "After all," she said later, "I had turned down a contract with Universal to do this show and wasn't taking chances on a nobody." Hopkins, a soft-spoken, persuasive man, changed her mind.

Gable would remark of his arrival in New York: "All my life I had been waiting for the chance just to plant my feet on the sidewalks that all actors have walked at some time. The Houston run gave me the confidence. Some money in my pocket and a good wardrobe did the rest."

Josephine was waiting for him in New York and insisted on being present during the four weeks of rehearsal, but Clark told her to stay out of his life. "He signed the contract with Hopkins," she would recall, "got himself a good agent, and phoned to say he was through with me. I said I was going back to California and that he had better become a good actor, as he could never be a man."

Josephine left New York before Clark made his debut on Broadway; he was on his own. "We had a tryout in New Haven," he remembered, "and I lost my nerve . . . got a horrible case of the jitters. I mumbled my lines and floundered around and lost all semblance of character. I tried too hard. The next day I told Hopkins to replace me, but he was an easygoing guy and told me to relax."

On September 7, 1928, *Machinal* opened at the Plymouth Theatre in New York. "I panicked," Gable later reported, "but dear old Hopkins told me to forget the house was full of people and to play it the way we rehearsed it. The last thing Hopkins said was that he'd be sitting in the back where he always did. I felt better."

Clark walked on stage with confidence, and he gave a superb performance. "I had heard a lot and read a lot about the New York critics," he would recall, "and how they could make or break an actor. I sure wanted to meet them, from the other side of the footlights—scared to death, you understand, but anxious just the same. I wanted to see exactly what they would do to me."

The Morning Telegraph said, "Gable is young, vigorous and brutally masculine."

The New York Times reported, "Gable is an engaging adventurer who played the casual good-humored lover without a hackneyed gesture."

The New Yorker referred to him as an "excellent lover."

Overcoming her initial reluctance, Zita Johann told Clark that he was very good in his role and thereafter supported him completely. "I wasn't attracted to him at all," she would later report. "We got along well and I liked him. He insisted on walking me home, but only as far as the door. I wouldn't let him go any farther. He invited me to supper, but I declined. He had impact on the stage, but no impact on me."

During the run of *Machinal*, Gable lived the high life after the curtain went down. A cast member recalled, "Clark was always out with women. I don't know where he slept, because he was never in his own bed."

By now, Gable had established his pattern with women: running around until he landed, without even searching, in a golden nest. Women came to him without invitation or coaxing.

"We noticed there were several players from Houston in the cast of *Machinal*," Ria Langham later explained. "My brother, who was also an actor, knew them and suggested we go backstage after the play. We did, and Clark went to supper with us."

When they met, Clark Gable was twenty-seven years old; Ria Langham was forty-four.

Josephine Dillon swore that Clark and Ria first encountered each other at a society party in Texas, and that Ria moved to New York to be with him. Other accounts suggest that it was Ria's influence in Houston that made it possible for Clark to get lead parts with the Gene Lewis Players and his two-hundred-dollar-a-week salary. But Ria's daughter Jana said, "I was a big fan of Clark Gable's in Houston, but I never saw him with my mother until she introduced us in New York." This was Ria's version, too.

When *Machinal* closed in January 1929, Clark concentrated on his relationship with the aristocratic, wealthy Mrs. Langham, who was in the process of shedding her third husband. Clark blended in nicely at formal dinner parties and intimate cocktail gatherings at her elegant apartment on Eighty-first Street at Park Avenue. New York was enveloped in a snowy winter, but when the country roads were passable, Clark and Ria would make their way to her Long Island mansion, where, in an elegant smoking jacket and ascot, he would snuggle up to her beside a marble fireplace.

Society has always been lenient toward its own kind. Divorce may be a bore, but it's a common bore for the very rich. Wasn't it a damn shame, the elite whispered, that Ria and Clark were both so anxious to be free of their spouses.

"Do you suppose that Gable chap is after Ria's money?"

"So what? She's madly in love with him."

"Everyone knows that. He can't get a job, but he wears a derby and carries a gold-headed cane."

"Ria can afford him. He's terribly handsome, isn't he?"

"Breathlessly so . . . except for his gold teeth. He paints them white, you know."

"How do you like that thin mustache he grew to make himself look older?"

"Dashing, darling. Dashing!"

Ria Langham wore her auburn hair in a fashionable wavy bob; she had ivory skin and soft, dark eyes. Five feet two inches tall, she bore some resemblance to Franz Dorfler, but Franz could not have afforded Ria's elegant wardrobe: matching hat, gloves, and shoes, tweed or wool suits, an heirloom pin holding a silk scarf in place. Always groomed to perfection, Ria was stately and proper, but plain; she might have been more attractive had she not dressed so conservatively. Photographs of her, however, do not do her justice, for by all accounts she was poised, graceful, handsome, and stylish, a gracious hostess and a devoted mother.

Born Maria Franklin on January 17, 1884, in Kentucky,

Ria was raised in Macomb, Illinois, where she married William Prentiss at the age of seventeen. Four years and one son later, Ria divorced Prentiss and moved in with an aunt and uncle in Houston. She thrived on the single life until millionaire contractor Alfred Thomas Lucas, twenty-two years her senior, proposed. Theirs was an ideal marriage. Ria had two children by Alfred, lived in a palatial home, and became the belle of Houston society. After ten years of wedded happiness, Lucas died, leaving his fortune to Ria. In 1925, she married Denzil Langham; she left him two years later.

Though Ria was an active and admired member of Houston's closely knit elite, she was a homemaker, mother, and wife above all else. But Ria was not one to rough it or lower her standards to suit the occasion. The status she had attained as Mrs. Lucas was ingrained in her.

Ria was well read, fluent in the arts, and surrounded herself with people of refinement. Clark wanted to fit into her gracious life, and she was eager to show him how. Though he was usually famished after her delicate meals, he acclimated himself to the tiny portions of poached sole or filet, usually served with small round potatoes and tiny green peas that he found impossible to manage. With one gulp he'd finish a petit four, wishing he had a big portion of apple pie à la mode to dig into instead. He might have taken a long walk from Ria's swank apartment to the Automat, but . . .

Clark was broke again.

Had his Broadway debut been the end of the line? He was living in luxury, wanting for nothing, but he missed the stage. Clark was honest with Ria. Should he give up acting? He was twenty-seven and going nowhere. Was he washed up?

Ria was willing to do anything for him, say anything to make him feel better. "You're a fine actor," she said, "but surely by now you know the rewards of patience. There is something more important than your career right now."

What was that? he wanted to know.

Josephine, she reminded him. For a hundred dollars, though, he could get a quickie Mexican divorce.

Clark kissed Ria good-bye and boarded the Twentieth Century Limited for Los Angeles. Of course, Josephine already knew all about Ria Langham; she was sure that Clark had been involved with her in Houston, and he'd never convince her otherwise. "In Texas he had met the right people and I was told to step aside," Josephine would recount. She considered his wanting to marry Ria no different than his wanting to marry her five years earlier. Both women had, at least for a time, what he needed and wanted: Josephine had the knowledge to make an actor of him; Ria had the money to give him the luxury he craved.

"Clark had one of those Mexican divorce papers that he wanted me to sign," Josephine related. "I refused to enter into any such affair, knowing that the next woman he married would find herself in a legal mess if she trusted herself to Mexican marriages and divorces. So I filed for divorce in March 1929, on grounds of desertion. I could have added all the other things, but I was protecting Clark. I asked for nothing—no settlement, no alimony. *But* he would have to wait a year before the divorce was final."

Clark returned to New York, where Ria encouraged him to find work in the theater. Two months later he was offered the lead in George M. Cohan's *Gambling*, which opened in Philadelphia. Clark's first-night performance was terrible, and he was fired the moment the curtain went down. Cohan himself replaced Clark in the lead. Then came a play called *Hawk Island*; it closed in only four weeks, but the *New York Herald Tribune* said, "Gable was the most competent in the cast."

A Broadway producer who remembers Clark in *Hawk Island* said, "I don't know if it was fear or determination, but on matinée days he made the rounds in costume and makeup. He wanted to line something else up before he was out of work. My memory of him is vivid because he used white paint on his gold teeth, and sometimes the paint streaked."

After another flop, *Blind Windows*, Gable was out of work again. "At least I was in New York," he would recall, "and could go to the theater to observe other actors and study their technique. I remember Katharine Cornell in *Dishonored Lady*, Constance Collier in *The Matriarch*, and Francine Larrimore's *Let Us Be Gay*."

Without Ria, Clark could not afford this lull. His financial slump began after *Machinal* closed, but watching him stroll down Fifth Avenue with Ria, stopping for lunch at the Plaza after an exhausting shopping binge, no one would have suspected he was in debt.

Though he didn't know it at the time, Gable's last appearance on the Broadway stage was to be in *Love, Honor and Betray* with Alice Brady, George Brent, and Glenda Farrell in the lead roles. It opened on March 12, 1930, and closed eight weeks later.

In April, Clark's divorce from Josephine became final. He and Ria were married shortly thereafter, but exactly when and where remains a mystery because they did not at first admit to being man and wife. Their secretiveness might have been inspired by Clark's not surprisingly strained relationship with Josephine, who, if she had chosen to do so, could have told the press about her husband's Houston adultery, a revelation that might also have presented problems for Ria, who was having legal difficulties with her ex-husband Denzil Langham. They might have also wished to avoid insulting remarks about the seventeen-year age difference between them and Ria's living with and supporting Clark.

In later years, Clark admitted to having married Ria in 1930, but the wedding that was publicized occurred in 1931, when MGM discovered that Clark's New York marriage to Ria was not valid in California. The couple was rushed into a second ceremony that, for publicity purposes, was considered Gable's official marriage to his second wife.

When Clark finally signed with MGM, no information, with the exception of his Broadway credits, was given about where or how he had lived in New York. This was highly unusual, as MGM's publicity staff almost invariably took great pride in rehearsing the lives of the studio's major stars and describing, truthfully or not, where and how they had suffered during the bad times. Clark Gable's two years in New York were carefully skimmed, the studio emphasizing his stage appearances without providing the usual sympathy-inducing decriptions of cold-water flats and sleeping on park benches.

Married or not, Clark was a happy gigolo in New York, and for the time being, he had no intention of leaving. Life with Ria was perfect: he didn't have to worry about money in between jobs, and her optimism and constant praise meant a great deal to him as any mother figure's devotion would. But Clark nevertheless continued to make the Broadway rounds.

Then Lillian Albertson MacLoon of the West Coast Players called Clark from California. "We think you'd be perfect in the part of Killer Mears in *The Last Mile*," she said. "Spencer Tracy is playing it on Broadway. I'd like you to see it and let me know if you'd be interested in doing it out here in Los Angeles."

Clark saw the play and was in awe of Tracy—which is why he decided *not* to accept the offer. "How can I follow a guy like that?" he asked MacLoon.

She laughed. "You won't have to be that good out here."

"I'll think it over and call you back," he said.

Clark discussed the offer with Ria, who wanted him to accept. "I'll join you when the children are out of school."

"That won't be necessary. I'm sure the damn play will close before that," he scowled.

Clark refused to go to Hollywood until the last minute. It took a good deal of convincing by both Lillian MacLoon and Ria to change his mind. "I hate California," he insisted, "but the only thing that'll keep me going out there will be knowing my agent here in New York will be working like hell to find me a good play." Very reluctantly, he headed west.

Clark had only four weeks to rehearse *The Last Mile*, a powerful drama about death-row prisoners and a desperate escape attempt. He played the role of a heartless, vicious, venom-spitting killer; audiences were in awe as his big hands grasped his cell's bars, and his sunken, evil eyes screamed out for freedom and revenge. *The Last Mile* opened at Los Angeles's Belasco Theatre on June 7, 1930; it was Clark Gable's greatest triumph to date.

The *Los Angeles Times* said, "Gable literally knocked everyone in the audience between the eyes with the fierce, bloodthirsty, vindictive and blasphemous way he tore the part open."

Eventually, the show traveled to San Francisco, where Louis MacLoon, producer of the West Coast Players and Lillian's husband, ran off with the box-office receipts after a six-week run. He had left behind only enough money to pay the cast's way back to Los Angeles. Clark laughed off the whole scandal, saying he'd hitchhike, if necessary. He was and always would be just one of the boys.

The talent scouts were hounding Clark for films, but he told them, "I've got some plays lined up in New York and I'm going back." He wanted nothing to do with agents, either, until he met Minna Wallis, sister of producer Hal Wallis. Unlike other agents, Minna didn't try to fill Clark's head with big ideas; she never mentioned a screen test, and she was frank with him about the liability of his inexperience. Clark liked her refreshing approach and, considering the money the studios were paying extras in those days, he knew he'd be a fool not to give her a chance.

Minna took Clark to Pathé, where star William Boyd was making *The Painted Desert*. She did all the talking. When the casting director said that Gable fit an offered part very well and added, "I assume you can ride a horse," Clark's mouth dropped open, but Minna blurted out, "He certainly can!" The deal was closed; Clark was to be paid $750 a week. Clark went ashen; Minna took him by the arm and led him out of the studio before he fainted. "I can't ride a damn horse," he said with a dry mouth.

"So what?" she said casually. "You can learn."

Clark went to Griffith Park Riding Academy and told Art Wilson, the instructor, his problem. The lessons began. "I don't think the guy believed me," Clark recalled, "'cause I mentioned living on a farm once but it just wasn't my thing to ride. He took the small horse and me to the top of a hill and said, 'Get on and meet me at the bottom where we came from.' I hung on, and that little horse didn't know how to do anything but run. I made it, though. Every day I took lessons, and by the end of two weeks I could ride fairly well."

Minna was not only Clark's agent but his good friend. She and her mother invited him for dinner almost every night before he left for Arizona to make *The Painted Desert*.

He was still sore from his riding lessons, and he wasn't thrilled about shooting a B western in the desert. "The whole thing was a mess," he later recounted. "Something went wrong with the mine I was supposed to blow up, and it exploded just as we were chargin' in. One man got killed, and several others were injured. I got hit by falling rocks but wasn't hurt. It was depressing and very discouraging."

When Clark got back to Hollywood, Minna told him that Pathé was almost bankrupt. "We can't rely on them for a contract," she said. "But don't worry. I'm negotiating with Warner Brothers to test you for *Little Caesar*. We'll use a scene from *The Last Mile*."

"*Little Caesar?*"

"It's a gangster film."

"That's right up my alley," he said, grinning.

But studio head Jack Warner took one look at Gable's screen test and howled with laughter. "What the hell am I going to do with a guy who has ears like that?"

Clark didn't learn why Warner Bros. had turned him down until years later, when Jack Warner saw one of the actor's better films and exclaimed, "That's the guy with the big ears! I don't believe it! He must have had them fixed."

Clark brooded over his bad luck with Pathé and Warner. He wanted to take the next train back to New York, but Ria had already settled down in Los Angeles for the winter with her two children. Seventeen-year-old Jana and eleven-year-old Alfred liked Clark, who thought of himself as their friend rather than their stepfather. With little else to do with his time, he took them on picnics, to ball games, and on drives through the country.

But Clark was a loner by nature, and not one to spend his time entertaining others, particularly children. He was a hustler, a go-getter, an opportunist. He had no intention of wasting his time at garden parties with Ria and her wrinkled lady friends. He preferred talking to Minna about the movie business.

Hollywood had changed considerably in the two years Gable had been away. The silent film had been made obsolete by sound. For the major studios, sound was a new beginning, and a profitable one. In 1927, when silent films were dominant, moviegoers paid a total of sixty million dollars at the box office; in 1929 the take doubled, despite the crash of the stock market in October.

But by the time the sound film was perfected, the careers of many silent-screen stars had already been ruined.

John Gilbert's effete "I love you" in his first talking film, *His Glorious Night* (1929), made audiences laugh although his voice wasn't actually as bad as legend has it. Some old-timers claim that L. B. Mayer tampered with the film's sound track to destroy Gilbert because the two men had once had a fistfight. Whatever the actual reason, the highest-paid screen lover of the twenties was finished. Among the most famous heartthrobs who did not make the transition was Ramon Novarro, whose voice did not fit his personality.

The studios, desperate for actors, were sending talent scouts everywhere in search of good-looking men who could be nurtured and trained for the screen.

Clark was worried, and with good reason. Despite Josephine's rigorous training, his voice was still high-pitched. Minna, however, was not wasting any time, despite Clark's intense dislike for Hollywood. "I haven't made one friend here except you," he told her. "No one paid any attention to me while I

was making *The Painted Desert*—like I was an outsider and
didn't belong there. In the theater, people are friendly. We
knew and liked each other. Isn't that the way it's supposed to
be? Shit! I dreaded coming back here, and it turned out like I
thought it would. This is not my racket. It stinks!"

Ria was content anywhere, as long as she had Clark, and
she was willing to see him through another slump. He had her
loving and financial support. She left her close friends in New
York and Houston to be with him. In Los Angeles, Ria
Franklin Prentiss Lucas Langham Gable was just another wife
and mother. Her social connections meant nothing in a city of
movie celebrities. She was nudging fifty and wanted roots. She
forgot her own problems and focused on her husband.
Without Ria and Minna, Clark admitted his defeat. "My life
reminds me of riding that little horse at the riding academy,"
he said. "Downhill all the way and ending up where I
started."

Clark wasn't far from wrong. Gloria Swanson would write
in her memoirs that he had been considered for the leading
role in her 1929 film, *The Trespasser*. "Gable tested very
well," she wrote, "but he was not at home in white tie and
tails. The part called for a well-bred gentleman, but Mr.
Gable looked like a truck driver and spoke like a private
eye."

MGM's vice president of production, Irving Thalberg, had a
different impression of Clark when they were introduced by
Minna at a dinner party. Thalberg thought Clark would be
perfect for a small part in *The Easiest Way*, which was to star
Constance Bennett and Robert Montgomery. Clark played the
laundryman husband of Anita Page. The story revolves
around Gable's character's gold-digging sister-in-law (Bennett), who dangles two rich men on a string, loses them, and
ends up a prostitute.

Before *The Easiest Way* was released, it was sneak-
previewed at the Alexander Theater in Glendale to get the
audience's reaction. Viewers answered questionnaires that
would tell MGM how to revamp the film before its official

premiere. Thalberg was at the sneak and saw for himself how people reacted to Clark Gable. "I think we have ourselves a new star," Thalberg told an associate.

On December 4, 1930, Clark signed a one-year contract with MGM for $650 a week. Ria threw her arms around him and rejoiced, "I knew it would happen! Minna and I never gave up hope."

Leary of camera close-ups, Clark had his teeth capped again, compliments of Ria, who was more thrilled by her husband's new success, perhaps, than he himself was. He had yet to be convinced that a film career was what he wanted, but there would be little time to fret over it. There was no doubt, however, that Clark had landed at the most powerful studio in the world. Metro-Goldwyn-Mayer was considered the Tiffany of Hollywood. Everything was done with class, and money was no object.

There was friction between Clark Gable and L. B. Mayer from the outset, because it was Irving Thalberg, of whom Mayer was less than fond, who had discovered the future King of Hollywood. Later, Mayer even gave the impression that *he* had brought Clark Gable to MGM. Thalberg, a gentle and brilliant young man, paid no heed, but Clark resented Mayer's taking the credit.

Of Clark Gable's arrival at MGM, head of publicity Howard Strickling would recall, "I was amazed when I set eyes on Clark for the first time. He was tremendous. I was afraid of his strength, frankly—that he'd hurt someone. He never did."

Clark liked Howard Strickling at first handshake, and they quickly became friends. This was a good start for the thirty-year-old actor, who hadn't had a permanent job since his days in the lumberyard. Odd that Clark should make so close a friend so soon in his film career, especially a friend like Strickling, who had worked with Rudolph Valentino, John Barrymore, Greta Garbo, Joan Crawford, and Norma Shearer, to mention only a few. Howard was a master at handling temperamental stars. He understood them as unique

individuals with their own fears, quirks, desires, habits, and
limits. He often accompanied them on their honeymoons, and
he was frequently called upon at all hours of the night to go to
the scene of an accident, a fight, a suicide, or a murder if an
MGM player was in trouble. In short, Howard Strickling
made sure there was no scandal connected with Metro-
Goldwyn-Mayer's family. He was a man to be trusted, the
man responsible for maintaining peace. Gable later said, "If it
hadn't been for Howard, I never would have lasted."
Strickling always went to bat for his stars, and he was one of
the very few on the Metro lot who could handle boss L. B.
Mayer.

When Strickling and Mayer working in tandem were unable
to save a falling star, it was not for lack of trying. Billy
Haines, for instance, ignored Mayer's order to stop flaunting
his homosexuality and to get rid of his sweetheart, Jimmy
Shields. When incriminating blind items appeared in gossip
columns, Strickling worked overtime to publicize Haines's
love for and proposal of marriage to actress Pola Negri.
Photos of their king-size alleged wedding bed were planted in
fan magazines. But when Haines was caught in a raid at a
YMCA, there was nothing Strickling could to to save him.
Mayer fired Haines, who opened a decorating business.
With the help of industry friends like Joan Crawford,
Claudette Colbert, and Jack Warner, Billy Haines became a
very successful interior decorator in Hollywood.

6.

"Ars Gratia Artis"

Metro-Goldwyn-Mayer was the studio that had "more stars than there are in heaven." Louis B. Mayer, a former junk dealer, and Irving Thalberg, fourteen years Mayer's junior and chronically frail from a weak heart, were the driving forces that made the MGM lion roar.

Behind the scenes were the industry's top experts in diction, makeup, hairstyling, drama, fashion, set design, music, and dance. These people helped create the individual images of the Metro stars, who were groomed, pampered, tutored, protected *and* ordered about: they were told what to do, how to do it, and when to do it.

There was a morality clause in each studio contract that gave MGM the right to suspend or fire a player who did not behave in public. Of course, the clause was not enforced casually: if a star was worth millions at the box office, he could certainly get away with an indiscretion or two. It's safe to assume that Billy Haines could have been saved had MGM wanted to "prove" he'd been framed in that YMCA raid. But Billy's popularity was waning, and he was of no further use to Metro.

The morality clause could be interpreted in any number of ways, depending on various definitions of "scorn, ridicule, insult or offend." The majority of contract players were more than willing to obey the rules. Sanctioned exceptions were carefully guarded by Strickling's staff, and occasionally given a verbal spanking by Father Mayer.

MGM stars were never photographed in nightclubs until cocktail glasses and bottles of liquor were removed from the table. Actresses were provided with handsome escorts, and actors were seen with lovely starlets. The studio arranged their players' dates and provided their wardrobes and limousines. Their phone calls and mail were carefully screened. All photos, interviews, and fan-magazine articles had to be approved by the publicity department.

Stars were made or remade by the studio, and Clark Gable was no exception. In *The Easiest Way*, he looked much younger on the screen than he actually was—he was almost pretty. But Irving Thalberg was not particularly interested in what Gable looked like in the film—nor that his look was inappropriate to his tough-guy role—because Clark Gable had yet to be molded into an image, a distinctive personality like no other. Six days a week, Clark reported to the studio at 6:00 A.M. to pose for pictures, work out in the gym, learn how to fire a gun, control a fishing rod, and perfect his stance on a horse. Howard Strickling later commented, "We were showing him how, but Clark was a natural. He loved to fish and hunt, but hated posing for pictures and being interviewed. Clark wanted to learn. He wanted to be a star. He wanted to be a success. So he cooperated and always had a smile. The guy had charm. He really did. I saw it the first time we met and so did Irving Thalberg."

Clark was concerned about his protruding ears and wanted to know how to face the camera at the appropriate angle so as not to call attention to them. He was self-conscious about his hands, too. Cameramen who worked with him in the early stages of his career said that Clark learned quickly how to de-emphasize his shortcomings. If Josephine taught him how to walk and talk and Ria showed him how to be a gentleman, it was MGM's dream makers who put the pieces together into one stick of dynamite. His past and present were glamorized, though there was little the studio could do to glamorize Ria, who would hardly be the public's concept of Mrs. Clark Gable. Of course, her social status was an asset, when she was mentioned at all, but on the rare occasions when she and Clark were photographed together, Ria looked, unfortunately, like his mother. Fan magazines said she was a "bit" older than he; when pressed for how much older, they'd admit to only ten instead of the actual seventeen years.

In any event, MGM preferred their male stars to be single and available to the millions of women who might convince themselves they had a real chance, or at least enough of a chance to buy a ticket at the box office and dream of what could be. So in later years, Ria would be referred to as Gable's "sponsor," in much the same way that Josephine had been called his "teacher," with no emphasis on or even mention of marriage.

But his past caught up with Clark—or perhaps it was Clark trying to catch up with his past—when he heard that Franz Dorfler had moved to Los Angeles. He found out where she was living, called her, and the two frequently had dinner at her apartment. Franz did not try to hide her love for him, and Clark took advantage of this, as he always had. "You're the only friend I have in this town," he moaned. Franz, who as yet knew nothing about Ria, asked why Clark's marriage to Josephine had ended. "She did a lot for me," he admitted, "but she was forever preaching, and too domineering. She was always right. Guess I can't be with any woman for too long."

Clark gave Franz the impression that Hollywood had not

accepted him. "I'm a very lonely guy," he said with head bowed. Franz asked about beautiful Constance Bennett, who had appeared with Clark in *The Easiest Way*. "She didn't know I was alive," he complained.

Franz was caught in Clark's web once again. They saw each other often; then he dropped her, as suddenly as he had back in San Francisco. Franz read about Ria in an article and was devastated once again. Clark hadn't lied, exactly. He had merely omitted the facts.

Clark had proved himself in *The Easiest Way*, and it was now time to cast him opposite a well-known actress. "I was terrified the first time we met," Joan Crawford would recall, "because he was a stage actor, and that gave him an edge. Their training is far superior to the studio's drama school. I thought he'd make me look bad without trying and that he'd laugh behind my back."

But Clark was the one who was really petrified: "My God," he moaned to Howard Strickling, "she's a major star! She knows everything there is to know about making movies. I'll feel like a jerk, and probably look like one, too. I hope she doesn't laugh in my face." Gable had more to be concerned about, too. Crawford was married to Douglas Fairbanks, Jr., her in-laws were Mary Pickford and Douglas Fairbanks, Sr. Ria would have sold her soul for an invitation to the Fairbanks' home, Pickfair, Hollywood's Buckingham Palace, and an "audience" with America's Sweetheart and her swashbuckling husband. The star on Joan Crawford's dressing room door was impressive enough, but as one of the royal family, she attended the exclusive and elegant dinner parties at Pickfair. Crawford had guts and took it in her stride. She fought for the roles she wanted—and for the men she wanted.

Crawford eagerly gave interviews because she wanted to give her loyal fans a monthly treat in the movie magazines. She was one of the few stars who did not rely completely on the publicity department. She could talk around her past cleverly. She said her career as a dancer showed her the things she should avoid. Crawford admitted that she had been snubbed in Hollywood at the outset, and that she'd taken to snubbing back. "I'm still learning how to differentiate between being used and being needed," she commented. Yes, she learned a lot about men, but how else could she learn to judge for herself the one man she could trust—the man that could satisfy her, heart and soul?

Crawford was a poetic sob mistress, a passionate harlot, and a tough broad. But she represented everything that a Hollywood star was meant to be. Her enemies bowed to that.

While Joan Crawford reveled in her heavenly marriage to Douglas Fairbanks, Jr., she met Clark Gable on the set of *Dance, Fools, Dance*. Crawford's character, a rich girl who falls into poverty during the Depression, becomes involved with a racketeer, played by Gable. "In the scene where he grabs me and threatens to kill my brother," Crawford said later, "I felt such a sensation, my knees buckled. He was holding me by the shoulders and I said to myself, 'If he lets go, I'll fall down.' He had more animal magnetism than any man in the world, and, goddam it, every women knew it."

In 1931, Gable was featured in twelve films—three with Joan Crawford. "We were attracted to each other instantly," she recalled. "Instantly! I had what he wanted and he had what I wanted. Call it chemistry, call it love at first sight or physical attraction. What's the difference? The electricity between us sparked on the screen, too. It wasn't just acting. We meant every damn kiss and embrace. God, we both had balls in those days!"

Joan Crawford was born Lucille Fay LeSueur on March 23, 1905, in San Antonio, Texas. Her stepfather owned the local opera house, where she learned to dance. She didn't know her real father, who had abandoned the family when Lucille was a baby. Her mother succeeded in driving away Lucille's stepfather, too. "I never forgave my mother," Crawford would recount. "When she got married again, her husband didn't want me around, so I was sent to boarding school. Sounds fancy, but it was hell. I had to clean all the rooms, do

the cooking, and take care of the younger children. When I
didn't do something just right, I was beaten with a broom-
stick."

At the age of sixteen, Lucille left school to work in a
department store, where she wrapped packages until she had
saved enough money to go to Chicago, Detroit and New York,
where she appeared as a dancer in *Innocent Eyes* in 1924.
Spotting her in the chorus line, an MGM talent scout gave her
a screen test, and she went to Hollywood. After her fourth
movie, a fan magazine used her in a "rename the star"
contest, and Lucille LeSueur became Joan Crawford.

In 1928, she happened across a script called *Our Dancing
Daughters*, swiped it, and went to producer Hunt Stromberg.
Crawford begged for the lead and got it. "This was a Clara
Bow part," she later said, "a flapper, wild on the surface, a
girl who shakes her wind-blown bob and dances herself into a
frenzy—a girl drunk on youth and vitality."

Crawford lost twenty pounds in Hollywood to accentuate
her cheekbones, and to emphasize her already athletic-looking
shoulders, she became the first film actress to wear shoulder
pads on the screen. Her bust was firm and abundant, her hips
were slim, and her legs have been described as "fantastic."
She had big blue eyes, full lips, and a classic nose that
blended better with her other features as she matured.

Crawford was twenty-one when she met the charming and
brilliant Douglas Fairbanks, Jr., who introduced her to good
books, the theater, and proper manners. They eloped to New
York on June 3, 1929, and quickly became Hollywood's ideal
couple. Two years later she said, "Doug didn't want me to
work. Isn't it strange? A man marries a woman for certain
qualities and then wants to change them."

He socialized and she worked. In 1931, Fairbanks made
$72,790. Crawford earned $145,750. She was disappointed by
his lack of professional enthusiasm and bored with the titled
rich who lounged around the couple's swimming pool while
she worked at the studio twelve hours a day. "We were never
alone," she complained.

The passion between Joan Crawford and Clark Gable during the filming of *Dance, Fools, Dance* was limited to the set. She gave her all and he reacted like a man, but still, he did not want to offend this top star by taking anything for granted. Besides, MGM kept him so busy he had no time to flirt. He still had her perfume in his blood when Jean Harlow's flowed through his nostrils during the filming of *The Secret Six*, in which Gable played a reporter investigating gangland killings, but if he had any ideas about Harlow, they were forgotten when he was rushed into *The Finger Points*, with Richard Barthelmess, Fay Wray, and Regis Toomey. Gable portrayed a crime boss and sported a derby. *Film Daily* said, "Gable again scores with his fine voice and magnetic personality in *The Finger Points*."

When Clark had the time to have a quiet dinner with Ria, he was learning lines in a new script. "I got another one coming up with Crawford," he told her, "called *Laughing Sinners*. Johnny Mack Brown had the part of a Salvation Army captain who saves a cabaret dancer—that's Joan—from suicide. They finished the damn movie and decided to replace Brown with me."

"Why would they do that?" Ria asked.

"Dunno. The brass didn't like Brown, I guess."

"Why you, darling?"

"Joan asked for me."

"How very odd. She's famous and you're a novice."

"Trying to give me a break, I guess. . . ."

"In that case," Ria said, smiling, "perhaps we should show our appreciation by taking Miss Crawford and her husband out to dinner."

Clark scowled. "I don't think so."

"But, darling, don't you want to meet the family?"

"The family?" he mumbled, engrossed in a script.

"Mary Pickford and Douglas Fairbanks. Pickfair appeals to anyone with an ounce of class."

"That's why it does *not* appeal to me, my dear."

Laughing Sinners had originally been called *Complete*

Surrender. Sneak-preview audiences had not been impressed, so Irving Thalberg decided to replace leading man Johnny Mack Brown. Crawford asked for Gable, who was quickly fitted into a Salvation Army uniform and, in the reshot, retitled film, saved Crawford's soul. Reviews were mixed, but Crawford fans, forever loyal, flocked to see the film. Her torch song, "What Can I Do?—I Love that Man!", was sung on-screen to actor Neil Hamilton, but it was meant for Clark.

When Crawford found out that Gable was going to work with her again, she was at the studio early. "Clark had presence," she said. "I knew when he walked on the set. I didn't know what door he came through, but I knew he was there. I was falling into a trap that I warned young girls about—not to fall in love with their leading men. Boy, I had to eat those words, but they tasted very sweet."

Crawford made her desires known to Gable during the filming of *Laughing Sinners*, and their long affair began without interference or suspicion. Her Doug was busy with his ritzy friends, and Ria understood her husband's working late.

Crawford told this author how she and Gable were united by their pasts. "We were unhappy kids and had to bum around for food and friends. We were nobodies transformed into somebodies by Hollywood, and married to people who tried to change us. We asked for it, bought it, and had to live with it, but we were scared shitless. He was relieved to know I felt the same, even though I was a star and he wasn't. God, how we talked and sometimes cried. Could we hold on to what we had achieved? Would the public see through us?

"Clark was the first one I could talk to candidly in Hollywood. He never—and I mean *never*—talked about me [publicly]. It took me a long time after he died to open up and tell the beautiful truth. In the beginning, he told me it wasn't his thing to get involved with a married woman. I was the exception. Later, we were both in and out of affairs, marriages, and divorces, but we outlasted them all."

Gable felt more confident shooting his next film, *A Free Soul*, despite his having to make love to Norma Shearer, Irving Thalberg's wife. Gable played a tough racketeer again, and Shearer was a spoiled rich girl who likes rough sex and gets it from Gable. At one point, Shearer makes fun of Gable's bad manners and flashy clothes. Outside the bedroom, she jabs, he's not good enough for her. He knows that, but when she says it once too often, he sweeps her up in his arms. She coos, but he throws her on the couch, making sure she stays there while he tells her what a rotten brat she is. Shearer stands up to protest but is pushed back down—"where you belong!" Gable tells her.

Audiences loved it. Here was a poor guy trying to make a crooked buck (who cared during the Depression?), and here was a rich dame who changed her furs as often as she changed her stockings. She wanted a good time, and he obliged. That was fair enough, but her tearing apart his position in life gave him every right to shove her around. Gable rebalanced the tipped scale of the sexes, too long weighted toward respectful, ardent swains pursuing maidenly heroines. *A Free Soul* was the beginning of Gable's rough-diamond image—the man who was raw and crude but had a heart of gold. If Gable couldn't get his woman, he either booted her in the fanny or carried her over his shoulder to the cave she would never leave and would never want to.

Men cheered, women swooned, and MGM raised Gable's salary to $850 a week. He wasn't a star yet, but he was the most talked-about movie actor in the country. Thousands of letters were addressed to MGM about "the guy who slapped Norma Shearer." People often exaggerate when they're enthusiastic. Gable *doesn't* slap Shearer in *A Free Soul*, but the nonexistent blow remains a legend to this day.

The lovemaking between Gable and Shearer in *A Free Soul* was so passionate that rumors spread about a romance *off* the set. Thalberg did not appreciate such talk about his wife, but the publicity was worth it. He had never seen Norma react to any of her leading men as she had to Gable. At one point, Gable remarked to director Clarence Brown that Shearer wasn't wearing any underwear during the shoot. Was she trying to tell him something? he wondered. "She must be one hot lay if she can behave like that with the cameras turning." It was common knowledge that Thalberg's heart condition meant a limited sex life for Norma, and she showed her frustration in Gable's arms. In response, some critics lauded a new and vibrant Norma Shearer. True enough, although *A Free Soul* is chiefly remembered now for establishing Gable's Hollywood stardom.

Come Oscar time, *A Free Soul* was nominated for best picture, Shearer for best actress. Neither won, although Lionel Barrymore walked off with his only Oscar for his portrayal of Norma's father. Barrymore was superb in a courtroom scene defending Leslie Howard, the nice guy in his daughter's life who killed bad boy Gable.

Hanging up his Salvation Army uniform and slick gangster duds for a chauffeur's livery, Gable was hastened into *Night Nurse*. Costar Joan Blondell remembered, "When he showed up the first day, Barbara Stanwyck and I had to sit down. There was something about him that was overpowering." In this melodrama, Gable is in on a plot to slowly starve two children to death and steal their inheritance. But a nurse (Stanwyck) hired to care for the children's rich, drunken mother gets wise to the scheme and confronts Gable, who socks her on the jaw. This time, he *does* hit the heroine. Eventually, the whole mess is straightened out, and once again, Gable gets his comeuppance in the end.

Ahead of its time, *Night Nurse* was condemned by critics as lurid and "unpleasant in theme." But MGM wasn't thinking about taste: they simply wanted to put Gable in as many films as possible to build up his image and keep his face before the public. Irving Thalberg said, "Gable's the man every woman wants and the man every man wants to be."

Minna Wallis watched and listened, and then made her move. She wasn't satisfied with Gable's raise in salary. Letters were *pouring* into MGM about her client, she reminded Irving Thalberg, and though the executive had nothing but praise for

Gable, he refused Wallis's request for more money. Fine, she said: there were other studios that wanted Gable, so he and Wallis would simply ride out the last five months of his contract. L. B. Mayer blew his stack, but he knew that Gable was a potential box-office draw, and Thalberg reluctantly agreed that the actor had that indescribable "it" worth millions. "All right," Thalberg told Wallis, "we'll give him five hundred dollars more a week, which will be put in trust." This was a ploy to make sure that Gable did not sign with another studio.

"Deal," Minna said, figuring Ria was paying the bills anyway, and recognizing that MGM was being tough but fair.

Gable next played a crooked gambler in *Sporting Blood*, with Madge Evans. *Time* magazine described it as "Horses and nonsense." And it was, but there was something significant that flashed across the screen: STARRING CLARK GABLE. No more "with," or "and." From now on, even when Gable's films were run-of-the-mill, he would rate top billing.

Skeptics said Gable had no competition as a leading man; all his rivals had retired, died, or been eliminated by the microphone. But had Valentino lived, had Gilbert's voice pleased the public, could either have held his own against the rugged, dimpled grin of a fellow who expected dames to light his cigarettes and open doors for him?

In most films of the early thirties, it was the man who chased the girl. With Gable it was the other way around, and though the men he played were often cruel, everyone wanted him to get the girl at the end. When he didn't, MGM had to kill him off.

It's hard for us today to realize the popularity of movies in this era, before television and videotapes. Most people went to "the picture show" at least once a week. Fan magazines sold out the minute they hit the stands, and movie stars set the pace for national trends in clothes and grooming. Gable thrived in this film-crazy world, and the timing was right for a new kind of star. And Josephine, by the way, was proven wrong once and for all. Gable never had a serious problem in

the movies with the pitch of his voice, "unless I get lazy," he
admitted.

While Ria kept herself busy looking for a house befitting a
movie star, Howard Strickling explained to her how the studio
system worked. Until Clark was firmly established, he said, it
was best that the public did not know too much about his
personal life. Mystery is part of the attraction. Once Clark's
name blazed from the marquees and remained there long
enough for moviegoers to want more, Strickling would see to
it that Ria was included in a few of his public appearances.
Meanwhile, she must be understanding and patient.

Before Strickling and his staff had a chance to work their
plan, MGM found out that Clark Gable was not legally
married to Ria Langham. To head off a scandal, Ria and
Clark were quickly and privately remarried in a civil
ceremony on June 19, 1931. As they were leaving the
courthouse, the "newlyweds" were attacked by reporters
armed with incriminating questions. Had Clark met his bride
in Houston? Or was it in New York? Why had they married
again? Had they divorced in the meantime and decided to give
it another try? Was Ria *the* Mrs. Langham of Houston and
New York society? Why had they eloped? Were they going on
a honeymoon? How long? Where?

Ria broke down completely. She pleaded with reporters not
to print anything about the wedding. She had three children,
she said. "What *about* your children?" the newsmen asked.
With that, she began to cry hysterically, sobbing her pleas
while MGM officials helped her into a waiting car. Clark,
expressionless and composed, followed. Ria was mortified at
having lost control. What a dreadful introduction to the
press. What else would they say, other than that Mrs. Clark
Gable lacked poise and self-confidence? What had happened
to the sedate and serene socialite? Where was her class and
presence of mind? "I'll never forgive myself," she wept.
Howard Strickling told her not to grant any interviews. "Be
firm and friendly and blame it on me," he said with a smile.

Ria was to be included, briefly, in press releases, the publicity department decided, but only when absolutely necessary; and there were to be none of the expected "at home" pictures of the Gables in fan magazines. Strickling thought that if the studio played Ria down, Gable's fans might forget she existed. MGM hoped so, anyway. And not being forced to appear with Ria in public gave Clark the freedom he wanted.

Strickling planned Gable's publicity campaign very carefully—feeding reporters just enough to get rid of them, but not enough to satisfy them. When the news leaked out that Greta Garbo wanted Clark Gable for her next film, *Susan Lenox—Her Fall and Rise*, the press dug deep into his past to find out for themselves who and what he was. They didn't have far to look.

Josephine Dillon Gable, a nobody six months before, was suddenly besieged by callers pounding at her shabby front door. She was cooperative until she realized that the newshounds wanted to know about more than her acting techniques that had worked magic for Hollywood's newest star. When they asked for intimate details of her marriage to Clark Gable, she was appalled. But the question that echoed in Josephine's ears, haunting her day and night was: "Why are you so poor if your ex-husband is so rich? Why does he have everything while you have nothing?"

Josephine tried to interest the press in stories about the bony kid she had sent to a farm for his health, about the hours of Shakespeare and deep breathing, about her determination to make him a success. Newsmen yawned. "Did you live together in Portland?" they asked. "How about Los Angeles? Was he a great lover? Are you still in love with him? Do you feel used? Cheated? Forgotten? Deserted?"

The press brought the hurtful truth to the surface for Josephine. She had tried to bury her feelings and leave Clark alone. But that would be impossible now that she had been made a fool for all the world to see.

Two months after Clark's "official" marriage to Ria

Langham, L. B. Mayer received a letter from Josephine Dillon Gable, who, in a polite and dignified manner, stated her plans to sell her story about her life with Gable. Because Clark had never made an effort to repay any of the money she had spent on him, and because she was now financially desperate, there was no alternative. Hers would not be a pretty sketch of Gable, she hinted; it might endanger his career. Moreover, the press was making it impossible for her to live a normal life. She was trying to make a go of her drama school, but the publicity was ruining her.

MGM wasted no time settling the matter. If Ria was a disappointing image of Mrs. Clark Gable, Josephine was even further below expectation. Mayer, long since used to threats and demands, deemed the situation annoying but not serious and acted as go-between when Gable, who felt that his ex-wife had humiliated him enough by contacting MGM, flatly refused to negotiate with Josephine.

Even Strickling was unable to calm Gable. Finally, though, the star was convinced to ward off adverse publicity by settling. Gable, who was close with his money, offered two hundred dollars a month, provided Josephine did not talk about him to the press. She signed the agreement while Gable fumed. Would he never be rid of her? Would she never stop using his name to bind them together?

Gable was under a great deal of pressure at this time. He had done nine films in just a few months, sometimes filming two at a time, and the troubles with Ria and Josephine added to his anxiety. Then he read in a newspaper that he was to play opposite Greta Garbo in *Susan Lenox—Her Fall and Rise*. Minna Wallis had assumed he'd be thrilled to know that Garbo had requested him, and Howard Strickling had taken it for granted that Gable would consider *Susan Lenox* the chance of a lifetime. Instead, Gable was livid.

His reaction was no doubt a blend of vanity, anger, and fright. Vanity because a film with Garbo was a *Garbo* film, no matter what. Anger because no one had consulted him. Fright because Garbo was the biggest star in the world. Her beauty, superb acting technique, and concentration were unequaled. Gable felt intimidated before shooting began, and in the completed film he is scarcely himself: his voice is, for once, shrill and forced, his movements awkward and stiff.

Garbo played a girl on the run from her brutal father, who wants to marry her off to a rich farmer. She meets and falls in love with Gable, but flees again when her father pursues her. In the end, she is reunited with Gable and they live happily ever after. *Variety* wrote, "Teaming with the great Garbo, of course, marks the peak of Gable's vogue."

There were no sparks between Gable and Garbo, though their clinches are the most believable scenes in the picture. Throughout, she dominates the screen. Gable later said that he was uncomfortable working with Garbo, who walked out on the film six times because she didn't like the script. But, he said, "Every actor should work with her. She gets what she wants and goes home every day at six, regardless of what is going on. It's in her contract." Gable would harbor the memory of Garbo's privileged status until the time came when he could demand a similar clause in *his* contract. Yes, indeed, he was very impressed with the power Garbo wielded.

In the summer of 1931, Ria and Clark moved into a rented house on San Ysidro in Beverly Hills. Their next-door neighbors were Fredric March and his wife, Florence Eldridge, and Pickfair was just around the corner. Though Ria was delighted to be able to entertain at last, Clark resented having to dress up and make small talk after working long hours six days a week. Dining with Norma and Irving Thalberg was no less of a job than seeing them every day at the studio, he complained; and Pickfair was stuffy and Fairbanks *père* a bore. In addition, Clark didn't think that sitting in a breakaway chair and landing on the floor was funny. Fairbanks was an inveterate practical joker. Nor did he appreciate picking up what he thought was a salad fork, stabbing a green, and finding out his fork was made of rubber. Then there was the hot-seat-at-the-dinner-table trick, once played on an elegant lady who'd been seated next to Clark.

"Didn't you feel anything?" Fairbanks asked, laughing, after the woman had endured the prank with no more reaction than a smile.

"Well, yes," she replied, "but I thought that's how you felt sitting next to a movie star."

Mary Pickford scolded sweetly, "Oh, Douglas, you've done it again!"

Evenings at the Goldwyns or the Selznicks and weekends at William Randolph Hearst's San Simeon castle were no more amusing to Gable, but at least Hearst's mistress, actress Marion Davies, also invited Joan Crawford and Doug junior to her parties. Crawford and Gable would settle for any occasion to see each other. Crawford confided the details of her affair with Gable to her dear friend Billy Haines, who in turn told her about his 1925 encounters with the young actor. And he teased Crawford about Gable's long-ago affair with Pauline Frederick.

"She's old enough to be his mother," Crawford snapped.

"So is his wife," Haines said with a laugh.

"How do you know so much about Clark and Pauline?"

"Oh God, Joan. It was common knowledge that he was at her mansion every night after the play."

"I've been told I resemble Pauline."

"But are you as exciting in bed?"

"I'm the best!"

"So I've heard."

"Besides, I'd like to look like Pauline when I'm her age, and still be able to lure young bucks into my bed."

"Me, too," Billy said, smiling.

7.

For the Love of Joan

hough MGM did not allow
Gable to meet the press by himself, he had nevertheless
developed a friendship with Hearst reporter Adela Rogers
St. Johns, who moonlighted as a Metro screenwriter. She had,
in fact, written *A Free Soul*. When this bright and
sophisticated lady met Gable in 1930, he was learning to ride
a horse for *The Painted Desert*. St. Johns was touched by
Gable's humility and transfixed by his handsome masculinity.
He in turn knew that he could always count on her as a friend
and loyal supporter.

When Josephine Dillon tried to take credit for Gable's
talent, St. Johns wrote articles denying Dillon's claim and
describing the actor's ex-wife as "an old lady schoolteacher."
Their feud continued because Josephine refused to see St.
Johns, who did her best to protect Clark. As was the case with

virtually every woman who knew Gable well, rumors arose about St. Johns' relationship with the star. Fifteen years after Gable's death, St. Johns was asked during a TV interview whether she had loved him. "There's a difference between loving and being in love," she replied. And what about the rumor that she'd had his baby in the thirties? St. Johns smiled. "What woman would deny that Clark Gable was the father of her child?"

Joan Crawford told me that St. Johns had coached Gable during the filming of *A Free Soul*. "If it hadn't been for her," Crawford insisted, "he wouldn't have been the actor he became. He was ever grateful. You wouldn't know it to look at her, but Adela had more men than I did. She used to cover up for Clark and me so often. That's the kind of friend she was."

Gable did, however, have an intimate relationship with St. Johns, who allegedly said that she was not stimulated by his lovemaking unless she kept her eyes open: "Looking up and seeing Clark Gable's face did it for me."

Adela Rogers St. Johns was a respected, well-liked, and brilliant journalist. When this author spoke to her about MGM, Taylor, Turner, and Crawford, she was fascinating company, never at a loss for words. She carried the conversation with funny stories about Hollywood, her admiration for Valentino ("Rudy") in *Blood and Sand*, Robert Taylor in *Magnificent Obsession* and Clark Gable in *A Free Soul*.

"They were such fine young men and so vulnerable. Well, maybe not Gable. He was such a big guy. Imposing, really. Acting can often be a liability in the movies. I think if he had tried to be anyone other than Clark Gable, it wouldn't have worked out. L. B. Mayer referred to his kind as a 'personality.' Clark's dialogue was written for films as he would express himself off the screen. For example, he called everyone 'babe,' and we wrote that into his dialogue. Also 'Listen' and 'Oh, yeah?'. Clark needed Howard [Strickling] because he always clashed with Mayer and couldn't depend on Thalberg."

Though reliable sources say there was never anything serious between Gable and St. Johns, they remained friends and lovers for many years. Like Gable's two wives, St. Johns was plain, diminutive, and at least ten years older than he.

Though Gable knew he was on the verge of success in 1931, he was not a happy man. Ria would recall that he was quiet, moody, cranky, and sullen at home. She had no idea what he was thinking, except when he expressed his concerns about money. "I'd feel better," he said, "if I had twenty thousand dollars in the bank." Ria had supported him for three years and was not about to pinch pennies. Nor did she intend to use her own money to build Clark's bank account.

Gable had no idea how long he would last in films. Being typecast as a leading man was dangerous, he said. The public was fickle. One day they'll stand in line to see a star, and the next they won't come at all. "I worked three months straight without a day off," Gable said at the time. "If this is what it's like to be a success, when will I have a chance to enjoy it?"

The answer: while shooting *Possessed* with Joan Crawford. She played a poor factory worker; he was the influential lawyer-politician with whom she falls in love. The excitement on the set when the cameras were not rolling was even more intriguing and romantic than the film. Several weeks into production, Hollywood was buzzing about the Gable–Crawford affair. They lunched together in her dressing room, held hands on the set, stared at each other with longing, and did their love scenes with sizzling passion, as if no one else were around.

Crawford said she cried every morning on her drive to the studio and wept all the way home. She feared for her future, she feared for her marriage, and she feared for her love for Gable. "I no longer enjoyed parties and small talk," she confided. "There were times I wanted to get into my car and race through the night." Sometimes she took drives along the ocean and found passing contentment. Occasionally she met Gable on the beach. Despite his own concerns, he sat listening to her for hours.

Ria had noticed a sudden change in her husband. In the past, the breakneck pace of going from film to film without a break had caused Clark to drag himself to the studio every morning and begin studying his script as soon as he got home. He was like a new man while filming *Possessed*, however.

Crawford said that she and Gable discussed marriage. "I suggested it jokingly, but Clark was quite serious. He thought we should both start divorce proceedings right away."

When *Possessed* was released, moviegoers were thrilled by Gable and Crawford's screen romance and clamored for more. L. B. Mayer was happy to accommodate them, but he had no intention of condoning an affair between a married ex-lumberjack and an ex-flapper married to a Fairbanks.

Ria was accustomed to gossip about her husband, but the rumors of an affair with Crawford were too intense to dismiss, and the clues indicated the worst. She kept her mouth shut and her eyes open. Ria did not attempt to discuss the obvious with Clark. He'd deny it or keep quiet. Ria knew that confronting her husband would be playing into Joan Crawford's hands. And above all, Ria did not want to drive her husband away. She knew that Hollywood was a world of extramarital affairs that often ended as quickly as they started. Making movies sometimes meant falling in love with one's costar. The motto in Hollywood was "Don't marry your leading lady until you've made at least one more film."

Ria decided to take her children to New York for a while, and she cleverly asked MGM to make the arrangements, thereby making clear that she was traveling as *Mrs. Clark Gable*. Though Ria had been catered to in the past, the attention she received as a movie star's wife was unprecedented. On the train east, Ria signed autographs and made herself available for interviews. She was divinely happy living in Hollywood, she told reporters, but had business in New York. Clark was so busy making one film after another, you know. She missed him terribly, but she wanted to see the new plays on Broadway because Clark was so interested in what was happening in the theater since he'd given up the stage to make films.

En route, Ria more than made up for her hysterical performance at the courthouse after she and Clark were married. She was cooperative, smiling, cheerful, and gracious. By the time she arrived in Chicago, the whole country knew precisely who Mrs. Clark Gable was. She had a marvelous time basking in her husband's fame, dropping his name at restaurants, department stores, box offices, and hotels. If Ria was worried over having left her husband alone with Joan Crawford, no one would ever have known it from her optimistic demeanor.

Gable considered his wife's trip a separation, and he saw Joan Crawford day and night. Fairbanks was also having a very active social life. Everyone involved was doing nicely until L. B. Mayer decided it was time to step in. He summoned Gable to his office.

Sitting behind his massive desk on a built-in platform, Mayer stood up and shook hands with Gable, who was forced to look up at his boss during their conversation.

"You did a fine job in *Possessed*," Mayer said. "How do you feel about it?"

Gable shrugged.

"The role's a serious one. . . . That's what I was referring to. . . ."

"Are you trying to say it's not for me?"

"Not at all. I was pleasantly surprised."

"Is that all?"

Mayer motioned for Clark to remain seated. "I haven't finished." There was a moment of silence before the little man behind the big desk announced his distress about Gable's performance offscreen: "Louella Parsons is ready to break the news in her column. She wants a scoop, but we can't let that happen, can we?"

"If you mean my divorce . . . Well, it has to come out in the open sometime."

"Does it?" Mayer asked harshly.

"Doesn't it?" Gable spat out.

"Have you any idea what we had to contend with when your first wife made herself known publicly? What I had to go through personally to shut her up?"

"I'm paying for it."

"If you think two hundred dollars a month is payment due, my friend, you're all wrong. You're getting away with murder. If she had been a smart woman, Josephine would have gotten herself a lawyer, put you on the front page of every newspaper in the country, and be living in a decent neighborhood right now. Fortunately, I was able to reason with the lady, but I don't think the present Mrs. Gable is going to be that innocent and stupid."

"That's *my* problem."

"As long as you work for MGM, it's my problem, too. Get that through your head."

"I'm not going to live with a woman I don't love."

"Why not?" Mayer asked.

"That's fairly obvious, isn't it?"

"Suppose you spell it out so I'll understand."

"I'm in love for the first time in my life."

"Who's the lucky lady?"

"Joan Crawford."

"She's no lady!" Mayer pounced.

Gable clenched his fists and glared.

"I know her better than you do, Clark, and she's good for only one thing. What about the others you've been sleeping with?"

"Joanie and I are in love, and we intend to get married."

"I'll extend my congratulations now, because when *Possessed* is finished, you and your Joanie are fired."

Clark smiled. "I don't think we'll have a problem."

"Neither of you will work for any other studio in Hollywood again. I can make 'em and I can break 'em. It's as simple as that. Don't put me to the test."

"I don't understand you. . . ."

"When you were a kid, did you understand your father?"

"No, and I still don't."

"That's all in the past, my boy. MGM is your family now, and I'm your father. If you can't abide by the rules, get out."

"What about people in love?"

"They don't exist in this town," Mayer announced. "I won't waste your time discussing the exceptions, because you're not one of them. You like women, and none of them can keep you in one bed for very long, and that includes Joan. The wife you have now is superior to anyone in Hollywood. She's been very understanding. Think about it."

"I don't have to," Gable exclaimed. "My marriage is over."

"You'll get on the goddam telephone and beg your dear wife to come back. You miss her."

"She won't buy it."

"It's what she wants to hear," Mayer said, "and her heart will take over from there."

"Then what?" Gable asked.

"You'll take her out in public and pose for pictures with a loving smile on your face."

"Then what?" Gable repeated.

"It will convince everyone that your affair with Crawford meant nothing. Maybe it never existed at all. You don't have to say anything to Joan. I'll do it. She and I speak the same language."

Gable called Ria in New York; she immediately began packing to come home. But before he had a chance to see Crawford, Mayer had already summoned her to his office. He praised her on her fine performance in *Possessed*. She cooed, "L. B., how sweet! Clark and I are good together."

"To put it mildly."

"What's next?"

"That depends on you." Mayer smiled.

"Are you giving me script approval?" she asked eagerly.

"I have the script, but I don't need your approval. It's *Grand Hotel*."

"Holy shit! With Garbo and Barrymore?"

"*If* you stop fucking around with Gable."

"Oh, that. . . ."

"How can you sit there and be so casual . . . as if he took you out for an ice-cream soda!"

"L. B., calm down! Clark and I are in love, that's all."

"*That's all?*"

"I mean . . . it's not shady or dirty. It's real and beautiful and—"

"You're talking to me, Joan. Do you want a list of girls he's been laying?"

"If he married me, that would stop," she said.

Mayer pointed a finger at her. "Give him up or you're fired, Joan. Give him up or you'll be blackballed from movies. That goes for your cocksman, too."

Crawford sobbed bitterly. Mayer waited for the appropriate moment, then got up from his desk to sit beside her. "You were MGM's first creation," he said softly. "A delightful, blessed experiment. You're a vision. An actress. A lady."

"I'm so confused," she sobbed. "So *very* confused."

"Take my advice," Mayer said, dabbing her cheeks with his handkerchief. "I warned you about Fairbanks. I wanted to get you out of that one. Goddamn it, Joan, I can't let you get hurt again. I'd rather destroy you myself than see you ruined by scandal."

Crawford moaned and wept. Mayer handed her the script of *Grand Hotel*. "Read this and you'll feel better," he said. Crawford read a few pages, then leapt from her chair and screeched, "My character's a fuckin' whore!"

Mayer pretended to be shocked. "I prefer to think of her as a stenographer with ambition."

"Who goes around screwing sick old men?"

"Why don't you discuss it with your girlfriend, Billy Haines?"

Joan grabbed her purse and the script and glared at Mayer. "Don't you ever lose?"

"Pray that I don't. When I lose, everybody loses."

Joan and Clark were shaken but not defeated. Mayer was

very, very serious, make no mistake about it. Ria and Doug were suspicious, and Hollywood columnists had their pencils sharpened, but the lovers found a way to be together.

Crawford later said, "What Mayer would never believe is that Clark and I gave each other the courage to go on and laugh at our defeats and mistakes. The next few months were very hard for us. Very tough. Nothing went right."

After *Grand Hotel*, Mayer sent Crawford to Catalina Island to film *Rain* for United Artists. Crawford hated her performance as Sadie Thompson and commented afterward that she hoped the film would be destroyed. *Rain* was a flop, and Crawford went into Hollywood seclusion. Doug, meanwhile, dashed off to Mexico for some fun.

Gable's last movie in 1931 was *Hell Divers*, and he hated every minute of it. Telling of two naval pilots (Gable and Wallace Beery), it was not a movie that interested women. Beery received top billing and praise from the critics. Gable was ignored.

Clark's nerves were frayed, his mood was black, his outlook was sour. He found solace in gin and long talks with Minna Wallis. "I can't take it anymore," he told her. "I'm tired and have nothing to show for it. Not much different than working on the farm—up before dawn and home after dark, but MGM's making hay, not me."

Ria was back in California, just in time to see her husband through this crisis. Clark had lost almost twenty pounds. He was nervous, depressed, and ready to crack. "I'll go along with anything you want," Ria said, but before he had time to think it over, MGM scheduled him to costar with Marion Davies in *Polly of the Circus*. Mayer spoke to Gable personally about the assignment. "We're doing this as a favor to my dear friend William Randolph Hearst."

"Who will do anything for his mistress," Gable said, scowling.

"Do you have a problem with that?"

"No," Gable mumbled, looking over the script. "But I'm not playing a goddamn priest!"

"Hearst will give you a bonus. He's a very generous man."

"I won't play the part."

"How about a goddamn minister?" Mayer fumed.

Clark grimaced. "The story is terrible. . . . Pretty trapeze artist falls in love with clergyman, who's dismissed for marrying a circus performer, who pleads with the bishop, who reinstates minister. It stinks."

Mayer spoke to Hearst, who spoke to his writers, who tried to oblige Gable, who walked off the set and hid out in Palm Springs while Minna Wallis tried to make peace. She told Mayer it wasn't only the picture that was bothering Gable. "Clark wants more money," she said.

Mayer raged, "You tell him if he's not on the set tomorrow morning, he's suspended without pay and he'll never work again at this studio or any other in Hollywood!"

Wallis phoned Gable. "L. B. means it," she said. "You'd better come home."

"The hell I will!" was the reply.

Gable would surely have been suspended had it not been for the intercession of Marion Davies, who with her famous stutter cried to Hearst, "I'm v-v-very h-h-h-hurt. Please d-d-do something."

Hearst convinced Mayer that Gable deserved a raise, and on January 22, 1932, Gable signed a two-year contract with MGM for two thousand dollars a week, thanks largely to Davies, who was "s-s-so h-h-happy to have C-C-Clarkie back." As might have been expected, *Polly of the Circus* was awful, but Mayer, who needed the backing of the powerful and influential Hearst newspapers, was satisfied.

The thirty-five-year-old Davies was deemed off limits to her leading men because of her liaison with Hearst, but the fun-loving blond ex-Ziegfeld girl *was* discreetly naughty on occasion. She lived in Santa Monica, while Hearst preferred his massive castle, San Simeon, built on top of La Cuesta Encantada, "The Enchanted Hill," a couple of hundred miles north of Los Angeles.

Hearst, worth at his acme some three hundred million

dollars, was thirty-four years older than Davies; their famous affair lasted more than three decades. He worshiped her and she sincerely loved him, but Davies found it difficult to resist flirting with men like Gable. Still, there was rarely any gossip about her, except that which concerned her presence on an ill-fated weekend cruise in 1924 aboard Hearst's 280-foot yacht, *Oneida*. Also along for the trip was producer–director Thomas Ince, whose sudden death that weekend has never been explained. (Ince was conveniently cremated before an autopsy could be performed.) Newspapers controlled by Hearst attributed Ince's death to "acute indigestion," but at least one witness claimed that Ince had been shot in the head. Had Hearst found Marion Davies with Ince and taken revenge? Or had a blameless Ince been mistaken for Charlie Chaplin, whom Hearst suspected of making love to his mistress?

Another guest, Louella Parsons, managed to get off the yacht without being noticed by the press, and denied ever after that she'd even been on board. Hearst gave her a lifetime contract with his newspapers shortly after the incident.

Ince's wife claimed she was at her husband's bedside when he died. If so, why did Hearst then set up a sizable trust fund for her?

Many Hollywood insiders accepted the theory that Hearst shot Thomas Ince, and perhaps that was enough to scare off any actor thinking of trying his luck with Davies; but Clark Gable was not just any actor. He frequently accepted Davies's dinner invitations to her beach house after work on *Polly of the Circus*, and the two would stroll arm in arm down Ocean Front Walk to the Venice Amusement Park, where they'd ride the roller coaster.

Davies, a heavy drinker, had discovered a devoted companion in Gable, who found solace in sharing the bottle with a genuinely friendly and radiant woman. Precisely when she gave him a piece of very valuable property in Palm Desert isn't recorded. Money always bought silence where Davies or

Hearst was concerned, and their names were *never* linked in the newspapers; to whisper about Marion Davies was to defy a man more powerful than the president of the United States.

Gable's cozy dinners with Davies were certainly romantic, but he also appreciated her delicious sense of humor and lightheartedness. There were so few women in Hollywood like Davies, who always had a smile and was forever poking fun at herself. Gable never let her forget that she'd once told everyone in a screening room that he looked like boxer Jack Dempsey. "You were sitting with Thalberg," Gable recalled, "and you said I couldn't play a society boy, remember?"

"Yes." Davies blushed. "And Irving said you were going to be the b-b-biggest sensation in the world."

"I heard him." Gable smiled. "But he'd never say it to my face, 'cause I'd ask him for another raise."

"What kind of a woman do you think an actor should marry?" the reporter asked Clark Gable.

"The kind of woman I'm married to—my wife. I am the star, and Ria is my wife. I could not and would not be married to an actress, because one professional ego is enough in my house. Neither would I want to marry some sweet young thing many years my junior. A younger girl wouldn't know what it's all about. She'd be jealous, suspicious, and resentful."

This was a portion of an interview for *Modern Screen*, and the MGM publicity department wrote the text. Gable is pictured with Ria at an exclusive nightclub. He wears a tuxedo, and has a gardenia in his lapel. Ria is decked out in a low-cut satin gown with flowers bunched at the cleavage and a white fur draped over her shoulders. One hand on her hip, she is a lady of confidence.

The article went on to say that Gable considered his wife a wise, sane, and balanced woman who did not believe rumors that he was stepping out and "having an affair with a star." In the upper left-hand corner of the page containing the denial was a photo of Gable and Joan Crawford embracing. Printed underneath the photo: "Mrs. Gable never visits the set to check up on Clark's big clinches, such as this one with Joan Crawford. Mrs. Gable is content to remain in the background, serene in the knowledge that she is first in his private life."

Gable wasn't the only husband in Hollywood who was trying to prove how happy he was with married life. Another article, "Four Rules of Married Love," credited to Douglas Fairbanks, Jr., was a shocker in the thirties.

"I don't think married people ought to be conscious of the fact that they're married," Fairbanks supposedly wrote. "They ought to live in sin, so to speak. . . . I mean that after marriage you should keep up the relationship that existed before marriage—to keep on courting your wife. Why take her for granted?"

And what were the four rules for a happy marriage?

"Be honest with yourself. Preserve the essence of comradeship. Never hurt the person you love. Never take anything for granted."

Crawford and Gable still managed to see each other, but now refrained from any discussion of divorce. She said later that they were smothering from lack of satisfaction in their marriages and careers. Both were caught up in the web of Hollywood society, which Crawford described as "emptiness." She cried on Gable's shoulder, and he leaned on her for comfort. Maybe they would make it—if, that is, there was a way to be together without rocking the boat.

There wasn't.

"Joan, dear, why do you persist in hurting me?" Mayer asked with tears in his eyes.

She responded, casually, "Clark and I are just friends now."

"Then make new ones."

Crawford knew that Mayer's tears were fake; she cried, too. "I haven't been the same since *Rain*."

"What you need is a nice long vacation."

"Well . . ."

"A second honeymoon with Douglas."

"Who?"

"Your husband."

"Where?"

"New York and Europe. Compliments of MGM. You have reservations on tomorrow's train east, so run along home and pack."

"I want to say good-bye to Clark first."

"He's having a script meeting with Jean Harlow."

"Harlow?"

"Very sad what happened," Mayer said, wiping away a tear. "John Gilbert was going to star with her in *Red Dust*, but he's back on the booze, so I'm replacing him with Gable."

"You son of a bitch!"

"She's a bride, Joan. Just got married to Irving's friend Paul Bern."

"He's not man enough to stop that harlot from massaging her tits in public!"

"Wait until you see what I have planned for you and Douglas." Mayer beamed. "Your fans will make you feel like a million. Leave it to me. And when they're not kneeling at your feet, you and Doug will be sipping the finest champagne and nibbling on caviar in the very best hotel suites in the world."

The Fairbankses' second honeymoon was, it turned out, a series of public appearances—too many fans and too little time alone. Mayer may have arranged for Clark Gable to fall in love with Jean Harlow, but his plans to save Joan Crawford's marriage failed.

8.

Superstar

*J*ean Harlow, known affectionately at MGM as "The Baby," was born in 1911 in Kansas City. She attended private schools; at sixteen, she eloped with a wealthy Chicago boy but the marriage didn't last. Harlow moved with her Christian Scientist mother and stepfather, Marino Bello, to Los Angeles, where she worked as a movie extra in films.

Howard Hughes took a chance on her in his three-million-dollar 1930 film, *Hell's Angels.* Harlow was terrible as the British girl who seduces the entire Royal Flying Corps, but the film was a success and Hughes put Harlow under contract for $250 a week. After several loanouts to other studios, MGM bought her contract from Hughes for sixty-thousand dollars two years later.

Harlow detested underwear but gave in to panties. "I'll

never wear a bra," she told the press. Harlow rubbed ice cubes on her breasts and nipples to make them stand out. She usually did this before facing the camera, to the delight of any male who was nearby. Harlow walked, talked, and dressed like a sexy dish, but she wasn't often seen in public with men. "All they care about," she said, "is getting their hands underneath my dress."

Harlow was at the peak of her career in 1932. Her choice of husband shocked MGM, but she had made up her mind to marry a man twenty years her senior—MGM executive Paul Bern, short and balding, with a Hitler mustache. Known on the lot as Father Confessor, Bern was a gentle man with a brilliant future as Irving Thalberg's assistant.

He began his courtship of Jean Harlow by asking her to lunch. Harmless enough. Then dinner, but no passes in the backseat of his limousine. Harlow was impressed that he asked her to the opera but skeptical when Bern invited her to his apartment. Harlow expected the worst, but he played classical music, talked about good books, and did not insist on a good-night kiss. "At last I've found a guy who isn't just interested in my body," she said after accepting Bern's marriage proposal. He was in desperate need of this sex goddess. His sanity was at stake. On their wedding night, the impotent groom, who had the genitals of a young boy, expected a miracle to happen. If Jean Harlow couldn't arouse him, who could?

Irving Shulman wrote in his 1964 biography, *Harlow*, that Bern failed to consummate the marriage, got drunk, and beat Harlow across the back with a cane. To avoid scandal, they decided to remain together until MGM felt it was the appropriate time to divorce.

It was Bern who recommended Gable for *Red Dust*, but he soon regretted it. When he found out that Harlow had refused to wear a bathing suit during her on-screen bath in a rain barrel, he stayed away from the studio. Bern was well aware of Gable's reputation with women, and now Jean was flaunting her nude body in front of the notorious lover.

If Joan Crawford and Clark Gable had sizzled *on* the screen, Gable and Harlow were even more passionate *off* the screen. They were constantly kissing, hugging, giggling, and whispering in a corner. Director Victor Fleming said they were like two kids getting ready to play doctor. Gable found in Harlow a little girl who loved her body and found pleasure in sharing its beauty. She liked to tease men she could trust, and most assuredly, she could trust Gable to be discreet. An affair with Harlow, Gable knew, could be far more dangerous than his liaison with Crawford.

Did Harlow and Gable have a fling? Most likely. Everyone on the set of *Red Dust* was rooting for it to happen. Costar Mary Astor recalled, "They seemed to be wrestling all the time. He was holding on to her or Jean was hanging on to Clark, pulling, tugging, and romping . . . always touching each other."

A close friend of Harlow's said that the actress wasn't particularly interested in sex: "She was married at sixteen and described her wedding night as 'messy.' Jean was practically a virgin, because she didn't play around. She had a tough life. She supported her mother and stepfather, who was rumored to have molested her. Jean adored Gable, and she needed him. He was a devil, but a harmless one with her . . . harmless in the sense that he'd never hurt Jean. I think they shared an intimacy that was therapeutic."

On Labor Day weekend, 1932, Paul Bern supposedly shot himself in the head with a .38 caliber pistol. His nude body was found by the Berns' gardener, who called MGM. Jean Harlow had spent the night of Bern's death at her mother's after a quarrel with Bern.

So much has been written about Bern's death, and much of it is false. In his effort to protect Jean, L. B. Mayer was partially responsible for the confusion. But crucial evidence has surfaced in recent years. The so-called brief suicide note, in which Bern apologized for a "frightful wrong" and referred to the evening before his death as "only a comedy," may not have been written on the night he died. It was not dated and was, in fact, found in a diary by L. B. Mayer, who used it as Bern's written farewell to Jean.

Bern's brother clashed with Mayer over the impotency theory and announced that Paul had had a common-law wife, Dorothy Millette, who would testify that Paul had had no sexual deficiencies. But a few days after Paul Bern's death, Millette's body was found floating in the Sacramento River. Letters from Paul were found in her room.

In the midst of this confusion, police informed Mayer that they were going to charge Jean Harlow with murder. In desperation, Mayer ordered Bern's doctor to tell the police about Bern's underdeveloped genitals. With this "evidence," and the coroner's report that the bullet wound and powder marks clearly indicated suicide, the police did not arrest Harlow. Bern's bigamy prompted some scandal, but Mayer was greatly relieved that Harlow re-emerged as an innocent victim. Bern had apparently picked a fight with his wife to get her out of the house, knowing that Dorothy Millette would shortly arrive for a showdown.

One recent theory is that the deranged Millette shot Bern. Neighbors remembered a veiled woman arriving at the Bern house in a limousine that night and saw her sitting by the pool with Bern. When she left, the limousine screeched off into the night at top speed.

Gable and Marino Bello were on a fishing trip the day of Bern's death and did not find out about it until that evening. Gable didn't see Harlow until the funeral, which was a nightmare. As the mourners were asked to pay their last respects to Paul Bern, the open coffin was put onto an electrical contraption that swung it around and tilted it up; it was a dreadful moment as Bern's corpse appeared to sit up for a last look at his friends.

Gable got blind drunk that night.

Harlow returned to the set of *Red Dust* and Gable's consolation. He made her smile again, helped her through each day, and was with her when the news broke that Dorothy Millette had committed suicide.

Gable's devotion to Harlow got her through the filming of *Red Dust*, which told of a prostitute (Harlow) who is stranded on a rubber plantation in Indochina with Gable. Their romance is interrupted when an engineer (Gene Raymond) and his wife (Mary Astor) arrive. Gable has a torrid affair with Astor but turns noble at the end, and Harlow stays with him in the jungle. (If the plot sounds familiar, Gable also starred in the 1953 remake entitled *Mogambo*.)

Red Dust was one of Hollywood's biggest money-makers of 1932. Audiences loved the nude Harlow bathing in a rain barrel and telling Gable, "Scrub my back." When *Time* magazine criticized the film's brazen immorality, the lines at the box office got longer. *Red Dust* was labeled the epitome of sexual daring. (Thanks in part to the runaway success of *Red Dust*, MGM was the only Hollywood studio that did not lose money in 1932. In fact, their profit that year was eight million dollars.)

Meanwhile, Gable had taken it upon himself to discontinue his monthly payments to Josephine because she had violated their agreement by granting interviews. To get even with him, Josephine talked to anyone who would listen. She chose her words carefully, but the message was there. She insisted that without her guidance, Gable would not have become a big star. For a time, Josephine was getting more press coverage than her ex-husband. Her "open letters" to Gable in a fan magazine commented on his acting technique, offered advice on how he might improve his voice, and suggested that he not "play up to the girls on the screen."

MGM would not allow Gable to respond directly, but they thought it might be helpful if he met the press briefly. Reporters were disappointed when Howard Strickling told them not to ask anything of a personal nature.

What makes a star? they wanted to know.

"It isn't looks," Gable began, "and it isn't experience. It isn't ability, because everyone knows there are stars who can't act worth a damn. The public makes the stars, but they don't know what they want. You can't explain a damn thing in this business.

"When you get to Hollywood, you find yourself in lots of chains of accidents. If it turns out all right, you're a star. If you're a gambler, move to Hollywood. You want to be a movie star? Maybe you'd like it, and maybe you wouldn't like it. You might not be happy at all."

What set him apart from the ones who failed?

"Damned if I know," he said with a shrug.

Why did he avoid the press?

"I'm paid to work, not think."

How did he like his new house?

"It's a hell of a lot better than the dump I lived in before," he replied.

That was the last interview Gable gave for a long, long time. Mayer demanded that he not talk to reporters under any circumstances. Gable snapped, "It's all bullshit anyway."

With his new raise in pay and no longer feeling obligated to pay Josephine, Gable felt he might finally save that twenty thousand dollars' worth of security. Ria, however, eager to entertain the upper crust, was on a spending spree. Recognizing that it was MGM and not Clark who had wanted her to come home—everyone in Hollywood was aware of it, too—Ria set out to prove that her marriage was authentic. She wanted to redecorate the house, buy a new chic wardrobe, hire servants, and plan elegant dinner parties. Above all, it was crucial that Mrs. Clark Gable live like a star's wife.

Joan Crawford had returned from Europe and made up her mind to divorce Douglas Fairbanks, Jr. She kept her decision to herself, however, and made the social rounds, including dinner with the Gables, in the company of her husband. Surprisingly, Joan and Ria got along well and often had lunch together, Joan always making sure to introduce Ria in public as "Mrs. Clark Gable."

Gable, meanwhile, was having many casual flings, more than he could count; still, he stayed away from girls who talked. When asked why he had turned down an offer to spend an evening with a particularly sexy actress, he replied, "Because she has a big mouth. I know I'm not the greatest in the sack, and she'd blab it all over town."

Gable's next picture was *Strange Interlude*, adapted from the Eugene O'Neill play. Norma Shearer played a woman, married to an impotent man, who falls in love with the family doctor (Gable), becomes pregnant, and allows her husband to think the child is his own. Though Shearer hopes to run away with Gable, her husband has a stroke, and the thwarted lovers find themselves tending him.

Strange Interlude was well received by both moviegoers and critics. Gable thought his role too serious, not even one smile in the whole film, and he expressed his feelings to L. B. Mayer, who said, "Hell, you're knocking up Norma in this one instead of knocking her in a chair. They'll love it!"

If was for *Strange Interlude* that Gable first grew his mustache, which afterward became a crucial part of his virile image.

Gable's last movie in 1932 was *No Man of Her Own*, for which MGM loaned him out to Paramount. Gable, like most of the MGM players, did not appreciate being traded off to another studio like a piece of merchandise, but Marion Davies had wanted Bing Crosby, who was under contract to Paramount, for her film *Going Hollywood*, so in return, Paramount got Gable. Gable's *No Man of Her Own* leading lady was Carole Lombard, who was, at the time, married to actor William Powell.

No Man of Her Own was a fluffy movie about a big-time gambler (Gable) who marries a small-town girl (Lombard) on a bet. She finds out the truth and leaves him. He reforms, and she takes him back. The movie made money because people enjoyed light comedy during the bleak days of the Depression.

As for Gable and Lombard, they worked well together, and Gable enjoyed his costar's frequent pranks. Energetic and ambitious, Lombard was difficult to catch, but Gable, for the

moment, wasn't chasing. As a parting gift, she gave him a ham
with his name on it, and Gable grinned broadly for the
photographer as Lombard presented it. Later, she told her
cronies at Paramount, "I'm one leading lady he didn't
seduce!"

MGM Christmas parties were always a blast once Louis B.
Mayer wished his "family" a happy holiday and departed.
Writer Anita Loos referred to it as "the Orgy," adding that it
was "given to cement morale, break down class distinctions,
and keep workers happy throughout the coming year."

Musicians, electricians, stars, secretaries, and executives
drank bootleg booze, embraced, danced, and watched stag
films in the screening room. Christmas Day was a bleary haze
of "What happened?" and "Where am I?" Some wanted to
forget, while others couldn't remember. (Gable was perenially
asked not to attend the annual celebration for fear that the
studio's female employees might tear him apart.)

At the 1932 party, Irving Thalberg enjoyed himself more
than usual and subsequently had a near-fatal heart attack.
The MGM contractees sobered up fast, fearing life under
Mayer without the gentle and understanding Thalberg to
make peace. For stars like Gable, who had been discovered
and groomed by Thalberg, a Mayer régime would be
especially tough going.

Norma Shearer barred all visitors from her husband's
hospital room. She stood in front of the door, arms
outstretched, glaring at an enraged L. B. Mayer, who left
determined to replace Thalberg should he attempt to return to
MGM.

Though Mayer had vowed that his son-in-law David O.
Selznick, who had worked at MGM in the twenties, would
never return to the lot, Selznick was brought in during
Thalberg's convalescence to supervise an independent production unit. Gable could not relate to Selznick; Selznick, in
turn, did not understand Gable's image. This was made
apparent when Gable was cast opposite Helen Hayes in *The*

White Sister, a sad tale about lovers separated by war. In the film, told that Gable is dead, Hayes enters a convent and takes her vows. Gable returns and abducts Hayes, but quickly realizes he's too late. As he bids farewell to her at the convent, he's shot and dies in her arms.

The White Sister received excellent reviews but failed to entice moviegoers. Clark complained to Ria that he could not make good films with saintly women.

"L.B.'s in your corner, darling," Ria offered.

"Or backing me into one" was Clark's retort.

"David O. Selznick seems like a nice chap. By the way, what does the 'O' stand for?"

"It stands for nothing, my dear. He put it in there to give his name rhythm, to be like Mayer with his goddamn 'B.' Which stands for 'bastard,' far as I'm concerned."

"Shh. Not so loud, darling."

"We moved into this house to get away from my fans. Now I can't talk because the guards and servants might hear me."

"This is going to be a divine year," Ria suddenly exclaimed. "President Hoover says Prohibition will be over, and . . ."

"And *what*?"

"Your father's coming to live with us!"

If Clark had a few too many drinks the day Will Gable appeared at the smart Colonial house in Brentwood, he would need many more in the coming months. The MGM publicity department claimed that Gable had been searching for his father a long time, which is undoubtedly untrue. Will, broke and in bad health, made first contact, and Ria took it from there. She may have meant well, but she also needed an ally. And what better ally than a father-in-law?

Filling in the void of Clark's inattention, Ria took charge of Will. She renovated a section of the house for his comfort, helped him select a new wardrobe, and made sure he had a thorough medical checkup. Clark had no choice but to offer his father a home with all the fringe benefits: cook, maid, butler, flashy cars, and a star's discarded expensive clothes.

On the work front, L. B. Mayer decided to put Clark into
Hold Your Man, another film with Jean Harlow. Gable plays
a con artist, and Harlow is a hussy. He accidentally kills her
boyfriend and allows her to take the rap. But when Gable
finds out that Harlow is carrying his baby, he attempts to
marry her and is arrested. In the end, mother and son are
waiting for Gable at the prison gates.

London Film Weekly wrote, "Being themselves is the job at
which Harlow and Gable have made good. . . . It is as a pair
of charming toughs, hard as nails, and superbly imprudent,
that we have come to know them on the screen. . . ."

Once happy-go-lucky, Harlow and Gable were anything but
on the set of *Hold Your Man*. There were few giggles and no
wrestling. Both had become bitter about Hollywood. Harlow
complained that her mother and stepfather were spending
money faster than she could earn it. Gable was drinking and
maudlin. "I'd like to get out of this business," he said.

"So would I," Harlow sighed.

"You know we haven't one chance in hell to save a buck,
don't you?"

"Save?" she laughed. "I'm in debt!"

"Don't let them getcha, baby."

"Look who's talking."

"A sucker," he said, watching Jean pinching her nipples.
"One big sucker!"

Joan Crawford disliked Harlow intensely. They were not
invited to the same parties, nor did they share friends.
Crawford felt that Harlow was a threat to her, both with
Gable and with MGM. "That frustrated bleached-blond vamp
with the loose-hanging cow tits is bedding him down,"
Crawford said. "She's a frustrated tart." To add insult to
injury, Harlow's latest reviews had been superior to Crawford's. That one was a comedienne and the other a dramatic
actress didn't matter: if there was only one MGM, there was
only one MGM queen. (Garbo was not in competition. She was
in a class by herself.)

Gable wasn't interested in Crawford's opinion of Jean

Harlow or willing to be dictated to by her. While Crawford was busy buying Ria hostess gifts, Gable was busy reveling in the freshness of Jean Harlow.

Gable, who was known to keep bootleg gin in his dressing room, drank plenty of it to get through *Night Flight*, a David O. Selznick project starring Lionel and John Barrymore, Helen Hayes, Robert Montgomery, and, in a small role, Myrna Loy. Critics complained that there were too many stars doing nothing: Gable sits in the cockpit throughout the film until he's killed when his plane goes down, while wife Helen Hayes sits home waiting for him.

Night Flight was a nothing film, and its star-studded cast could not save it. Gable would never trust Selznick's judgment again. "Such a waste of money, time, and talent," he complained.

When Clark read his next script, *Dancing Lady*, he was upset: his part was small and unimportant. How could Selznick *and* Mayer have put their heads together and come up with such a dud? Though costarring with Joan Crawford was a plus, Gable considered Franchot Tone's part far superior to his own. He also complained about getting second billing to Crawford. "So what?" she said. "I have to dance with some puny guy named Fred Astaire, who's making his film debut. I gotta help him out, not to mention some new singer, Nelson Eddy. Why do I always have to baby-sit?"

In *Dancing Lady*, Clark plays a stage director, Crawford is a dancer, and Tone is a rich playboy who tries to lure her away from Gable. The movie was lively and made money for MGM. But Fred Astaire, whose role was scarcely more than a cameo, wanted nothing more to do with Metro. "When I die," he said, "just bury me in a Crawford–Gable picture!" (Astaire returned to MGM, a star, in 1940.)

After Joan Crawford announced her divorce, she reminded Gable of their plan to marry. "I kept my part of the bargain," she said. "When are you getting off your ass?"

"Ria will destroy me," he growled.

"She's loaded!"

"Your divorce won't be final for a year. Besides, I don't want to hurt the kids."

"*Her* kids?"

"I've grown very fond of them."

She laughed. "You don't even know their names."

"Joanie, I know Ria will take me for everything. And now my father's spongin' off me. The timing's all wrong for me to get a divorce."

"In that case," Crawford sighed, "we'll have to wait. . . ."

In June 1933, Gable was hospitalized for what was reported to be an appendectomy. During his two-month absence from the lot, his rotten teeth were removed. While he waited for his gums to heal before being fitted for dentures, Gable joined the Masons. Later, stories circulated that he would not go to bed with a girl if anyone in her family was a Mason. Several close friends of his swear this is true.

Gable returned to work in September 1933, immediately demanding that Mayer give him better pictures. "Do you hate Irving so much you'd ignore common sense?" Gable bellowed. "Seems to me you're blackballing every one of his projects."

"If you're so faithful to Thalberg," Mayer retorted angrily, "maybe you'd like to work in one of his films."

"It has to be better than the shit I've been shoveling."

Mayer *had* to punish Gable now, and he knew precisely how to do it. L.B. called Harry Cohn, head of Columbia Pictures. "I owe you a favor," Mayer said. "How would you like Gable for *Night Bus?*"

"I thought we agreed on Robert Montgomery," Cohn said, chewing on his cigar.

"He turned it down like every other actor in town. Gable's been a bad boy, and I'd like to show him who's boss."

Night Bus, eventually retitled *It Happened One Night*, was to be directed by Frank Capra, who had been working with Thalberg. But after Thalberg's heart attack, Mayer told Capra to take his scripts back to Columbia Pictures. Harry

Cohn wasn't thrilled by "that bus thing," but he gave in when the title was changed.

Casting Gable as the newspaperman lead was only half the battle. Capra needed a good actress for the part of the bratty runaway heiress. Myrna Loy and Margaret Sullavan flatly refused. Miriam Hopkins said, "No! Not if I never play another part." Constance Bennett told Columbia to go fly a kite.

Capra considered canceling the project, but Cohn declared, "We can't do that! Mayer wants Gable to know how it feels to be in a Poverty Row picture. We *have* to do that bus thing!"

Capra decided that the heiress role needed revising, so writer Robert Riskin softened the script, making the female lead less tough, less unsympathetic. Then Capra made an offer to Claudette Colbert, who was packing for a vacation in Sun Valley. "No, no, no," she said, then added, "However, if you double my salary and promise I'll be finished in four weeks, okay."

Capra thought fast. He had a budget of only $325,000, and Colbert wanted $50,000. "It's a deal," he said, trying not to choke on his words.

Colbert said at the time that she took the part for the money, but she had another reason, too. "I'd never met Gable," she later admitted, "but like every other woman in the country, I thought he was divine. I jumped at the chance to work with him every day and get paid for it."

Gable couldn't have cared less about Colbert or anyone else at Columbia. He stormed home and told Ria, "I'm getting out! I'm quitting!"

"What about your contract?" she asked.

"Let them sue me!"

"If it will make you happy, go ahead. But maybe you should do the movie and give it all you've got. See what happens, and then make a decision about your career."

Gable had a few bourbons and headed for the door. "I have an appointment with the director," he said, "in the bowels of this city."

"Where's that?"

"Gower and Sunset," he raged, slamming the door behind him.

"Oh, how awful," Ria sighed.

In his office, Frank Capra heard Gable climbing up the creaking stairs and watched with horror as the star lurched in. "He was plastered!" Capra would recount. "Loaded. He slurred his words and belched loudly every once in a while. He said, 'What's the poop, Skipper, 'sides me?' Before I could answer, Gable spurted out, 'That son of a bitch Mayer! I always wanted to see Siberia, but, damn it, I never thought it would smell like this!' And he belched again."

Capra offered to go over the story line. "Or would you like me to read it to you?"

"Buddy," Gable slurred, "I don't give a fuck what you do with it."

As Gable made to leave, Capra didn't think he would see the actor again. "But he put the script under his arm and stumbled out singing 'My Gal Sal' like a drunken sailor," Capra said. "I told Cohn that Gable probably wouldn't report for work, which meant his career in films was finished. But Clark did show up, and cooled down. He had a lot of fun. We all did."

Capra forged ahead against all odds. His tools were weak—one bourbon-slugging leading man and a prissy leading lady who refused to show her leg in the film's now-famous hitchhiking scene. Replaced in the car-stopping close-up by a model, Colbert viewed the shot and changed her mind: "My legs are better than hers!" she said. During the shoot, there was plenty of ad-libbing and last-minute changes, which gave the finished film an almost unprecedented relaxed and buoyant quality.

It Happened One Night was filmed in four weeks. Colbert finally headed for Sun Valley, telling her friends, "I just finished the worst picture in the world." The film opened at Radio City Music Hall on February 23, 1934, with no fanfare; after one week, the movie was released to theaters all around the country. It was a smash! *The New York Times* thought

Gable was at his very best. *London Film Weekly* urged, "Go and see for yourself how Capra and his players conjure amusement out of practically nothing."

Gable was subsequently approached by Capra's agent, Berg-Allenberg, the biggest and best in the industry, and decided to sign with them. Minna Wallis did not try to stand in Gable's way, though she was, of course, deeply hurt. She said afterward that she let Gable go because she adored him, and though Berg-Allenberg insisted that Wallis's "letting go" cost them twenty-five thousand dollars, she denied this. Gable continued to see Wallis, who, friends say, was one of his "dear loves."

Gable's women had one common attribute—the bond of secrecy. He has proven to be the rare exception to all that is traditional. If he was unique on the screen, he was incomparable in his personal life. His protection by MGM defies that of the president of the United States, with the exception of John F. Kennedy, whose sexual prowess burst forth like the Fourth of July until the fireworks bored us. Perhaps it was the quantity and not the quality that lacked impact. Both men had charisma—an indefinable magnetism that was not easily forgotten. Unlike Kennedy, Gable was not a rooster. He did not hit and run. He was faithful to all his women at the same time and willing to come back for more. Gable was also a warm lover, who made all his affairs important.

Women made themselves available to him, so it's fair to say he did not take advantage of them. Though Minna Wallis was his agent, this did not make her any less a woman. She understood Clark's need for a prestigious agency to handle his career. Most assuredly it would be an insult to compare her to Josephine, but both made personal sacrifices for Clark, and neither shared his curtain calls.

If in 1932 Gable's life story had been sketched on a blackboard, with the names of those who had helped him along the way written beside it, at this stage we might see him holding an eraser that he used at his own convenience for personal and professional satisfaction. With hate in his heart, Gable might have wiped the slate clean.

9.

Superstud

able returned to MGM
assuming his "probation" was over. It wasn't. Mayer cast him
in the role of a dedicated intern in *Men in White*, with Myrna
Loy. "No," she said, years later, "we weren't lovers. He
wasn't my type, even though I found him extremely attractive.
I heard he was always on the make at the studio, snapping
garters left and right."

In her memoirs, Loy said that she met Gable for the first
time in 1933, when Minna Wallis offered her a ride home from
the Mayfair Ball with the Gables. After Wallis was dropped
off, Gable began snuggling up to Loy in the backseat of the
limousine, with Ria sitting right there. "When he escorted me
to the door and I was unlocking it," Loy wrote, "Clark bent
over and gave me a 'monkey bite.' It left a scar on my neck
for days." Loy shoved him off her front porch into a hedge.

He laughed, waved and got back into the limousine.

Gable was cool to Loy during production of *Men in White*, in which she portrayed his heiress fiancée, who resents Doctor Gable's dedication to medicine. Gable finds solace in the arms of a student nurse (Elizabeth Allan), who dies aborting his baby. On her deathbed, Allan pleads with Loy to forgive the affair.

Gable did not talk to Loy off camera. "He developed a pretty serious thing with Elizabeth Allan," Loy recalled. "He was punishing me. That Dutchman just wasn't taking no for an answer."

Men in White was a good film, and Gable was applauded by the critics. *Motion Picture Herald* said that Gable had done a remarkable job of acting. *Film Daily* commented, "This is the beginning of a new Clark Gable. Watch for him in a new kind of hero roles."

MGM sent Gable on his first publicity tour to promote *Men in White*. This was an experience never to be forgotten. Yes, he had already made twenty-two movies, not counting his extra work. Yes, he was the guy who put Norma Shearer in her place and socked Barbara Stanwyck on the jaw. Yes, he was the guy who kissed Jean Harlow so passionately that the screen ignited. But Clark Gable had never met his public face-to-face. He had been hungry, broke, married, divorced, remarried; he had made love to the most beautiful women in Hollywood and taken many of them to bed; he had a head shaped like a sugar bowl, a wife who was seventeen years older than he, and three stepchildren. Yes, moviegoers knew all about Clark Gable, but they had never seen him in the flesh.

For the record, every major star was introduced to the American public in New York City this way. Elaborate arrangements were made by the studio and the publicity grossly exaggerated, but unless one has been mobbed and kissed and grabbed and poked and stripped of buttons and cuff links and sleeves and shoes and hunks of hair, one cannot possibly imagine the terror and the reality of what one has become during the long months locked up inside the studio walls with one's peers. Suddenly the doors of the outside world open, a billion eyes stare, and a billion hands reach out to touch their idol, their god.

Gable was completely bewildered and confused. There was no adjusting to the public's adoration of him after his exile by Mayer. The contrast was too startling—the true meaning of it all was beyond his comprehension. Ria accompanied her husband to New York, but she was kept out of sight for the most part and rarely mentioned in press releases. Never alone, Gable had little time to think—to put who and what he was in perspective. On a merry-go-round of premieres, press fêtes, dinner dances, cocktail parties, Ria's society dos, and MGM's gala affairs, Gable had no peace. He was mobbed while walking down Fifth Avenue, browsing in department stores, and dining in restaurants. He attended the theater, but the audience watched him instead of the show. People stared at him everywhere, asked for his autograph, fainted, cheered. He smiled until his dimples ached and laughed until his dentures wobbled as hard as his knees.

Women, women, women everywhere, and they were all his!

Ria hoped that this proof of his popularity would lift his ego, put him in a tolerable mood for a change, and reduce his drinking, but the imbalance of his worth increased his hatred of Mayer and set him on a binge of women and bourbon. Ria tolerated his disappearances because he always came back, in need of her understanding and sound advice. She was the mother figure who listened and never let him down when he was wounded and discouraged. She did not allow his attention to other women get her down. More than once, she walked into their New York hotel room and caught Clark kissing and fondling a girl; Ria pretended to be nearsighted. Her worst fear was a serious romance, à la Crawford. Ria was over fifty and had no illusions about her ability to compete with lovely young women who would settle for just one hour with her husband, but she also knew that it would take a very, very special woman to take him away forever. She knew Clark better than anyone else and would recognize the symptoms.

Ria thought of him as a thirty-three-year-old kid getting his feet wet in an ocean of publicity, as loyal fans slept in stairwells of the Waldorf, jumped into his limousine, and chanted for him from the sidewalks far below his hotel window. His cigarette butts were worth more than gold.

When Gable returned to California, everyone was talking and reading about *It Happened One Night*—that silly movie about a rich brat who lifts her skirt to hitch a ride, a newspaperman without an undershirt munching on raw carrots and dunking doughnuts, piggy-back rides, and corny goings-on in a cheap motel room with a blanket hanging from a clothesline separating the stars' twin beds and her lingerie flung over the "Walls of Jericho."

Clark said that the big deal about his not wearing an undershirt was easily explained: "I couldn't afford two rooms, so the brat and I had to share one. She was stubborn, so I started taking off my clothes. Removing an undershirt can't be done without effort, so I left it out. The idea was my looking half-naked and scaring the brat into her own bed on the other side of the blanket."

But the sale of men's undershirts in America dropped to almost nothing. Apparently, Gable gave the impression that going without was a vital sign of a man's virility.

Thalberg was back at MGM, and tension was building. Gable kept a low profile and accepted his role as the gangster Blackie Gallagher in *Manhattan Melodrama*, another film pairing him with Myrna Loy. Mickey Rooney began his long association with MGM in the film. Carole Lombard's husband, William Powell, costarred; he would soon be teamed with Loy in *The Thin Man*, the first of the very popular Nick and Nora Charles comedy-mysteries.

In *Manhattan Melodrama*, Gable and Powell play child-hood buddies who wind up on opposite sides of the law. Loy is torn between the two men, but when Gable is executed for murder, she's relieved of having to make a choice.

Loy wrote in her memoirs, "Clark suffered so much from the macho thing that love scenes were difficult. He was afraid to be sensitive for fear it would counteract his masculine image. I always played it a little bit rough with him."

The *Hollywood Reporter* said, "Gable's back to the type of role he does best, a do-gooder gangster. And he comes off great."

In the spring of 1934, Joan Crawford was considering marriage to Franchot Tone when she found herself costarring with Clark Gable in *Chained*. Their mutual attraction had not dimmed. "We grabbed every chance to be alone," Crawford remembered. "When we did *Chained*, that's exactly what we were—chained by a studio that possessed us body and soul. It's no wonder our personal lives were all fucked up!"

Gable told Crawford that he had made up his mind to leave Ria. "She brought my father out here to make our family a cozy one," he complained, "but I'll be damned if I'll let him call me a sissy in my own home, so I bought him and his new bride a house of their own."

"Ria tells me her daughter is getting married in Houston," Crawford said, "and she may stay there for a while."

"Yep, and that's when I make my move. But," he said, lighting a cigarette to avoid having to look into Crawford's eyes, "I'll never get married again. Never."

"I'm not so sure I will, either," Crawford sighed. "Mayer ruined it for us, but you're the guy I love."

"Yeah, babe, you're the only dame for me. I think about you all the time."

"Then why did you call Mary Pickford for a date?"

"I didn't ask her out!"

"That's right. You wanted to see her at Pickfair on the servants' day off."

"I didn't want to impose. . . ."

Crawford smirked. "And Carole Lombard?"

"She doesn't have any servants."

"As soon as you heard she was getting a divorce from Bill Powell . . ."

"Dames need consolation at a time like that."

"Carole told you to shove it, right?"

He scowled. "Who told you?"

"She told Billy Haines and—"

"And Billy told you."

Crawford laughed. "I just wanted to hear it from you that two beautiful women actually turned you down."

"When they change their minds, I might not be interested."

In later years, Mary Pickford said that she did not agree to see Gable because she was devastated over her pending divorce from Douglas Fairbanks, Sr. "Clark wanted to stay home, if you know what I mean," Pickford said. "I made myself unavailable but regretted it later. I must have been out of my mind."

Gable never fell out of love with Joan Crawford. They were soul mates who sought comfort, advice, and sex from each other for thirty years. There was never a need to put on airs—they understood each other, and often sounded in conversation like a waitress and a truck driver.

On the screen, of course, they were dynamite together. In *Chained*, Crawford is the mistress of a rich, elderly man. When his wife discovers the truth, he sends Crawford on a cruise until things can calm down. She meets and falls in love with Gable, but leaves him when her lover gets a divorce. It is out of gratitude that Crawford marries the old man, who lets her go when he realizes how deeply she and Gable love each other.

The New York Times said, "So long as Miss Crawford and Mr. Gable are in a picture, it is as inevitable as the coming of night that the characters they impersonate will not be disappointing in the end."

Gable's last movie to be released in 1934 was *Forsaking All Others*, a comedy with Joan Crawford, Robert Montgomery, and Rosalind Russell. The plot was simple and silly. Montgomery jilts Crawford at the altar. She turns to Gable, who loses her when Montgomery returns. Another wedding is planned, but Crawford runs away with Gable instead.

Moviegoers and critics enjoyed watching Gable clown and wisecrack his way through the picture.

MGM took advantage of Clark's success in comedy and rushed him into *After Office Hours*, released in 1935. Gable plays a newspaperman who crashes high society to solve a murder. Helping him with clues and laughs is Constance Bennett. The critics liked it, and needless to say, light comedy went over big during the Depression.

Though it was a tough year for Gable personally, he made the list of the ten most popular movie stars of 1934—he was number two; Will Rogers was number one. Joan Crawford came in sixth, and Norma Shearer was tenth.

John Gilbert put an ad in the *Hollywood Reporter* stating that MGM would not offer him work or release him from his contract. The woman he had once almost married, Greta Garbo, demanded that he costar with her in *Queen Christina*, but despite his fine performance, the public would never accept Gilbert again. He became a hopeless alcoholic and died in 1936.

Because many in Hollywood believed that Mayer had purposely destroyed John Gilbert, the fall of this great star was not only tragic but frightening. Gable may have been scared, but he had no way of knowing that the public had more power than Louis B. Mayer, and that they were exercising it by flocking to see his films.

MGM picked up Gable's option and raised his salary to $3000 a week as a result of his Oscar nomination for *It Happened One Night*, of which Gable commented, "It was sheer luck."

Despite all the good things coming his way, Gable grumbled about having to give his father an allowance of $500 a month. "Every time I get more money," he complained, "something comes along to take the gravy."

Ria wasn't trying to figure out her husband's strange moods any longer; it was a long time between smiles. Then one night, shortly before Christmas, Gable came home grinning from ear to ear. "After the holidays," he said, "I'm going to Mount Baker, Washington, to do *Call of the Wild*. You know how much I like Jack London!" Ria was happy if he was, and it turned out to be their best Christmas together. She assumed he was excited about taking his guns and doing some hunting in Washington. Or was it the sheer joy of getting away from Mayer?

While Gable was on location, Ria heard rumors that he was having an affair with his costar, Loretta Young. Without identifying the stars, gossip columnists hinted at a hot combination in the state of Washington that should have melted the ice and snow.

Gable returned to Hollywood in time for the Academy Awards dinner at the Biltmore Hotel on February 27, 1935. At the last minute, he announced, "I'm not going. Who wants to sit around and smile, watching someone else win?"

He was in such a nasty mood that Ria was almost afraid even to plead with him, but she managed to convince Clark to put on his white tie and tails. He grumbled about having to sit around all evening in formal clothes and said that he hated "putting on the dog" for those who would destroy him.

Gable was also aware that Hollywood took it for granted that his marriage was over. He and Ria had not been out together in a long time, nor had he attended her dinner parties, now much smaller and less frequent than in the past. There was no outward sign of a marriage whatsoever, and Gable knew all eyes would be on them. The only way he could get through the night was to fortify himself with bourbon. A lot of bourbon!

Gable's competition for best actor was Frank Morgan in *Affairs of Cellini* and William Powell in *The Thin Man*.

Claudette Colbert, nominated for best actress, was up against Grace Moore in *One Night of Love* and Norma Shearer in *The Barretts of Wimpole Street*. Colbert was so sure she wouldn't win that she was skipping the presentation and taking the train to New York that evening.

Nominated for best picture: *It Happened One Night*,

Flirtation Walk, The House of Rothschild, Imitation of Life, The Barretts of Wimpole Street, One Night of Love, Viva Villa!, The White Parade, The Gay Divorcee, Here Comes the Navy, Cleopatra, and *The Thin Man.*

Dinner at the Biltmore was scheduled for eight o'clock. While dessert and coffee were being served, Columbia officials dashed on board the New York-bound train, retrieved Colbert, and delivered her just in time for her to receive the best-actress award. Embarrassed in a beige traveling suit, she wept, clutched the statue, and was whisked back to the waiting train.

It Happened One Night was voted best picture, Frank Capra was named best director, and Robert Riskin was cited for his screenplay. By the time host Irvin S. Cobb read the nominees for best actor, the crowd of a thousand was rooting for Gable to make it an *It Happened One Night* sweep. He did. In a daze, he expressed his thanks and left the podium, mumbling to himself, "I'm still gonna wear the same-size hat . . . the same-size hat. . . ."

Gable had, it seemed, beaten the system, Metro-Goldwyn-Mayer, and Metro's almighty dictator, Louis B. Mayer, who applauded as if he were responsible; indeed, he was. Thalberg cried. Crawford schemed. Ria clapped with gloved hands and knew her marriage was over. Columbia's Harry Cohn shot Mayer a quick "Screw you!" Gable was in a sweat. Making the film, he had defied all principles of acting, had lived on bourbon, had worked only four weeks, and hadn't made a pass at Claudette Colbert. All this had won him the award for best actor. If he was drunk when he accepted the Oscar, he went far beyond drunk once the Biltmore dining room closed.

Ten years later, he gave the statue to a little boy. "Having it doesn't mean anything," he said. "Earning it does."

Gable had been *very* eager to do *Call of the Wild* in Washington. He had been glad to get away from Mayer and Ria, but there was more to it than that. This episode in his life

has been a mystery for almost sixty years. The facts are hard
to pin down, and the witnesses are coy. It is apparent,
however, that Gable was involved with twenty-three-year-old
actress Loretta Young. Maybe it is a tender love story. Maybe
not. But Loretta Young played a memorable role in Gable's
life.

Born Gretchen Young in Salt Lake City on January 6, 1913,
she moved to Los Angeles with her mother, two sisters, Polly
Ann and Elizabeth Jane, and a brother, Jackie, when her
parents were divorced. Polly Ann and Elizabeth Jane became
popular movie extras; Gretchen seized her chance in 1927
when director Mervyn LeRoy called the Young home looking
for Polly Ann, who was not available. Gretchen went in her
place. LeRoy changed her name to Loretta, and at the age of
fifteen she was Lon Chaney's leading lady in *Laugh, Clown,
Laugh.*

At the age of seventeen, Loretta eloped with actor Grant
Withers, who was nine years her senior. They were divorced
the following year after a highly publicized court battle.

Though Young appeared in more than forty films in the first
six years of her career, her acting left a great deal to be
desired. Bosley Crowther, a *New York Times* film critic, once
said about Young, "Whatever it is that this actress never had,
she still hasn't got it." What lifted her to stardom was her
high cheekbones, big gray innocent eyes, and virginal quality.
Her figure lacked curves, but Young wore clothes with flair.
She knew how to accentuate the positive and eliminate the
negative with an irresistible innocence.

Grant Withers referred to her as "The Steel Butterfly," and
she was widely known as "Hollywood's Beautiful Hack," but
Young cared little what anyone said about her. She studied
the craft of performing before the camera and became a
symbol of beauty, class, and refinement. She made the
transition from silents to talkies with ease.

In 1933, Loretta Young costarred with Spencer Tracy in *A
Man's Castle.* They fell in love, and their names were linked
in all the gossip columns. He had not yet reached her star

status, but within weeks everyone recognized Tracy from widely published photographs of him and Young taken on the nightclub circuit. The cast and crew of *A Man's Castle* may have thought they had seen it all, but Young and Tracy's on-set romancing made them blush. Tracy moved out of his home and into a hotel. His wife announced the couple's separation on the grounds of incompatibility, but also announced that she hoped they would work out their problems.

A casual guy with a bitter temper when he was drunk, which, according to some acquaintances, was most of the time, Tracy got into numerous fistfights with reporters, smashing a few of their cameras, during his tryst with Young. The affair came to a heartbreaking end on October 24, 1934, when Young tearfully told the press she could not marry Tracy because they were both devout Catholics.

A few months later, Young was at the Mount Baker Lodge in Heather Meadows, Washington, five thousand feet above sea level. The expedition included two hundred players and technicians. Snowplows worked day and night clearing over sixty-five miles of road to make way for equipment. Blizzards extended production several weeks beyond the anticipated ten days. The unit was literally cut off from civilization, and when food ran short, crews had to make their way laboriously to the nearest town. The cold actually froze the oil in the cameras. Director William Wellman would recall, "We had trouble on *Call of the Wild*, big trouble, on top of a mountain. Gable wasn't tending to business, not the business of making pictures. He was paying a lot of attention to monkey business, and I called him on it, lost my easy-to-lose temper and did it in front of the company, a bad mistake.

"He was a big man. I am not, but there was a big something in my favor, his face. He made his living with it; mine [was] behind the camera. He might have beaten my brains out. I don't know [how a fight might have ended], but I do know that I could have made a character man out of him in the process."

Gable, who was usually prompt, showed up late on the *Call of the Wild* set and was not prepared with his lines. Gossip

had it that Gable and Young were passing time alone together
at the Mount Baker Lodge. The news leaked out to the press,
and gossip columnists printed blind items stating that two
Hollywood stars were "pitching woo" on location in the state
of Washington. As *Call of the Wild* was the only movie being
filmed there at the time, no guesswork was required.

A few months later, Loretta announced that she needed a
long rest and was planning a trip to Europe with her mother.
Reporters caught up to her in London. "I'll be back in
Hollywood in August," she said, "after seeing Paris and
Rome." Then Loretta Young disappeared.

Ria and Clark separated and reconciled several times in the
first months of 1935, but he was too busy at the studio to
think about his marriage. The Oscar afforded him a big
dressing room at MGM with all the star trimmings and his own
seat in the commissary. But when Irving Thalberg cast him in
Mutiny on the Bounty, Gable exploded. "That character is a
pansy!" he bellowed. "And I'm not going to be seen wearing a
pigtail and knickers!"

"Do this one for me," Thalberg said.

Gable gave in, but he was furious that he had to shave off
his mustache.

Mutiny on the Bounty won the Academy Award as best
picture of 1935; Gable, nominated for best actor, lost to
Victor McLaglen in *The Informer*.

Gable was reunited with Jean Harlow in *China Seas*, in
which he played the skipper of a tramp steamer who dumps a
floozy, Harlow, for the elegant Rosalind Russell. Pirates and
a typhoon bring Gable to his senses, and Harlow takes him
back.

In September 1935, Gable left Hollywood for a few weeks in
South America, where fans cheered and followed him from
one country to another. On his way home, Gable stopped off
in New York and was seen dining with several beautiful
socialites. He arrived home on November 18 and immediately
announced his separation from Ria.

Then Loretta Young returned to Hollywood on November 30, and gossip columnists and fan magazines, having only recently reported that she was seriously ill and wasn't expected to work for a year, found themselves trumpeting her remarkable recovery.

In later years, Loretta confessed that she had been very much in love with somebody before her twenty-fifth birthday. "But I had to learn the lesson of self-denial," she said. "The man I loved could not love me."

In May 1937, Loretta was said to have adopted a twenty-three-month-old baby girl, somehow skirting a California law forbidding single people to adopt children. "I fell in love with her in a San Diego orphanage," she said.

However, William Wellman later commented, "Clark and Loretta were very 'friendly' during the picture. We were all locked in our rooms trying to keep warm for weeks. He wasn't himself. Something was bothering him, and that's why we clashed. All I know is Loretta disappeared when the film was finished and showed up with a daughter who had big ears. She's grown up into a lovely woman who resembled her beautiful mother."

Anita Loos wrote forty years later that the son born after Gable's death was not his only child: "A short but hectic affair Clark went through with a costar when they were far from Hollywood on location had resulted in the birth of a baby girl."

Writer George Eels reported talking to a former coworker of Young's who claimed to be acquainted with a nurse who worked at the hospital where the actress gave birth to a daughter.

Loretta was not under contract to MGM, but she did occasionally make a film for them, and though she couldn't have avoided running into Gable or Tracy on the lot, she refused to be photographed with either of them. In 1940, Young married advertising executive Thomas Lewis, who adopted his wife's little daughter, Judy. Watching the child grow up must have been a fairy tale for the Hollywood romantics who would like to have believed that Gable was her father.

Loretta settled down to a marriage she had sacrificed so much to attain. She went on a campaign to abolish swearing, pornography, and immoral literature. On every one of her movie sets she had a "swear box." Monies collected went to a home for unwed mothers. Some actors handed her a ten-dollar bill and told her to "lay off." Robert Mitchum, who didn't play silly games, once asked her how much she charged. "Five cents for every 'damn,' ten cents for 'hell,' and twenty-five cents for 'goddamn,'" she replied.

"How much for 'fuck'?" he asked.

She smiled. "That's free."

Joan Crawford made at least one marvelous joke at the expense of Young's devotion to the church. During one of Crawford's parties, a guest was about to sit in a chair when Crawford grabbed him. "Can't sit *there*," she said. "Loretta Young just got up and it has the mark of the cross on the seat!"

10.

Married Bachelor

f Gable's marriage was hanging by a thread before he made *Call of the Wild*, his romance with Loretta Young cut the thread. Winning the Oscar gave him the confidence and power he needed to break away from Ria. He had the best agents in Hollywood, and Mayer was eating crow. Ria's role as mother and confidante was over, but no one could convince her of that. When Clark moved into the Beverly Wilshire Hotel, Ria bought a house in Beverly Hills rather than returning to Houston.

After Joan Crawford's divorce from Douglas Fairbanks, Jr., the actress told the press, "I'll never marry again as long as I live. There is no such thing as honesty or true love. If anyone ever catches me believing in anything, I hope they give me a good sock in the jaw." But while Gable was in South America, Crawford eloped with Franchot Tone on October

11, 1935. "Thank God I'm in love again," she cooed. "Now I can do *it* for love and not for my complexion." The newlyweds moved into the house Crawford had shared with Fairbanks. Tone had made only $50,000 that year, compared to Crawford's $250,000. Billy Haines did the redecorating and laughed out loud when Joan told him to change all the toilet seats. He would do this automatically after both of her subsequent divorces.

Tone intended to return to the Broadway stage. He'd got his start there in the late twenties, and almost convinced Joan that she too would be happier working in the theater. He filled her head with big ideas, and for a while, she lived in a fantasy world of opening nights and bowing to standing ovations. Tone was so deeply in love that he was willing to stay in Hollywood until she was ready to leave. This was his second mistake. The first was becoming "Mr. Joan Crawford."

Ria met with reporters and struggled to explain her husband to the press. "I understand what happened," she said. "Clark was under tremendous pressure. It was a combination of too much work, too sudden success, and the fact that women fairly threw themselves at him all the time. Basically he has good Dutch principles, and no one could be sweeter at times, but he could also be stubborn and perverse. I tried to make him see that his happiness would have to come from within himself."

Gable enjoyed his first Christmas in fourteen years as a married bachelor. He took advantage of his freedom with young starlets, extras, and high-priced call girls. When asked why he paid for something he could get free, Gable replied, "Because I can pay them to go away. The others stay around, want a big romance, movie lovemaking."

Years later, MGM press agent George Nichols explained, "Mayer might have been a bastard, but he knew his male stars were going to have casual sexual encounters, so he made sure they had a safe place to go. We referred to it as 'The Cat House.' Some of the girls were ex-starlets, and they were examined regularly for venereal diseases. Mayer was trying to [prevent] his leading men from getting into trouble such as adultery and blackmail. The most important thing to Mayer was the clean and beautiful images of his stars. He *was* like a father in this respect."

In early 1936, Gable was seen about town with the exquisite actress Merle Oberon. When they appeared together at the Academy Awards banquet, tongues began to wag. Both were unattached and renowned for their passionate affairs. Oberon had been the mistress of Joseph Schenck, chairman of the board at Twentieth Century–Fox, and was now enjoying the company of actors Leslie Howard and David Niven. The exotically beautiful Oberon was born in Tasmania of an Indian mother and a British father, but her mixed-race background was not revealed until after her death in 1979. Oberon claimed to be an aristocrat, educated in India and London.

When Gable became acquainted with her, she was twenty-five and on the verge of stardom. An intimate night with Oberon, however, might not have been his idea of raw satisfaction. Her approach to sex was elegance—champagne and caviar, candlelight, soft music, satin sheets, silk robes with ostrich trim, French lingerie, and incense. A banquet of love.

It's possible that Gable would not have had an affair with Oberon had he known her origins. The half-breed status was not accepted in society during the Golden Era. A half-caste was an outcast in 1936, and Gable had his principles in the bedroom. He had a fetish for cleanliness, often taking five or six showers a day, and he was known to shave his chest and underneath his arms. He had more than his share of women—ugly, fat, thin, flat-chested, busty, tall, short, young and old. But we have learned from those in the know that Gable would not bed down with the daughter of a Mason, so it's very possible he might have passed up the chance with a half-caste. Even one as gorgeous as Merle Oberon.

Joan Crawford would recall, "After Clark's separation

from Ria, he didn't stop when it came to women. I don't know
how he did it. Dolls and booze. He was like a kid in a candy
store, but he had his own way of picking out sweet delicacies.
At a party, he'd size up every woman in the room. Within
minutes he knew which one was leaving with him, and he
hadn't met her yet. At other times, he made his subtle
approach with a look only he had. He'd say something
flattering about her dress or maybe her hair, never taking his
eyes off her face. He didn't have to say anything sexy,
because he reeked of it. He was a huge magnet. Maybe he did
some chasing, but very few girls ran the other way. Clark
didn't appreciate coyness, but he understood shyness. He
knew the difference. He was a very happy and contented man
at this time. He wasn't looking for a wife, because he had no
intention of getting a divorce. I knew him well enough not to
wait."

In 1936's *Wife Versus Secretary*, Gable played opposite
Myrna Loy (his wife) and Jean Harlow (his secretary). In this
light comedy, Loy suspects Gable is having an affair with
Harlow but eventually finds out she is mistaken. Harlow toned
down her vamp image for *Wife Versus Secretary*. Her hair
was a shade darker and her role a shade tamer than usual. At
the time, she was being courted by the debonair William
Powell. Her second marriage, to cameraman Harold Rossen,
had ended in divorce. As for Myrna Loy, she went into the
film reluctantly and expected a cold shoulder from Gable.
Instead, he kept his hands to himself and they became good
friends.

With Gable, Harlow, and Loy on movie marquees, *Wife
Versus Secretary* made money for MGM. *London Film Weekly*
summed it up: "Here is one of the best films seen for a long
time in which next to nothing happens."

In 1935, Gable had signed a seven-year contract with MGM,
starting at $4000 a week, with a five-hundred-dollar-a-week
raise every two years. If he made more than three films a
year, he was guaranteed a twenty-five-thousand-dollar bonus
for each picture. But, as he had once told Crawford,

"Whenever I get more money, something comes along to take the gravy." This time the something was Ria, whom a judge awarded half of Gable's earnings. Without a doubt, he was angry about this, but he never said an unkind word about her and refused to discuss their separation. "Talk to the lady," he told reporters.

In December 1935, after a tiff with Marlene Dietrich over a visit from Greta Garbo, John Gilbert had a heart attack. Dietrich returned to his bedside, hoping to nurse him back to health. On the night of January 9, 1936, he was unable to sleep. His nurse gave him a shot, then left him alone. Gilbert choked to death on his own tongue. He was forty-one years old.

Hollywood was well represented at his funeral, though L. B. Mayer was conspicuously absent. Irving Thalberg wept over his friend's death. He himself would be gone in nine months.

On the night of January 23, 1936, the Mayfair Club of Hollywood held its annual gala at Victor Hugo's in Beverly Hills; Carole Lombard was the honorary hostess. As requested on the invitations, the ladies all wore flowing white gowns. Gable arrived with Eadie Adams, who provided the singing voice of many leading ladies at MGM. Ria attended with a group of friends, apparently undaunted by the presence of Loretta Young. Then Norma Shearer appeared, all in red. Scarlet, in fact. Lombard was furious. Her first impulse was to throw Shearer out, but one does not eject a Hollywood queen from a Hollywood party. Gable must have sensed trouble brewing, for he quickly approached Lombard for a dance. Still seething, she accepted, only to find herself on the dance floor trying, without success, to follow him. "I'm not much of a dancer," Gable said.

"No kidding," she cracked.

Gable could feel Lombard's tension. "Why don't we take a drive in my Duesenberg convertible?" he said.

"I'm in charge of this fuckin' party," she snapped.

"I think we could both use some fresh air," he said, taking her firmly by the arm.

Gable drove in the direction of the Beverly Wilshire Hotel, but Lombard wasn't buying it. "I haven't got time for this crap," she said. "Take me back to the goddamn party!"

Gable was the one who was seething now. He pressed down hard on the accelerator, driving Lombard back to Victor Hugo's in record time. But the fresh air had not cleared Lombard's head of Norma Shearer's gall, and she was ready for a confrontation. Indirectly attempting to avoid an embarrassing scene at the party, Gable drunkenly propositioned Lombard again. "Come back to my place for a drink," he said.

"I have a better idea," she smiled. "How about my place?"

Gable was delighted, but once home, Lombard began preparing for additional guests. "C'mon," she said. "I need your help. They should be here any minute!"

"Yeah? Well, I've got a date."

"Yeah?" she retorted. "With Loretta Young?"

Gable turned around and walked out. The next morning, he woke up in his suite at the Beverly Wilshire with a white dove cooing in his ear and six others fluttering overhead. A card revealed the sender, and he phoned her. "The birds can't stay in the hotel," he exclaimed.

"You can keep them at my house temporarily."

"I'll bring them right over!" he said, hopping out of bed.

"That won't be necessary," Lombard chirped. "I'll send someone to pick them up."

She had cleverly outfoxed him, but Gable was not one to give up. He called her often. And Lombard was always busy.

They did not see each other again until the "Nervous Breakdown" ball on February 7 at the mansion of millionaire John Hay Whitney. Though the party was called for noon, guests were expected to wear their finest formal attire. It was almost suppertime when the screech of a siren caused everyone concern as an ambulance pulled up to Whitney's front door. Four interns in white carefully removed a stretcher bearing the body of Carole Lombard, wrapped in a sheet. They carried her into the house, and for a moment the shocked guests, including Gable, were stunned. Lombard was motionless; her eyes were closed. When she sat up and laughed, Gable wasn't sure how to respond. He was mad at himself for worrying about her, but he had to admit that she had pulled off a great stunt.

There are many versions as to how this famous couple met and this is due, perhaps, to the parties that were so close together. But we know Carole and Clark did not melt into each other's arms at the Mayfair Ball. They were at odds, in fact. Either they exchanged insults or Gable *was* concerned about Lombard's spouting four-letter words at Norma Shearer, and took advantage of the situation by taking her back to his hotel room. She knew how he operated and wanted no part of his "quickies." Clark reacted like he did with Myrna Loy, but Carole was an unpredictable blonde spitfire with mischievous eyes and boundless energy. It's doubtful that Gable was angry over her ambulance gag. On the contrary. He thought it took guts and he envied Carole's spirit.

Though Lombard had avoided Gable after the Mayfair Club ball, she was attracted to him. Her strategy was not to let him know how much. With Valentine's Day approaching, Lombard wanted to send Gable a funny gift, and she came up with a gem. Knowing the inordinate pride he took in his Duesenberg, she bought a beat-up old Model T for fifteen dollars, painted it white with red hearts, and had it delivered to Gable at MGM on the morning of February 14.

"How about dinner and dancing at the Trocadero tonight?" he asked her on the phone. Lombard accepted, dolling up in a white beaded gown and fur wrap. She stepped out of her house to find Gable, dressed in a tuxedo, sitting behind the wheel of the Model T. The car's interior was a mess, but Lombard hopped in anyway. "I worked on this thing," he said, "and it runs pretty good." She cheered when he got the

car up to fifteen miles an hour. He chuckled, too. In fact, they
both howled with laughter all the way to the Trocadero.

They continued to date occasionally, but Gable was busy
filming *San Francisco*, and Lombard was working on *My Man
Godfrey* with her ex-husband, Bill Powell, at Universal. She
was also dating screenwriter Robert Riskin and was not
always available when Gable called. He was, after all, a
married man who was not seeking a divorce. When Gable was
asked whether he was serious about Lombard, he replied,
"No. I just like the way she wiggles her derriere in a tight
satin dress."

Confronted by the press, Lombard made light of her
"friendship" with Gable, and shocked reporters into complete
silence with a casual quip: "Clark's not circumcised, but
that's all right."

Gable did not want to do *San Francisco*. "She sings and I
listen," he said of the idea of working with Jeanette
MacDonald. "No thanks." But MacDonald had personally
requested Gable and was determined to have him. "I'll go off
salary," she said, "until Clark's available." Gable held firm.
"I don't like sitting around and having to react to someone
singing to me. Makes me feel like a lump!"

Spencer Tracy hadn't wanted to do *San Francisco* either.
Playing a priest bothered him. "Then I thought about it," he
would recall. "My father wanted me to be a priest, and I
figured he would have liked it." Once Tracy had changed his
mind, Gable changed his, too. "I never forgot Tracy's
performance in *The Last Mile*," he said. "I was in awe of
him."

In *San Francisco*, Gable portrayed a gambler, and
MacDonald was an innocent young opera singer who needs
money so badly that she lowers herself to a job in Gable's
saloon. Tracy is the priest who protects her virtue. Boy gets
girl, boy loses girl, but the 1906 earthquake brings everyone
together again.

Gable liked Tracy. Though they didn't mingle socially, they

had much in common. Both were heavy drinkers and had had
torrid romances with Loretta Young and Joan Crawford.
They had both started out on the stage and shared fond
memories of the theater. While they drank and exchanged
jokes on the set, MacDonald sat alone, with tears in her eyes.
Gable never took to MacDonald. She was one of Mayer's
favorites, which was a strike against her from the very
beginning. Moreover, Gable maintained a friendship with
Nelson Eddy, who had been teamed with MacDonald in two
very successful films. MacDonald and Eddy were very much
in love, but Mayer forbid them to marry. Even had Gable
been attracted to MacDonald, he would not have done
anything about it. Another redheaded pet of L. B. Mayer's of
whom Gable was not particularly fond was Greer Garson. It
might be worth noting here that Mayer did not have affairs
with his female players. If a young lady wanted to get ahead at
MGM, going to bed with the boss was not the way to do it.
Mayer admired beautiful, refined women, like MacDonald and
Garson, and the all-American types, like June Allyson and
Debbie Reynolds, who both called him "Pops." Mayer did fall
deeply in love with starlet Jean Howard, but strangely
enough, he never touched her. The saying at MGM was "If
L.B. were in a whorehouse, he couldn't get laid." He knew
how to get revenge, however. When Jean Howard married
agent Charles Feldman, Mayer blackballed him.

Gable was not worried about MacDonald complaining
about him to the boss. On the contrary. No one could report
back that he had made a pass at L.B.'s prima donna. Still,
the costars' on-screen love scenes were as believable as the
film's special-effects earthquake, and *San Francisco* reaped a
harvest of four million dollars at the box office.

Lombard would not rearrange her life to suit Gable. If she
was busy, he could "go screw himself," she insisted. When
they were out together and he flirted with other women,
Lombard would simply catch another man's eye and put on a
teasing performance herself. This was a first for Gable, who

· 138 ·

wasn't quite sure how to react. During Prohibition, Lombard nipped bootleg booze while playing poker with the boys, but she always wore a clinging dress to prove she was all woman.

She was born Jane Alice Peters on October 6, 1908, in Fort Wayne, Indiana. When Jane was six years old, her mother, Bessie, took Jane and her two brothers, Fred and Stuart, to Los Angeles on vacation and never returned home. Bessie and her husband, Fred, did not have a good marriage, and he elected to stay in Indiana.

The Peters were a wealthy family. One biographical account mentions that Jane's paternal grandfather founded the Horton Company in Fort Wayne after importing the first washing machine from Germany. On Bessie's side of the family, a great-grandfather of Jane's established one of the first electric companies in California, helped finance the laying of the Atlantic cable, and was a founding director of New York's National City Bank.

Jane was a spunky tomboy who tried to join her brothers' football team, was told to go home, but played anyway. There was no fence high enough to keep her out.

She was either spinning cartwheels or wrestling with her brothers on their front lawn when movie director Allan Dwan, who was visiting a neighbor, thought she was the high-spirited girl he was looking for to play Monte Blue's daughter in *A Perfect Crime*. Jane worked for two days, but afterward, there were no further offers. Bessie Peters tried her best to get Jane, who was only thirteen at the time, into films but finally decided a career could wait until Jane finished school. Jane, however, had already made up her mind to be an actress, and in 1924, Bessie went for help to her columnist friend Louella Parsons, who arranged an interview at Fox Studios. Shortly after her sixteenth birthday, Jane was signed to a one-year contract at sixty-five dollars a week; her name was changed to Carol Lombard. (The *e* originated in a billboard misspelling in 1930. Lombard liked it but told the press that she was adding the *e* on the advice of a numerologist. "I need thirteen letters for the right vibrations," she said. The public admired Lombard for admitting she was superstitious.)

When Lombard was eighteen, she was in a serious automobile accident. A sharp piece of glass cut into the right side of her face from nose to ear. She endured four hours of surgery, without anesthesia, while her face was being stitched. After the healing process, she underwent plastic surgery. The procedure was a long one, and Fox dropped her contract.

When she recovered, Lombard got a job with Mack Sennett, producer of the wildly popular Keystone Kops pictures. For two years she appeared in two-reelers, engaging in pie-in-the-face routines and other silly antics. Joseph P. Kennedy, who was then head of Pathé, offered Lombard a contract if she'd lose twenty pounds. "For four hundred dollars a week I'll do almost anything," she told him, "but you're not so skinny yourself, Mr. Kennedy."

In 1930, after Pathé chose not to pick up her option, Lombard signed a seven-year contract with Paramount for $375 a week. She made two films, *Man of the World* and *Ladies' Man*, with thirty-nine-year-old William Powell, then married him on June 26, 1931. After their wedding night, she wired a friend, "Nothing new."

Two years later they were divorced, and Lombard commented, "Our marriage was a waste of time for both of us. Bill liked quiet evenings at home, and it drove me mad. But after our divorce he took me out often, and we had a better time together than before."

Lombard's marriage to Powell had puzzled her intimates. Though he had a marvelous sense of humor, as one can certainly see watching his film performances, he was no match for Lombard's bubbly personality. His poise and graciousness smoothed over the rough edges of her mien, but he could not cure her of using curse words. "It's not easy to break a habit," she told him. "It puts me in a shitty mood."

Lombard had enjoyed profanity since her teens, but she carried her four-letter words with dignity. One of her friends recalled the first time Lombard rode a horse. "I don't know why the hell everybody thinks this is so great," Lombard exclaimed in front of a crowd. "It's like a dry fuck."

Carole never wore a bra and avoided panties. She was five feet one inch, one hundred and twelve pounds, and very wealthy even before she became the highest paid actress in Hollywood.

Yes, Lombard was raunchy, tough, romantic, strong-willed, sexy, sophisticated, and hell on wheels. She never thought of becoming a great actress or making a lot of money, and she rarely complained. At the beginning of her career, Lombard was suspected of being a lesbian, because she enjoyed the company of homosexuals, male and female. After her divorce from Powell, she lived with her business manager, Madalyn Fields, nicknamed Fieldsie, who was over six feet tall and weighed well over two hundred pounds. Whenever the rumors of lesbianism reached her friends, though, they laughed. One commented, "Carole is capable of trying anything, but she's straight as an arrow."

She was an excellent dancer and excelled at tennis. "Carole was good at everything," Bing Crosby once said. "She had a delicious sense of humor and was one of the screen's greatest comediennes. She was also very beautiful. The electricians, carpenters, and propmen all adored her because she was so regular, so devoid of temperament and showboating. The fact that she could make us think of her as being a good guy rather than a sexy mama is one of those unbelievable manifestations impossible to explain."

Lombard loved to start rumors about herself, and one story, that she kept a dildo in her dressing room, made the rounds, then got back to her. She pretended to be livid, but actually, she couldn't wait to show it to everyone.

Lombard's parties were the talk of the town. Marion Davies recalled, "Carole would tell us 'formal dress' and serve dinner in bedpans. At more intimate gatherings, we'd all sit around having a drink. Each had his own little table. We'd all be engaged in conversation without realizing dinner courses had been served one by one very quietly. Carole invented TV tables, actually. She was way ahead of her time."

Lombard was the first in Hollywood to hire Billy Haines as an interior decorator. No one else dared give him a chance. "After Carole's divorce from William Powell," Haines said, "she bought a simple, medium-sized house of her own and asked me to decorate it. I wanted to make her place reflect her personality, but with the same good taste underneath that spicy clowning."

Haines "blasted" bright shades of blue and purple against a background of white. This type of décor would become a fad in Hollywood, but Billy considered the lively contrast all Lombard. "She was one of the most beautiful girls on the screen," he said. "She photographed like a virginal princess, but she lived like a tiger and fluttered like a colorful butterfly. I accentuated the rooms with mirrors because Carole was a reflection of life. When the house was finished and Carole gave me a check, I refused it. She had taken a chance by putting her reputation on the line. Carole gave a party because her friends were dying to see the place, but when they arrived, the guests were stunned to see an empty house. All the furniture had been removed.

"Carole's mother, Bessie, was a great gal, too. She always had a numerologist and astrologer on retainer. They looked like a bunch of Gypsies playing poker every Saturday night . . . fortune-tellers, psychics, and mediums."

According to Haines, Lombard often changed clothes in front of him and walked around in the nude. The first time it happened, she saw the surprised look on his face and said, "I wouldn't do this if I thought it would arouse you, Billy."

Who would be crazy enough to marry Lombard? Maybe singer Russ Columbo, who fell in love with her after his hot romance with actress Pola Negri cooled. Columbo and Lombard became inseparable. He carried his cigarettes in a fifteen-hundred-dollar diamond-studded case, and gave Lombard similarly extravagant gifts. He lived with his parents in a mansion on Outpost Circle Drive, in an exclusive Hollywood neighborhood. When Columbo was twenty-six, he signed a lucrative movie contract with Universal after starring in *Wake Up and Dream*. On August 30, 1934, he and Lombard attended the premiere together. She was thrilled for him. "You wait, Russ," she told him. "I predict you're going to be a star."

Two days later, Columbo was visiting a friend who collected old guns. While they were admiring some Civil War relics, a pistol fired; the slug ricocheted off a table, struck Columbo just above the right eye, and lodged in his brain. Two hours later he was dead. Lombard was heartbroken. At the funeral she said, "His love for me was the kind that rarely comes to any woman."

Columbo's mother did not attend the funeral; blind and ill, she was thought too frail to withstand the shock of her son's death. Lombard then helped with a charade that was to last eleven years: Mrs. Columbo was led to believe that her son was away on a very successful European tour. A "royalty" check was sent to her every month, enclosed with a letter describing her son's exciting life abroad. Lombard visited faithfully, and Mrs. Columbo died never knowing the truth about her son. After she married Gable, Lombard once told a reporter, "off the record," that Russ Columbo was *the* great love of her life. And always would be. . . .

Though Lombard was not known for casual flings, she had dated Gary Cooper, known as "Studs," when she was sixteen and again, some years later, as his costar at Paramount. Certainly, Lombard gave Gable the impression that she had been involved with Cooper, who, unlike Gable, was *very* well endowed. As a result, Gable made sure ever afterwards that his cars and gun collection were bigger than Cooper's.

Rumors also linked Lombard to David Selznick and Howard Hughes; she was known to jest about these liaisons but, wickedly, never denied that they were true. George Raft, Lombard's costar in the beautiful film *Bolero*, was another alleged lover. Lombard's portrait was prominently displayed over Raft's bed, and he admitted being very much in love with her. Once, when asked who was Hollywood's greatest lover, Lombard replied, "George Raft. . . . Or did you mean on the screen?"

Lombard's relationship with Robert Riskin was serious, and their friends assumed they would marry, but after Christmas 1935, she was seen around town with Cesar Romero. Lombard never explained why her romance with Riskin faded other than to say that he didn't want children. His long-time associate Frank Capra said that Riskin brooded over Lombard for some time.

The great John Barrymore fell in love with Lombard, too. Initially, he hadn't wanted to work with "that dizzy blonde" in *Twentieth Century* because, he said, she couldn't act. "I felt sorry for her," Barrymore said, "and at the same time had no intention of lowering myself to appearing with what looked like a cute little flapper. Director Howard Hawks took me aside and told me to keep my mouth shut until we finished for the day, regardless of what happened. Carole caught me off guard. In [one] scene, she was supposed to fly off the handle . . . rave and rant at me. Well, she threw her arms in the air, kicked, screamed, and carried on like a madwoman. I recall instinctively covering my balls. We went through twelve pages of dialogue, too, without a mistake. We did that scene only once—just long enough for me to fall in love with her."

11.

King

*L*ombard's friends did not think that Gable was good enough for her. One of them said, "Gable didn't have much respect for women. He wasn't a warm and considerate guy. I thought he was too tough and lacked sentimental values. Carole deserved more affection and attention. She liked to hug and touch and embrace. He didn't. She remembered birthdays and anniversaries of all her friends. Gable remembered his own birthday. He was generous with food and booze, but gifts? Forget it. Carole would never have put up with this from any other man. She'd have booted him in the ass and explained the facts of life. I think Carole could tell he was hurting inside—that the gruff exterior was all an act—but he *did* take women for granted. Clark didn't give a hoot about much except hunting and fishing, whereas Carole liked frilly clothes, nightclubs, luncheons at the Brown Derby, and putting on one of her fashionable hats for cocktails with reporters. All of this bored Gable, so Carole pretended to like his hobbies. She bought britches and sport shirts and boots, learned to use a rifle, and went along with him 'for the fun of it.' Carole was out to catch him, and Clark never felt a thing."

Gable's friends weren't particularly fond of Lombard at the outset because he insisted on taking her along on camping trips that were usually for men only. She was able to keep up with the jargon and taught the boys some new raw lingo. Her jokes were the raunchiest, too. Gable thought she was cute and encouraged her. Lombard knew that Gable's pals were waiting for her to get fed up with the bad weather and the bugs. Instead, she was the first one up in the morning, and she reeled in the biggest fish.

When Lombard was asked once what she and Gable did to occupy their time in the bushes when the ducks weren't cooperating, she shrugged. "Sometimes we fucked. We did it twice in the rain."

Quizzed about his intentions, however, Gable insisted, "I am *not* getting a divorce because I have no intention of marrying again."

Following *San Francisco*, Gable costarred with Marion Davies in *Cain and Mabel*. He had been scheduled to do one more film with Davies, and despite a falling out between Hearst and Mayer, Thalberg honored the commitment. In the film, Gable plays a boxer and Davies is a musical-comedy star. They are linked romantically for publicity purposes and fall in love for real. Critics were bored. *Newsweek* said, "Clark Gable and Marion Davies fit into this picture like a fat hand squeezed into a small glove." *Time* wrote, "These two glorious people go off to a little rose-covered cottage in Jersey, and that's the end. It's the end of some very fine feelings about Mr. Gable and Miss Davies and musical comedy. See it at your own risk." Perhaps unsurprisingly, Hearst lost money on *Cain and Mabel*.

Clark next made *Love on the Run* with Joan Crawford and

her husband, Franchot Tone, who asked Gable why he didn't return to the theater. "Because I couldn't face an audience" was the response.

"Why?" Tone asked.

"Because I'm Clark Gable, and people would come to see me in the flesh and get a pound of it before they were through."

"I'm considering a stage career," Crawford said.

"Yeah? Well if you can tear yourself away from Stanislavsky," Gable said, "I want you to read a script."

"Which one?"

"*Parnell.*"

"Are you mad? Who the hell's gonna believe you're the uncrowned king of Ireland?"

"That's my problem. Will you be in it with me?"

"Get Loretta," she said.

"She's not available."

"You son of a bitch!"

Gable was livid, and wouldn't speak to Crawford for a long time. They did, however, score well in *Love on the Run,* in which Gable played a newsman and Crawford was a runaway heiress in a story of royalty and spies in Europe. *The New York Times* commented, "A slightly daffy cinematic item of absolutely no importance." Other reviews cited the fine performances of the lead players.

In the 1936 box-office polls, Gable held second place; Shirley Temple was first. (The others, in descending order: the team of Ginger Rogers and Fred Astaire, Robert Taylor, Joe E. Brown, Dick Powell, Joan Crawford, Claudette Colbert, Jeanette MacDonald, and Gary Cooper.)

Gable had no rivals. The new leading man at MGM was twenty-five-year-old Robert Taylor, who once said about himself, "I'm just a punk kid from Nebraska." Like Gable, Taylor was Pennsylvania Dutch, but unlike Gable, Taylor was a favorite son of Mayer's. Howard Strickling took Taylor under his wing, and Gable, too, came to like the wholesome, good-looking Taylor, who often accompanied Gable on hunting and fishing trips.

It was Thalberg's idea to costar Taylor and Greta Garbo in *Camille*. Taylor told Gable, "She was supposed to kiss me once, and do you know what she did?"

"Kiss ya twice?" Clark laughed.

"She kissed me all over my face."

"Yeah? What did you do?"

"Nothing. She's the aggressor in love scenes. Did you notice that?"

Gable scowled. "I don't remember much about Garbo except that she went home every night at six o'clock."

On September 14, 1936, shortly before *Camille* went into production, Irving Thalberg died of lobar pneumonia; the "Boy Genius" of cinema was thirty-seven. Hollywood went into mourning, and on the day of Thalberg's funeral, MGM closed down for the first time in its history. Out of respect, the other Hollywood studios were silent during the services at B'nai B'rith Temple. In tears, Grace Moore sang the Twenty-third Psalm while a congregation of fifteen hundred mourners wept. Clark Gable was a somber usher, and L. B. Mayer, whom many blamed for Thalberg's death, sat with his head bowed, refusing to acknowledge anyone. But after the services, in his limousine, Mayer looked over at his aide Eddie Mannix and smiled. "Isn't God good to me?" he commented. At long last, Mayer had MGM all to himself—his baby, his life, his reason for living. Those who had gone crying to Thalberg would now have to deal with Mayer. Thalberg was praised during his tenure with MGM; now that he was gone, even Mayer's enemies would learn to be appreciative.

Thalberg's projects—*The Good Earth*, *A Day at the Races*, *Maytime*, and *Camille*—went forward as planned, and *The Good Earth* would become the only film that ever bore Thalberg's name.

Gable's *Parnell* was not affected by Thalberg's demise. Mayer liked the source, a play by Elsie Schauffler, and had no objection to Gable's playing the Irish statesman. It might, Mayer thought, prove Gable's worth as an actor and improve his image. Was it possible that Mayer and Gable had finally agreed about something? The answer is "Yes, unfortunately."

Myrna Loy was probably the only person besides Mayer who thought *Parnell* was a wonderful idea. After Joan Crawford refused to play Gable's married mistress in the picture, Loy was cast in the part. At the end of the film, Parnell fails to obtain home rule for Ireland and dies of a heart attack. The movie died, too. *The New Yorker* said, "Among the notable invertebrates, I would list *Parnell*." *The New York Times* called it "pallid and tedious."

Gable received his requisite twenty-five-thousand-dollar bonus for completing *Parnell*, failure or no. Lombard had thousands of *Parnell*, stickers printed up; Gable found them everywhere he looked. Perhaps this was Lombard's way of reminding Gable that no one is infallible. But balancing the scales was not easy, because Gable *was* infallible. *Parnell* is a forgotten flaw; it didn't even leave a scar. Gable did, however, leave his footprints behind for posterity.

Sid Grauman, who owned a chain of movie theaters, once paid a visit to Mary Pickford and accidentally stepped into wet cement at the entrance to her dressing room. This mishap gave him an idea, and when Cecil B. De Mille's 1927 film, *King of Kings*, opened at Grauman's new Chinese Theatre on Hollywood Boulevard, Pickford became the first to "record" her footprints. Except for the Oscar, being asked to leave one's imprint at Grauman's Chinese Theatre was considered the most prestigious compliment to a movie performer.

In January 1937, ten years after newsreels of Pickford placing her tiny shoes into cement charmed the country, Clark Gable imprinted his big feet and huge hands and wrote the inscription "To Sid, who is a great guy." Gable drew the largest crowd in history to this event, and grinned broadly when Lombard whispered in his ear, "Wouldn't it be more appropriate if they took your cockprint, too?"

Lombard's risqué remarks did not make the newspapers, needless to say. In fact, she said very little to the press about her relationship with Gable. They were seen dating frequently, but always with propriety. MGM was very much keeping an eye on the affair. Gable did not have to be warned this time. There was too much money at stake. Ria may have been waiting for her husband to come back, but she was not sitting home nights. She occasionally ran into her husband and Lombard at banquets, but there was never an unpleasant incident. Ria later said that Clark never embarrassed her during their long separation. L. B. Mayer told Howard Strickling to make sure that everything concerning Gable and Lombard was socially acceptable.

Reporters and fans, however, lurked around Lombard's Hollywood home, affording her little privacy. She was at risk meeting Gable at his suite at the Beverly Wilshire. To avoid the glare of publicity, Lombard moved into an English Tudor house in secluded Bel-Air. When Gable got tired of commuting at all hours, he rented a house close to Lombard's. "Since our work schedules conflict," he told friends, "I decided it was the only way I could get to see her once in a while." This was quite an admission for a womanizer like Gable, who never went out of his way for any girl. For Lombard, it was another victory. Sneaking in and out of hotels was beneath her, and if there was one thing she refused to do, it was pave the way for an eternal affair.

MGM threw a birthday party for Gable in February 1937. L. B. Mayer asked fifteen-year-old Judy Garland to sing "You Made Me Love You" for Gable. She said, "Looking at him close up, my knees almost caved in." When Gable gave Garland a hug and kiss, she burst into tears, scurried over to Mayer, and sat on his lap.

Ten years later, Garland met Gable at a banquet. He told everyone at his table, "Judy ruined all my birthday parties. Just when I was startin' to have a good time, in comes this rotten kid with that song. She was a real pain in the ass!" But Garland later said, "When Clark teased, this was an expression of how much he liked you. I never got used to seeing him around the studio. It was always a thrill."

In April 1937, Gable appeared in a Los Angeles federal courtroom as a witness for the prosecution in the United States government's case against Violet Norton, an English-woman who claimed that Gable had fathered her fifteen-year-old daughter, Gwendoline. Norton claimed that she'd recognized her lover, "Frank Billings," when she saw *It Happened One Night.* She'd written letters to Gable, Walter Winchell, MGM, and, for some reason, Mae West. The district attorney of Los Angeles contacted Gable, who said, "I've never been in England."

"In that event," the district attorney said, "you'll have to prove beyond a doubt where you were in 1922."

"All over the Northwest. I was a drifter."

"You'll have to be more specific than that, and get witnesses to back you up."

MGM attempted to contact everyone who might have known Gable in 1922. The Silverton Lumber Company offered copies of Gable's paychecks. But the most important witness would be Franz Dorfler, who was living in Los Angeles.

On April 22, 1937, before an all-male jury, the trial began. It was established that Clark Gable had never been issued a U.S. passport. He took the stand and related his early years, from Ohio to Kansas to Montana to Oregon. Violet Norton insisted on taking a closer look at the man on the stand, to verify, she said, who he was. The judge said, "Everyone in this court can see the witness is Clark Gable! Your request is denied!"

Franz Dorfler was able to provide specific dates. She told the court that Gable had been staying with her parents on their farm in September 1922, the month Violet Norton said her daughter was conceived. After Franz testified, Gable assisted her down from the witness stand.

And Violet Norton was deported to Canada.

All smiles, Gable commented, "As affairs go, the one decribed was a long-distance project. It would have set a world's record."

With a straight face, Lombard retorted, "That's right. You have all you can do to make it at close range."

When Gable found out that his onetime fiancée wasn't doing well financially, he asked MGM to hire her for their stock company. But at the studio, Gable treated her as if she didn't exist. Her comment: "He married two women he didn't love to further his career. But then he did a number of things I didn't think were right."

Gable's next film was about horse racing. Originally, he had wanted Joan Crawford as his leading lady in *Saratoga*, but when it came time to cast, the two were not on speaking terms. In fact, he blamed the failure of *Parnell* on Crawford's refusal to do it. To Gable's delight and satisfaction, Jean Harlow was to be his costar. In *Saratoga*, a romantic comedy tinged with light melodrama, Gable played a bookmaker who wins and loses money and women while keeping one eye on the Thoroughbreds. It was a sparkling movie, dimmed only by the death of Jean Harlow. Filming one of her last scenes, she collapsed. Assuming it was the flu, the studio sent Harlow home to her mother. The following Monday Harlow did not show up for work. Her mother, Jean Bello, phoned the studio to say that Harlow would report for work the following day. When Harlow failed to apear on Tuesday and a studio messenger was turned away by Mrs. Bello, Gable took it upon himself to visit Harlow.
"I'd like to see Jean," he said.
Mrs. Bello smiled. "She's sleeping."
"What did the doctors have to say?"
"Someday," Mrs. Bello said, "I must introduce you to Christian Science, Mr. Gable."
Gable raced back to the studio and, through Howard Strickling, alerted L. B. Mayer, who arranged to have Harlow rushed to the Good Samaritan Hospital in Los Angeles. But it was too late. Harlow died on June 7, 1937, of cerebral edema, the result of untreated uremic poisoning. MGM went into

shock and deep mourning once again. They had lost a member of their family—the twenty-six-year-old star everyone called "The Baby."

Carole Lombard and a shattered Clark Gable attended the funeral. Jeanette MacDonald sang "Indian Love Call"; Nelson Eddy followed with "Ah, Sweet Mystery of Life." The flowers that filled the chapel were estimated to have cost twenty thousand dollars, almost as much as the platinum blonde had left behind. In her hand was a white gardenia with an unsigned note that read "Good night, my dearest darling." Obviously, it was William Powell's last farewell to the girl who had worn his sapphire engagement ring but had hesitated to marry him. After two divorces, perhaps Powell, too, was afraid of marriage. If he had wed Harlow and taken her away from her mother, The Baby might have survived.

Gable was too overcome with grief to comment. The terrible death of Jean Harlow brought him closer to Carole Lombard, much closer than he had ever thought possible. Hollywood wasn't what it was cracked up to be, was it? Life was shorter here than anywhere else in the world. Poor Irving, poor Jean, poor everybody else. . . .

Saratoga was completed. A double, seen only from the back, was used for Harlow's remaining scenes. Several of the young blond hopefuls who tried out for the part might as well have been auditioning for Gable's harem. He saw to it that candidate Virginia Grey was in many of his later films, and Mary Dees, who won the part, was another favorite of Gable's over the years.

Saratoga was released a month after Harlow's death, while the public was still in shock. Gable grieved for a long time. He was appalled that the studio was taking advantage of Harlow's death by exploiting her last film. He wondered if anyone realized how hard she had worked, even after she became ill. He remembered her collapsing, then trying to rise from her chaise to continue a scene. For a brief time, Gable understood why Mayer demanded to be kept informed about his contract players, why he insisted on knowing the details of their private lives, and why Howard Strickling stayed loyal to Mayer without betraying anyone's trust.

In 1934, Robert Taylor was the lowest-paid star in Hollywood history, making only thirty-five dollars a week and trying to support himself and his mother. Gable encouraged him to ask Mayer for a raise, and a shy Taylor gave it a try.

"Bob," Mayer said, "God never saw fit to give me the great blessing of a son. He gave me daughters—two beautiful daughters, who have been a great joy to me. They're now married to fine, successful fellows—top producers—Dave Selznick and Billy Goetz. But for some reason, in His infinite wisdom, He never saw fit to give me a son.

"But if He had given me a son, Bob—if He had blessed me with such a great and wonderful joy—I can't think of anybody I would rather have wanted that son to be than you. And if that son came to me and said, 'Dad, I'm working for a wonderful company, Metro-Goldwyn-Mayer, and for a good man, the head of the company, who has my best interests at heart, but he's paying me only thirty-five dollars a week, Dad. Do you think I should ask him for a raise?' Do you know what I'd say to my son, Bob? I'd say, 'Son, it's a fine company. It's going to do great things for you. It's going to make a great star of you. You'll be famous. That's more important than a little money. Don't ask for a raise, son.'"

As Taylor was leaving Mayer's office, Howard Strickling asked, "Did you get the raise, Bob?"

"No, but I got a father," Taylor replied.

Mayer might have been stingy with the young man from Nebraska, but he taught him how to budget what money he had. *Then* he increased Taylor's salary; less than a year after Taylor's unsuccessful attempt to get a raise, he was making $750 a week. "Mr. Mayer gave raises when it was appropriate," Taylor said. "He knew I couldn't live on thirty-five dollars a week, but he didn't want me to think I talked him into it."

Gable helped Taylor get through the ordeal of breaking off his engagement to actress Irene Hervey. (Mayer wanted Taylor to remain single). Taylor was crushed when she married singer Allan Jones. Hervey told this author, "I didn't want to wait until the studio decided it was all right for Bob to marry. Besides, I thought Allan had more star potential."

Gable might have suffered during his overheated affair with Crawford, but he did not regret their not getting married. Franchot Tone related his miseries after his divorce from Crawford. When his wife caught him making love to a young starlet in his dressing room, Tone told her, "I had to prove to myself I was a man. It was an honor for her to be seduced by talent." Crawford said that that was bullshit, but Tone did not get down on his hands and knees to beg forgiveness, as he had been forced to do earlier in their marriage. "With Douglas, I tried too hard," Crawford later said. "With Franchot, I didn't try hard enough."

And Billy Haines changed the toilet seats in Crawford's Bristol Avenue house once again.

Gable and Crawford were on speaking terms again. According to her, the affair continued because they lusted for each other. "I was one of the few women who could satisfy him," she said.

On the Hollywood merry-go-round, Franchot Tone was now dating Loretta Young, and Joan Crawford was seeing Spencer Tracy. Robert Taylor and Barbara Stanwyck were a steady couple, and Norma Shearer was chasing Tyrone Power, who was trying to make up his mind whether he preferred men or women.

While the talk around town was largely concerned with David Selznick's forthcoming film adaptation of Margaret Mitchell's *Gone With the Wind*, Gable teamed with Myrna Loy and Spencer Tracy in *Test Pilot*. Tracy called it, at least partially in jest, "just another Gable movie," but he did spend much of the shoot trying to steal scenes, as only he could. "Spence" and Clark were buddies and rivals, each wishing he had the attributes of the other. Tracy wanted Gable's no-effort magnetism, and Gable envied Tracy's acting ability.

In *Test Pilot*, Gable played the title role, Tracy was his mechanic, and Loy was the country girl who marries Gable. "In one scene," Gable later recalled, "Myrna and I were talking in the front seat of a convertible. Spence was sitting in the middle of the backseat. Myrna and I were having a 'hot' conversation, and Spence had one or two short lines, but the bastard was chewing gum. That did it! Nobody paid any attention to my trying to seduce Myrna, because all eyes were on Spence chewin' gum. He didn't get the girl, but he stole the picture with little effort."

For his death scene at the end of the film, Tracy lay in Gable's arms for what was meant to be a brief farewell. As he stretched it out, Gable shook him and cursed, "Die, goddamn it, Spence! I wish to Christ you would!"

Tracy, who had a drinking problem, went on benders between films. It was difficult for him to stay sober when he was working, but usually he did so, at least early in his career. Once, Gable and his close friend director Victor Fleming wanted Tracy to join them on a spree; Tracy refused. When Gable and Fleming returned to the lot, drunk and frisky, Gable headed in Tracy's direction, but Loy stopped him. "You know he has to be careful!" she exclaimed. "Where are your brains?"

Test Pilot was a big success. *Cue* said, "As a trio, Clark Gable, Spencer Tracy and Myrna Loy turn in probably the best performances of their careers." *Time* applauded the film, adding, "Director Fleming got what he wanted without coaxing." *Test Pilot* was nominated for an Academy Award as best picture of 1938; it lost to *You Can't Take It With You*, director Frank Capra's adaptation of the Kaufman and Hart play. Spencer Tracy won the best-actor award that year for *Boys Town*.

In the fall of 1937, columnist Ed Sullivan ran a "King and Queen of the Movies" contest. Twenty million voters participated. Clark Gable and Myrna Loy were the winners. (Robert Taylor and Loretta Young came in second.)

On December 9, before a crowded audience at the El Capitan Theatre in Hollywood, and untold numbers of radio listeners, Sullivan crowned Gable and Loy with tin-and-purple-velvet crowns. Gable said, in a prepared acceptance speech, "I've played reporters and miners and lots of other roles, but this is the first time I've ever been a king. I want to thank all those readers who made me one." Loy told the audience, "No queen ever stood beside such a good-looking king."

Lombard behaved herself at the coronation, though she did at one point turn to a friend and whisper, "If Clark had an inch less, he'd be Queen of the Movies."

Loy's crown has virtually been forgotten, but Gable's title remains with him to this day.

The American public did not need verification that Clark Gable deserved a crown. He had already been their king for several years. What most people did not know (or, perhaps, care about) was that Carole Lombard, earning $465,000, was the highest-paid star of 1937. Her new Paramount contract was worth $2 million all told and guaranteed her three films a year, beginning at $150,000 per. *And* she was able to free-lance. *Film Weekly* commented, "There is one very significant indication on a star's ranking—Hollywood's own opinion. Every producer and director mentions Lombard's name with that mysterious professional enthusiasm whose authenticity cannot be mistaken. And they all declare that she is as fine an emotional actress as she is a comedienne."

Though Lombard was making more money than Gable, he led in the popularity polls. But success came with a high price tag. Their living in separate homes was common knowledge now, their privacy practically nonexistent. With Howard Strickling's help, Gable took an apartment in the Chateau Elysee on Franklin Avenue in Hollywood. Here, Gable and Lombard were able to spend their spare time together in apartment 604 without fear of discovery. Other famous couples had sought refuge at the Chateau Elysee at one time or another—Gloria Swanson and Joseph Kennedy, Marion

Davies and William Randolph Hearst, Cary Grant and Randolph Scott. The Chateau had an elegant European-style dining room but provided room service to those residents who did not want to be seen. The owner of the Chateau Elysee was the widow of movie producer Thomas Ince. She'd built the place with the money W. R. Hearst gave her after that fateful weekend on the *Oneida*. Across the street, Hearst himself had built the Chateau Carlotta, where Louella Parsons, reputed witness to Ince's death, lived for a time. And so there was power and protection on Franklin Avenue.

For many women, sneaking about with a lover is romantic and daring. But secrecy was not Carole Lombard's cup of tea. Especially when her future with Clark Gable was uncertain. Though he wasn't publicly dating other women, she felt certain he was not faithful to her. Without an engagement ring on her left hand, Lombard had no hold on Clark; with one, she felt, he'd still resent any effort of hers to possess him. Gable expected every date to end in the bedroom, but Lombard dismissed him on occasion, especially if they were with a group. "Talk to ya tomorrow," she'd say, closing her front door gently in his face.

While Gable kept his distance from the press, Lombard made it a point to meet her favorite gossip columnists for an occasional lunch. "God knows I love Clark," she told them casually, "but he's the worst lay in town."

When Gable heard about the remark, he laughed. "Well, I guess I'll have to do a lotta practicin'!"

Lombard had a way of attracting attention without trying. Once, she was knitting something on a movie set, but no one could figure out what it was. Finally, she left it in Gable's dressing room with a note, and he showed it around. According to Victor Fleming, "It was a cock warmer—and rather small at that."

Gable was teamed again with Myrna Loy in *Too Hot to Handle*, an adventure melodrama about rival newsreel cameramen. Gable became a real-life national hero when an on-the-set fire went out of control and firemen prepared to rescue Loy, who was playing an aviatrix trapped in a burning plane.

"Keep the cameras rolling, damn it!" Gable yelled. "I'll get her out myself."

When he reappeared from the smoke with Loy in his arms, Lombard, who was watching the shoot, cracked, "You big ham!"

To get even with her for that remark, Gable held on to Loy, whose arms were wrapped around his neck.

"You can put her down now," Lombard said.

Loy wasn't ever sure whether she was really in danger or whether the publicity department had simply decided to capitalize on the incident.

Observers seemed more fascinated by Lombard's presence on the set; Gable had strongly objected to visitors in the past. Perhaps he was attempting to soothe Lombard's frustration by making her an exception. It was no secret that she wanted to get married. Whether he felt the same way at the time is anyone's guess, but there's no question that Gable couldn't yet afford a divorce. In later years, Lombard expressed her fear that Gable would always prefer older women; her zany antics aside, she mothered him and hoped he would need her.

As *Too Hot to Handle* finished production, Lombard was anxiously waiting to find out whether Gable would be offered the part of hoofer Harry Van in the film version of Robert Sherwood's play *Idiot's Delight*. When the assignment was definite, she volunteered to help him with his dance routines.

Joan Crawford wanted to play Irene, the heroine, a phony countess. When Mayer refused to discuss it, Crawford cornered Gable on the MGM back lot.

"Must you wash your teeth in the drinking fountain?" she scolded. "Suppose someone sees you?"

"It's no secret," he said, putting the dentures back into his mouth.

"What's doing with the Sherwood flick?" she asked, lighting a cigarette.

"Norma's doing it."

Joan got off her bicycle and threw it onto the ground. "Did I hear you right?"

"Yeah. It's a long story."

"Irving's dead, but that bitch gets the good parts!"

"Are you crying?"

"What if I am?" she sniffled, burying her face against his chest.

"Don't do that," he muttered, easing her away. "Carole's around here somewhere."

"Fuck Carole! I want to know why the Widow Thalberg's playing Irene!"

"Norma made a deal with Mayer, Joanie. Seems the mail's been pourin' in about her playing Scarlett."

"Scarlett O'Hara?"

"No," he scowled. "Scarlett Goldberg."

"Let's go to your dressing room. I need a drink."

"And I keep tellin' ya, Carole's on the lot. Will you sit down over here and listen?"

"Why do I have to sit down?" she asked, gritting her teeth.

"Because you'll be fallin' down otherwise. Now then, it seems Norma doesn't think she's right for Scarlett and officially declined."

"What?"

"That way, she'll pacify her fans and Mayer won't get lynched. Her reward is *Idiot's Delight*."

"What?"

"Don't get up yet, babe. Norma also got the lead in *The Women*."

"What?"

"You gotta remember, Irving left his financial interest in MGM to Norma. She's got Mayer by the balls."

"She rode into this studio on Irving's balls, didn't she?"

"You've been holding a grudge against Norma too long, and all because you made your movie debut doubling the back of her head."

"I'm tired of playing second fiddle to her. If Selznick thinks

I'll play Scarlett after that cross-eyed bitch turned it down, he's an ass."

"I don't cast 'em, babe, I just play 'em."

"When do we go over your dance routines for *Idiot's Delight?* Good excuse to get together, huh?"

"Carole's been helpin' me. . . ."

"Why didn't you ask me first, goddamn it?"

"Because I'd like to be around for my fortieth birthday."

12.

Rhett

*G*able had several dance numbers in *Idiot's Delight*—the most complicated with a chorus line of six blondes, to the tune of "Puttin' on the Ritz." (At the end of the number, the girls carry Gable offstage and dump him onto the floor.) Lombard worked with him at home and at the studio. She arrived on the set one morning and saw a chorus girl flirting with Gable. Without hesitating, Lombard screamed, "Get that whore out of here!"

The dancer was fired.

Lombard kept her eye on Norma Shearer, too. Thalberg's widow was ready for an affair, and she had always flirted outrageously with her leading men. Shearer had had her eye on Gable before, and now, she was putting all she had into their love scenes. After one particularly long kiss, Lombard snapped at Gable, "I hope you put extra glue on your dentures this morning."

The cast and crew of *Idiot's Delight* weren't tense over Lombard's presence because she was as thoughtful and witty as she was jealous. When Gable finished his final dance number, she presented him with a big bouquet of flowers, calling him "the prima donna." Gable ate it up like a piece of his favorite chocolate cake.

In *Idiot's Delight*, Gable first meets Shearer while they're working in an Omaha burlesque house; they have a brief affair. Years later, they meet again in Europe, but Shearer, posing as a Russian countess, claims she never met him in "Omaha-ha-ha." *Time* considered the film "first rate." *The New York Times* raved, "If you don't see it, you'll be missing one of the year's events." *The Hollywood Reporter* said that Gable and Shearer had given their best performances to date.

Shearer had not given up on Gable. She knew that there was a mutual attraction, and she blamed Lombard's presence on the set for preventing nature from taking its course.

Gable might have contemplated giving Shearer a tumble. His restraint may have been inspired by ongoing loyalty to Thalberg, but it's more likely he doubted Shearer's discretion. The whole town knew about her unrequited love for Tyrone Power. Shearer's affair with Victor Fleming was no secret, either.

Norma Shearer may also have been intimate with Billy Haines in the late twenties. Certainly, he bragged to friends about a liaison, giving the impression that Irving Thalberg's bride was so passionate even *he* couldn't resist.

According to Joan Crawford, Haines frequented Hollywood's gay bars. "I heard rumors that Clark did, too, in 1925," she said. "Billy didn't know that [Clark] wasn't gay or bisexual and suggested a few places where homosexuals got together. If it's true Clark made the rounds, that's how desperate he was for a job."

A former MGM electrician remembers the rumors about Gable and the gay bars. "It's logical," he said, "because big stars like Haines and Ramon Novarro were regulars. I never heard Gable went to these bars for sex. He went there to meet the right people, who just happened to be gay, like myself. That's how I got a job." This electrician, who now resides at the Motion Picture Country House and Lodge, prefers to remain anonymous because he feels that talking about Gable's escapades in the twenties might provoke his friends at the MPCH. He added, "Unless you've lived through this cut-throat business, it's impossible to have compassion for the sacrifices we had to make. I don't regret it, but I'm not proud of it, either."

Clark Gable didn't have to fight for the most sought-after male lead of 1938. Actually, he didn't want to play Rhett Butler at all, but moviegoers demanded it by writing thousands of letters to MGM. "I haven't read the book," Gable said, "but the readers obviously have their own conception of Rhett Butler. Suppose I don't live up to it?"

Margaret Mitchell sold the *Gone With the Wind* movie rights in 1936 to David Selznick for $50,000. He offered the project to Irving Thalberg, who turned it down, commenting, "Civil War movies aren't popular." Selznick didn't have the money to produce the movie on his own, but he still tried to avoid dealing with his father-in-law, L. B. Mayer, even though it was apparent as early as 1936 that Gable was the only logical choice for Rhett. A possible Warner Bros. version, with Bette Davis as Scarlett and Errol Flynn as Rhett, fell through when Davis refused to play opposite Flynn.

Eventually Selznick went to Metro because he needed the services of Clark Gable. Mayer agreed to distribute *Gone With the Wind* in exchange for half the profits plus 15 per cent of the gross to cover costs. MGM would provide one half of the financing—$1,250,000. Gable told Selznick, "Too big an order. I don't want Rhett."

Gable never had a choice, of course, unless he was willing to go on suspension without pay. As an MGM contract player, he was obligated to do any movie the studio told him to.

If Selznick and Mayer thought their major problems were

solved, they were wrong. In late 1938, *Photoplay* magazine published an article that shocked not only the magazine's readers but the movie industry as well. Entitled "Hollywood's Unmarried Husbands and Wives," the piece discussed such famous couples as Barbara Stanwyck and Robert Taylor, Paulette Goddard and Charlie Chaplin, Virginia Rice and George Raft, Constance Bennett and Gilbert Roland, and Carole Lombard and Clark Gable. "The altar record among Hollywood popular twosomes is surprisingly slim," the article confided, noting that Clark Gable was "still officially a married man. . . . Ria Gable is the only wife the law allows Clark Gable." *Photoplay*'s conclusion: "Nobody, even Hollywood's miracle men, has ever improved on the good old-fashioned, satisfying institution of holy matrimony."

This article was a number one scandal. The studios usually controlled what the fan magazines printed; this back talk rocked the likes of Louis B. Mayer and David Selznick. Gable's playing Rhett Butler was out of the question now.

Ria consented to an interview and chose her words carefully. "I've always told Clark he could have a divorce any day he asked for it. And he can. Today or tomorrow. But he's a businessman as well as a movie star."

Mayer cringed. The article was bad enough, but Ria made itclear that she was not standing in Gable's way if indeed he *really* wanted to marry Carole Lombard. (In truth, Gable's reluctance to divorce Ria was, in part, financial: he did not want to give Ria half the money that MGM had put in trust for him. Nor did MGM want to part with it; it was their security should Gable try to walk out on his contract.)

Gable's reputation was on the line; Mayer insisted that serious negotiations with Ria get under way. As popular as Gable was, the public in 1938 would not pay to see anyone involved in a scandal.

Gable's past was catching up to him even as letters continued to flood MGM insisting that no one else could play Rhett Butler. Selznick was on the spot, too. He had been preparing for *Gone With the Wind* a long time, and he was eager to begin production. He wanted to stick with Gable, but there was too much money involved to retain a leading man involved in a bitter publicized divorce.

Shortly after the *Photoplay* article was published, Gable made a simple announcement that he was going to divorce Ria, and lawyers on both sides began to confer.

Precisely when Gable proposed to Lombard isn't known, but he made it official in booth 54 at the famous Brown Derby. They began house-hunting in Bel-Air and Beverly Hills, though Lombard's home was deemed adequate for the time being. Gable said he wanted to "spread out" because he and Lombard enjoyed horseback riding, pets, and, above all, seclusion. Director Raoul Walsh told Gable that his twenty-acre ranch in the San Fernando Valley was up for sale. Gable had long admired the Walsh hideaway, eight miles from Hollywood. In 1938, the Encino property, filled with fruit trees and surrounded by mountains, was in the wilderness. The few ranches nearby were scattered and accessible only by a single canyon road.

The two-story white-brick Connecticut "farmhouse" was thirteen years old. The stables were big enough for ten horses, which fed on home-grown alfalfa and red oats. Beautiful orchards of oranges, lemons, peaches, figs, and apricots surrounded the house, while huge pepper and eucalyptus trees provided shade from the sun's rays in the hot valley.

Making Walsh's second home livable year-round took a great deal of work: installing furnaces, expanding the kitchen, adding servants' quarters, erecting a caretaker's cottage. It also took money—and Gable's was tied up, pending his divorce. "I've always wanted a place like this," he sighed. "It would be the first home I've had since I was a kid. Ma and I could be very happy here." (Gable and Lombard usually referred to each other as "Ma" and "Pa.")

Lombard laid out the $50,000 for Gable's dream; she was investing in her man. Her financial support was a well-guarded secret, of course. What if the public learned that

Gable couldn't buy himself a house? Whether he was rich or
poor, unknown or famous, there was always a woman to come
to the rescue when Gable needed help the most.

Lombard didn't care that she had to bankroll her lover.
They were happy, excitedly making plans, strolling through
the orchards, discussing color schemes, and looking at
tractors. Then Ria announced that her husband had no right
to "presume" anything regarding a divorce. She had been
insulted by his ungallant announcement and was going to
contest. Within days, Gable gave a prepared statement to the
press:

> I regret bitterly that a short time ago a story was printed to the
> effect that I would seek a divorce. After years of separation, it is
> only natural that Mrs. Gable should institute proceedings that will
> assure her freedom.

Ria simmered down and finally agreed to begin negotiating,
but Clark's lawyers warned him he would pay dearly for the
divorce. MGM was forced to intervene, and though Mayer was
usually in favor of the poor unfortunate wife in such matters,
he had powerful motives behind his generosity and understanding this time. There is no evidence that he ever
approached Gable about Lombard other than through
Howard Strickling, but if Mayer wasn't convinced Lombard
was the best thing that ever happened to Gable, he was the
only one. She had many ways of keeping Gable on his toes,
especially when he bragged about his previous sexual
escapades. "I even did it in the swimming pool once," he said
with a grin. "You know, it's hard to do underwater."

"Yes, isn't it?" she deadpanned.

Gable's mouth dropped open. "What kind of girl are you?"
he exclaimed. "Doing a thing like that and having the nerve to
tell me about it!"

Lombard did not, however, appreciate reading items in the
gossip columns that linked Gable to other women. Unable to
sleep one night, she was scanning a fan magazine and came

across a rumor about Gable. It was three o'clock in the morning, but she called him on the phone and screamed, "Our engagement is off, you son of a bitch! Here's one dame who isn't chasing you." Gable loved it when she got angry, and this time it was Lombard who received the white doves of peace.

Gable was still not convinced that he *had* to play Rhett Butler, and he kept trying to beat the system. In one last attempt, Gable spoke to Mayer about *Gone With the Wind.*

"I'll be tied up for a year!" he complained.

"Six months at the most," Mayer assured him.

"I want to know who's playing Scarlett."

"Ask my son-in-law."

"Frankly, I don't like Selznick."

"Neither do I."

"Don't I have a say in the matter?"

"No."

"I'm being bounced around like a tennis ball, and I don't like it. Besides, I know for a fact Selznick wants Gary Cooper."

"That's because my son-in-law's an ass."

"I'm second choice. Is that it?"

"Third. He couldn't get Errol Flynn," Mayer said with a straight face. "Do you think you're the only actor who can play Rhett Butler?"

"No, but you do. I'd like to see a list of girls making a screen test for Scarlett." Gable looked at the names and shook his head. "Tallulah Bankhead? Is Selznick out of his fuckin' mind? Lucille Ball, and Susan Hayward? Never heard of 'em. Loretta Young? She's not wicked enough . . . on the screen, anyway. Forget Miriam Hopkins. Lana Turner—is she the young blonde kid? Too cute. Joan Crawford, maybe."

"Paulette Goddard's the favorite," Mayer said, laughing. "But she and Chaplin are living together and can't prove they're married. She says the mayor of Catalina performed the ceremony."

"So?"

"Catalina doesn't have a mayor. If Paulette were under contract to MGM, we would have protected her."

"Yeah," Gable said with a scowl. Leaving Mayer's office, Gable still wasn't convinced that he was locked into *Gone With the Wind*, which was the talk of the town. As Joan Crawford put it, "All of a sudden every girl in Hollywood has a southern accent." Crawford campaigned herself for Scarlett, telling Gable, "It's just a matter of time before it's official and you're Rhett Butler. I was in the mail room the other day and saw literally hundreds of thousands of letters insisting on it."

"What were you doing in the mail room?" Gable asked.

"I answer every one of my fan letters personally. Don't change the subject."

"I'm sick and tired of this Rhett business."

"Not if I play Scarlett. We're dynamite together."

"Yeah."

"You'll insist?"

"Carole wants the part, too."

"Scarlett's not a blonde, for Christ's sake!"

"I wouldn't know 'cause I haven't read the goddamn book!"

While Gable was dodging Crawford at MGM, Lombard was fencing with Gary Cooper at Paramount.

"Tell them you'll play Rhett and then cancel," she told him.

"Why would I do that?" he asked.

"Because I'm the logical one at Paramount for Scarlett. When you back out, David O. will be forced to work with Mayer. Clark isn't anxious to play Rhett, but he's in demand."

"MGM publicity."

"Jesus!"

Cooper frowned. "One and the same."

"You hate Clark. That's it!"

"I don't hate him, but I don't like him much. The truth is, I think *Gone With the Wind* is going to be the biggest flop in Hollywood history."

"If you played Rhett," Lombard said, laughing, "it would be!"

At Warner Bros., Bette Davis was fuming. Without Errol Flynn as Rhett she was not a strong contender for Scarlett, a role she felt was written for her. Gable felt otherwise. His remark that Davis was not the kind of woman that Rhett would look at twice infuriated her. According to Lawrence J. Quirk's Davis biography, *Fasten Your Seat Belts*, Davis dug up all the dirt on Gable she could manage and went after him with a vengeance. "I can't stand a man who has fake store teeth and doesn't keep his uncircumcised cock clean under the foreskin," she was reported as saying. "I hear he shoots too soon and messes himself all the time. Great Lover? Great Fake!" Quirk offers a corollary story, that George Cukor's 1939 birthday present to Gable was a cake of Life Buoy soap and a bottle of Listerine "to clean beneath your foreskin and take away the smell."

Gable had no idea to what extent his divorce was related to *Gone With the Wind*. Once Mayer made up his mind to deal with Ria, he began production meetings with Selznick, and Gable was finalized as Rhett in August 1938. Ever close with a buck, Gable fumed that Ria would collect $286,000 over a three-year period. His contract and MGM trust fund would be dunned accordingly.

Gable struggled to read Margaret Mitchell's book, eventually concluding that he wasn't sure how to portray Rhett Butler, and that Scarlett O'Hara so dominated the story that *whoever* played the part would be a real threat to him. Furthermore, he was livid over the choice of director.

"Why George Cukor?" he asked Selznick. "Everyone knows he's a woman's director."

"He's the best" was the reply.

Meanwhile, six thousand miles away in England, a green-eyed twenty-four-year-old beauty was pining away for her married lover, who was making a movie in the United States. She had just finished reading *Gone With the Wind* and identified with Scarlett. They thought and looked very much alike, she believed. She made up her mind in a split second, called her boyfriend, and said that she was sailing on the next boat for New York, adding, "Your agent is Myron Selznick, isn't it?"

"Yes, darling. Why do you ask?"

"Is he David's brother?"

"Yes."

"I should very much like to meet him."

"Then I'll arrange it."

Laurence Olivier hung up the telephone and thought nothing more of the request; he was only delighted that the woman he loved would be in his arms within the week.

In New York, the woman boarded a plane for the first time in her life. During the fifteen-hour flight—with three stopovers to refuel before reaching Los Angeles—Vivien Leigh skimmed through Margaret Mitchell's book again and again, visualizing how she should dress and fix her hair for her first encounter with Myron Selznick. After one glance at Leigh, he took her to see his brother, who was filming the burning of Atlanta on the back lot. Myron Selznick took Vivien's hand, walked her over to his brother, and said, "I'd like you to meet Scarlett O'Hara." David Selznick said afterward that he never forgot that first meeting. "When you picture someone in your mind and then you see that person, nothing else is necessary."

Well, almost nothing else. Vivien Leigh was a married woman having an affair with a married man. David Selznick explained that the code in the United States was strict. Americans did not take kindly to blatant adultery. But to put the couple at ease, Selznick explained how Gable and Lombard were facing the same delicate situation. But, he underscored, they were not living together. Olivier was gracious about the matter, but Leigh was distressed that she and her lover could not share a hotel suite. At the time, Olivier was filming *Wuthering Heights*; afterward, he would leave for New York to do *No Time for Comedy* on Broadway.

Vivien hated Holywood, and without Olivier, she was almost sorry she had agreed to play Scarlett. She felt better, however, when she met George Cukor, who she quickly came to adore and admire. It was a relief to her, knowing he would direct *Gone With the Wind*.

David Selznick tested Melvyn Douglas and Ray Milland for the part of Ashley Wilkes after Leslie Howard, Selznick's first choice, expressed his desire to produce and direct films rather than act. Finally, Selznick made a deal: Howard could star in *and* direct *Intermezzo* if he would also play Ashley. Howard said yes for the deal and the money; he never read Mitchell's novel, and he hated his role in the film. "I'm not beautiful or young enough," he complained, "and it makes me sick being fixed up to look attractive." Furthermore, Howard said the film was "utter nonsense."

In December 1938, George Cukor requested that everyone in the cast begin their southern-diction lessons. Gable told Mayer and Selznick, "I'm not talking with a southern accent, and that's final." Mayer didn't quarrel with Gable, recognizing that the public paid to see Clark Gable walk and talk like Clark Gable. Mayer knew that Gable was, first and foremost, a personality, not an actor; Mayer had *built* MGM on a foundation of personalities. Good actors were a dime a dozen. If Selznick was annoyed by Mayer's backing Gable in the accent battle, he didn't let on. Ria had yet to sign any papers, and there was no specified date for her to begin divorce proceedings. Mayer kept this information to himself; he enjoyed watching his son-in-law sweat.

On January 26, 1939, shortly after Ria went to Las Vegas to obtain her divorce, production began on *Gone With the Wind*. Cukor shot the opening scene, in which Scarlett flirts on the porch of Tara with the Tarleton brothers; Melanie's (Olivia de Havilland) giving birth to Ashley's baby; and Scarlett's killing a Union deserter who is looting Tara.

Gable had not yet met his leading lady, who was certainly the most beautiful woman he'd ever been cast opposite. Regardless of Lombard and regardless of Olivier, many believed that Gable would charm Leigh into a hot romance.

The first day the two stars were set to work together, Leigh arrived late. Gable ranted and complained. As she walked onto the set, he could be heard cursing her tardiness; the feisty Leigh approached fearlessly, looked up at Gable, and said, ever so sweetly, "I quite agree, Mr. Gable. If I were a man, I'd tell that Vivien Leigh to go right back to merry old England."

He turned around and looked into her green eyes and between her breasts, taped together for cleavage. Neither said a word. What a glorious moment! He smiled, took her arm, and strolled with her around the set. Their first scene together was the one in which Rhett presents Scarlett with an expensive Paris hat. Then they shot the Atlanta Bazaar Ball sequence, where the widowed Scarlett, dressed in black, shocks the crowd by dancing with Rhett. Then, less than a month after production began, George Cukor was fired. When Leigh heard the news, she burst into tears and ran from the set.

Joan Crawford remembered Gable's utter unhappiness with the whole picture. "He hated making *Gone With the Wind*," she said. "He absolutely detested Cukor, who was a discreet gay. He was my favorite director, God bless him, but George and Billy Haines *were* good friends. In fact, George had recently given a birthday party for Billy. Clark was sure that George knew that he and Billy had a thing in 1925. To make matters worse, George called Clark 'dear' on the set. I tried to discuss it with Clark, but he was upset about a lot of things. He resented an English girl taking the part of Scarlett, and Vivien went by the book—Margaret Mitchell's. Shit! That's not how movies are made. Clark was stubborn, but he had the upper hand. He had power and he used it."

After consulting Gable, David Selznick brought in Victor Fleming, who was just finishing *The Wizard of Oz* (from which the original director, in this case Richard Thorpe, had also been fired). Under pressure from MGM and as a favor to his friend Gable, an exhausted Fleming took over as director of *Gone With the Wind*. Justifying the change, Selznick insisted that Cukor had gone ahead with his own ideas, which were different from those originally agreed upon.

Cukor said, "Perhaps Clark mistakenly thought that because I was supposed to be a woman's director, I would throw the story to Vivien—but if that's so, it was very naïve of him and not the reaction of a very good or professional actor. It is nonsense to say I was giving too much attention to Vivien. It is the text that dictates where the emphasis should go, and the director does not do it. Clark Gable does not have a good deal of confidence in himself as an actor, and maybe he thought I did not understand that."

Gable left the studio every night at six. Emulating Garbo, he had long since made sure that a "no overtime" clause was in all of his contracts. Leigh considered Gable's attitude "common." Factory workers punch time clocks, she said, not dedicated actors. The other players were amazed at Gable's ability to get anything he wanted—no southern accent for Captain Butler, a change of director, no late hours, and, eventually, a complete new wardrobe and tailor.

Gable wasn't seeing his leading lady after hours, but he was widely believed to be sneaking off with one of the female extras. Now that Gable was on the verge of divorce, Lombard's jealousy had increased. She wasn't quite sure what she'd do if she caught Gable with another woman. They were close to getting married, but Lombard had her pride. The rumors about his flirtations during *Gone With the Wind* upset her, and they fought about it.

Victor Fleming, whom Gable idolized, was a man's man. He was a big-game hunter, he raced cars, he'd been a photographer for the Signal Corps during World War I; he was a talented cameraman and a notorious womanizer. Part American Indian, he was tall and broad shouldered; he had salt-and-pepper hair and gray eyes. Like Gable, he was a magnet to woman (among his conquests were Norma Shearer and Clara Bow). Born in 1883, Fleming began directing films in 1919. A longtime bachelor, he impregnated a friend's wife and married her in 1933.

Considering his directorial accomplishments, Fleming has been sadly overlooked in Hollywood chronicles. His films include the 1929 version of *The Virginian*, *Red Dust*, the 1934 version of *Treasure Island*, *Captains Courageous*, *Test Pilot*, *The Wizard of Oz*, *Gone With the Wind*, the 1941 *Dr. Jekyll and Mr. Hyde*, and *Joan of Arc* (starring Ingrid Bergman, with whom he also had an affair).

Producer Arthur Freed once said, "Gable owes everything he was, his personality, to Vic. He modeled himself on him."

Though Fleming was a no-nonsense director, he had the sensitivity to direct *The Wizard of Oz* and to convince Gable to cry in *Gone With the Wind* when Rhett's little daughter dies. At first, Gable refused to, but Fleming knew how to handle the actor. "Hell, we probably won't use it, but let's give it a try," Fleming said casually. So Clark wept, and he was pleased with the outcome. Cukor, on the other hand, would surely have had a bitter fight with Gable over this scene.

Vivien Leigh did not respond to Fleming. She wept, and he stood his ground. Following days of tension, she asked him how to play what he considered a simple scene. "Ham it up," he said. Vivien retorted, "That's not the way George told me to do it." Fleming glared at her and exclaimed, "Miss Leigh, you can stick this script up your royal British ass!" Then he stormed off the set and did not report for work the next day. His wife said he had contemplated suicide and suffered a nervous breakdown. David Selznick talked to Fleming's doctor and was told otherwise. Director Sam Wood took over, but Fleming returned two weeks later to direct Gable's scenes.

It has been said that *Gone With the Wind* was a success *in spite* of David Selznick, who tinkered extensively with the screenplay and intrusively supervised the film's various directors. Cukor later said that he resented Selznick's interference.

As for Gable and Leigh, they managed to get through the shoot without clashing, although she did not think he was too bright or a very responsive actor. Fleming disagreed: "Clark was unique at responding. That was his secret. He was an intent and genuine listener on and off the screen. I preferred giving the good lines to someone else because he was a genius at reacting—sometimes with a dumb look on his face or a smirk. It's not clear to me what Vivien meant. She attended the Royal Academy of Dramatic Arts, was a polished actress and an artist, but Clark knew his limitations. He didn't try to pretend to be anything he wasn't. They were very well matched on the screen but were worlds apart when the camera wasn't rolling."

What Leigh resented most about Gable was his bad breath, caused, apparently, by his false teeth. He also reeked of liquor, which nauseated her. In his biography, *Vivien Leigh*, Hugh Vickers wrote, "he [Gable] later confessed that when obliged to kiss on screen he normally thought of a steak."

The film was near completion when Fleming filmed the scene in which Rhett carries Scarlett up a long staircase to their bedroom as she thrashes him with her fists. Leigh managed to do something wrong in each take, and Gable had to repeat the strenuous business ten or eleven times. Just as his exhausted star was about to blow his stack, Fleming quipped, "The first take was perfect, Clark, just perfect. The others were for laughs."

On June 27, 1939, having cost approximately four million dollars, *Gone With the Wind* was completed. Selznick also had to pay a fine of $5000 for the use of the word "damn" in Gable's famous exit line. Within a year, the film had grossed fourteen million dollars. Five years later, Louis B. Mayer bought out Selznick's entire share of *Gone With the Wind*.

The Making of a legend.

Clark and Ria Langham, his second wife.

Clark with Carole Lombard in the film *No Man of Her Own*, 1932.

With Lombard after their 1939 marriage.

Gable and Vivien Leigh in *Gone With the Wind*.

Gable earned his wings in the Air Force during World War II.

The Crawford–Gable chemistry work[s]
on and off the screen. Their affa[ir]
lasted thirty years.

Clark and Lana Turner in *Honky To[nk]*
made wife Lombard jealous.

Grace Kelly fell in love with Gable during the filming of *Mogambo*.

able was patient and loving with the notionally unstable Marilyn Monroe during the *Misfits*.

Clark's marriage to Lady Sylvia As
was a disaster.

Clark finally found happiness with
fifth and last wife, Kay Spreckle

13.

Ma and Pa Gable

When the notorious "Hollywood's Unmarried Husbands and Wives" article was published, MGM immediately announced Robert Taylor's engagement to Barbara Stanwyck, and began coddling Ria Gable. Taylor had been in England, shooting MGM's first overseas film, *A Yank at Oxford*; he returned to Hollywood in January 1939. Gable kidded him about the *Photoplay* article: "Babe, betcha Carole and I beatcha to the preacher." Taylor took the bet.

On March 8, 1939, Gable's divorce from Ria was final. "I was thinkin'," he told Lombard, "maybe we'd get married on my first day off."

"I'll do my best to make it, Pa."

"What?"

"I'm scheduled to do *In Name Only* with Cary Grant. Suppose we don't have the same day off?"

"Because Vic and I devised a plan. Big doin's in San Francisco for the premiere of *The Story of Alexander Graham Bell*. Everyone wants to go, so Vic is plannin' a four-day weekend."

"I wouldn't miss that premiere for anything!" Lombard said with a straight face.

"Well, if you change your mind, Ma, we could head in the opposite direction ... say, Kingman, Arizona, and get married. Howard can arrange it so that if we drive down there and back in twenty-four hours, no one has to know about it."

"I promised Louella an exclusive."

"You were that sure, huh?"

He got a pillow in his face, but before he could throw it back, she was in his arms.

At 4:30 A.M., March 29, 1939, Lombard and Gable left on the 357-mile drive to Kingman, Arizona. To throw off reporters, Gable's personal public-relations man, Otto Winkler, drove the couple in his own car. They took along a large picnic basket for the ten-hour drive so as to avoid having to stop and be recognized in restaurants. Winkler himself had been married in Kingman just the week before, so he knew precisely where to go. After obtaining a marriage license at the county clerk's office, Lombard and Gable were married at the First Methodist Episcopal Church by the Reverend Kenneth Engle.

When Howard Strickling got the phone call from Winkler saying that it was safe to release the news, he set up a press conference for the next day. Lombard called her mother but was unable to reach Louella Parsons, who was in San Francisco. By the time the columnist finally received Lombard's telegram, the news was already out. (Parsons was livid and broke her friendship with Lombard.)

At 3:00 A.M. Sunday, April 2, the newlyweds returned to Lombard's home. Her brothers and her mother, Bessie, were there to greet them with a champagne toast. Weary from the long drive, the Gables retired to separate rooms. Bessie Peters asked her daughter, "What's going on?"

"Clark's tired," Lombard explained, "and he has enough trouble performing under the best of circumstances." Later, she crawled into bed with her snoring groom and snuggled up to him. This was the ultimate for Lombard. Lying beside Gable was nothing new, but it had meaning this time. There was no sex on her wedding night and that made it all the more romantic, even though Gable's dentures were lying on the bedside table.

The following day, the newlyweds held a press conference. He was in a navy suit and white tie, and she wore a simple gray flannel suit. Lombard was all smiles, but she did not have a juicy remark for eager reporters, who were used to a flippant, outspoken Lombard. Gable beamed but had little to say, which was no surprise. Reporters asked whether the couple planned to have children. Lombard looked proudly at her husband and let him respond. "We'd rather not answer that," he said.

The press reported Lombard's "new personality"—a quiet softness, a coy giggle, a gentleness about her that oozed happiness, and an obvious determination to take "second billing" to Gable in their marriage.

Louella Parsons, who wielded a good deal of power in Hollywood, was still furious with Lombard, but the actress tried to make up by promising a scoop when she became pregnant. Parsons took her revenge, anyway, and excluded Gable's name from her list of favorite performers in 1939.

Press agent George Nichols recalled, "When Parsons went to Europe, Carole had Louella's bathroom redecorated. This was the only way to get around the columnist. Every Christmas, Parsons got truckloads of presents from studio moguls and stars. If anyone forgot her, she forgot them in her column. But Louella was hooked on Gable. She was a clever woman who was not easily taken in. He was an exception."

Parsons later said that Gable's charisma was a form of hypnosis. "He could cast a spell on anyone. Clark wasn't chivalrous, cultured, or polished, but whatever the good Lord gave him—potency, might, vigor—was enough. As close as we were, I was never immune."

Columnist Sheilah Graham was, however. In 1936, she had written, "Clark Gable threw his handsome head back and exposed a neckline on which a thin ridge of fat is beginning to collect." He never spoke to Graham again.

The press had always relied on Lombard for gossip and laughs; then she married Gable. *Modern Screen* wrote, "Carole has long been the pet of the boys and girls who write stories about the stars because she was always cooperative, because she always gave honest, swell copy, told the truth and didn't blue-pencil every word she spoke that was more pithy than a nursery. These days there is an un-Lombardian evasiveness." *Modern Screen* also hinted that Lombard had been counseled to be difficult and aloof, advice, the magazine said, which neither fit nor "becomes a good fellow who is Lombard." Indirectly, *Modern Screen* was pointing a finger at MGM, which had control over their stars *and* their stars' spouses.

Adela Rogers St. Johns, who had always come to Gable's rescue, defended Lombard. "Clark told his wife that if anyone was going to do the swearing, he'd do it. He didn't want to hear any of it again from her, and he didn't." Friends say that statement was for public consumption, that Gable liked Lombard the way she was. In public, however, she conducted herself as the wife of an MGM star should.

Lombard's attitude toward her life as Mrs. Gable was not the least bit complex or bewildering. Nor had she changed. "Adjusted" is a better description, and she had done so wisely. She had married a man who was known to chase every girl in town but needed a mother. Lombard was not the type to let him get away with much or sit at home wondering if he was coming home for dinner. Gable knew it, too. Lombard fit into his life and enjoyed it. Everything revolved around him because that made her happy. She sent a red rose to his dressing room every day when he was working, and gave him other mementos of their love. Some were romantic; others were tools or rifle attachments or, as Clark was regularly making arrangements for their next outing, the latest thing in camping equipment. One of their favorite trips was to go sixty-five miles south of the Mexican border to the La Grulla Gun Club. Gable frequently had the urge to go deeper into the mountains, or farther south for duck and geese. Often they had to take a private plane to these desolate places. More than once, the hunting party nearly crashed on takeoffs or landings. Occasionally, their station wagon broke down on lonely roads. Lombard took these inconveniences in her stride. She felt, as Gable did, that if anything awful happened, at least they would be together. Lombard's philosophy was "One has the ability to work out personal problems, but if it has to do with cosmic influences, ignore them and go about your business." But if a near accident occurred in an airplane, Carole said they should never travel in separate planes.

She was most contented having him all to herself, snuggling with him in a sleeping bag and dining on canned beans, or roughing it in an isolated cabin by the Rogue River, or fishing from a cabin cruiser in the middle of a small lake full of trout. Lombard endured rattlesnakes (she stepped on one once), walked into a hornet's nest and was stung, waded in mud up to her waist, and learned how to cook over an open fire.

Did Gable make sacrifices for Lombard? Maybe so, but they were too insignificant to mention. He admitted wanting to share his outdoor hobbies with her and delaying trips when she was working. He wasn't enthusiastic about his wife's big annual parties or the few she gave in between, though she tried to make the latter as informal as possible. Dinner parties for Hollywood big shots were always formal, however, and Lombard enjoyed putting on a slinky long dress and playing hostess.

The Gables' annual party was an outdoor event. The Brown Derby catered the festivities in a large tent erected on the couple's lawn. The best food in town was served on checked tablecloths, however. Candles and wine bottles and flowers were on each table; a hot-dog stand was nearby, and a dance floor was set up for those who were willing to put up with a band consisting of friends who were exercising their musical talent for the first time since high-school days.

Always a topic of conversation were the famous white doves, which had multiplied and were penned for sentimental reasons.

There was a serious side to Lombard, though she seldom revealed it, even to close friends. "Clark hasn't had a very happy life," she once confided. "He needs someone to look after him, but don't tell him that."

Clark rarely talked about the hardships of his youth. Will Gable was willing to take his son's money now, but he did not consider Clark to be a successful man in a respectable trade, and he never pretended otherwise. He attended his son's premieres, but never in formal attire, and he always went in the back way to a regular seat.

There would never be a genuine closeness between father and son. If the early years had been strained, Clark now had to live with the fact that Will knew the details of his "useful" marriages to Josephine and Ria. In his father's eyes, Clark was not only a sissy but a gigolo, as well.

Though Clark Gable often referred to himself as "Mr. Lucky," he had little to show for his success aside from his ranch. Ria and taxes regularly claimed the bulk of his wages. Carole Lombard hadn't done much better. In 1937, she paid 85 percent of her wages in taxes. Characteristically, she said, "I don't mind. I'm proud to be an American."

The Encino ranch was modest by Hollywood standards, but not for the lack of or concern about money. The Gables preferred comfort to luxury. Clark often looked at the orchards and fields of oats in awe. After being owned and operated by MGM, he finally had something that belonged to him. Yet he was terrified that his appeal would fade and, with it, his beloved property. He needed Carole's strength because she had no fears. She attributed this to her belief in astrology,

numerology, and the occult. (Her Libra and his Aquarius
were compatible.)

Though Gable later said that he never would have lasted in
films but for *Gone With the Wind*, as 1939 came to an end, he
wanted to forget that Rhett Butler existed. Mayer kept Gable
busy with Joan Crawford in *Strange Cargo*.

"*Idiot's Delight* was terrible," she said. "Old beady eyes
gave the worst performance of her life!"

Gable scowled. "You weren't so professional in *The
Women*."

"You saw the rushes?"

"I'm referring to what happened on the set, babe."

Crawford had fought for and won the role of Crystal in the
film version of Clare Boothe's play *The Women*; her costars
were Norma Shearer, Rosalind Russell, Paulette Goddard,
and Joan Fontaine. Crawford played a seductive perfume
salesgirl who steals Shearer's husband. George Cukor
directed.

"I heard all about the knitting-needle episode," Gable
teased.

"The afghan isn't for you, darling."

"You know what I'm talkin' about—tryin' to distract
Norma when you were feedin' lines to her."

"Can I help it if she's slow? I was knitting, that's all!"
Crawford exclaimed.

"Yeah, with needles the size of elephant tusks."

Crawford smirked.

"What did you put in the telegram to Norma?" he asked.

"George wanted me to apologize. I told her off instead. I
told her she'd be a shit extra around here if it hadn't been for
Irving . . . that she had only two expressions on the
screen—with her eyes open and with her eyes closed."

"I don't believe you did that."

"I made up my mind to show her who's queen around here.
She knows the score now."

"Sure!" Clark laughed. "I saw what happened the day you

were late for that photo session with Norma. The whole studio knows about it."

"I wasn't going to be the first one there."

"Joanie, your dressing room was right across the street from the photographer!"

"So?"

"So why did you need a limousine?"

"It's in my contract."

"For a U-turn?"

"You got it."

By now, Gable was howling with laughter. "Round and round you went with Norma's car in front of yours. Jesus!"

"Behind mine."

"Yeah," he hooted. "Strickling turned out to be the traffic cop who made you both pull over. I saw it but couldn't believe it."

"You're to blame!" Crawford announced.

"Me?"

"You got Cukor fired and they gave him *The Women*. He wanted me to apologize. Me! Because he was so goddamn upset about being kicked off *Gone With the Wind*."

"Your Georgie was where he belonged—with a bunch of cackling dames and their knitting needles."

In *Strange Cargo*, Gable played a convict and Crawford was the prostitute who gets mixed up in his escape from prison. In the jungle, they encounter another convict (Ian Hunter), a Christ-like figure who carries a Bible. Gable returns to the penal colony when Crawford promises to wait for him.

Strange Cargo was released three months after *Gone With the Wind* and received excellent reviews, proving that the Gable–Crawford team was still box-office magic.

Gable did not want to attend the Atlanta premiere of *Gone With the Wind* on December 15, 1939. David Selznick had chartered a plane, but Gable had his name taken off the passenger list. Lombard tried to convince him that this was no ordinary premiere. It was a historical event, she said, and his absence would make him look shabby. "I won't go without Fleming," he announced. "And Vic is positively *not* going."

"Why?" Lombard asked. "He's the only one who's getting screen credit for director."

"Yeah, but Selznick has the whole town believing *he* was responsible—that *he* directed it."

"Look, Pa, let *them* fight it out. Please don't disappoint all those people, because they're really celebrating you. Not Rhett. Not David. Not even Scarlett. You can't disappoint all those people who love you, Pa."

With Howard Strickling's help, Lombard convinced Gable to attend the premiere. They chartered their own plane and were greeted at the Atlanta airport by thousands. Lombard, wearing black with sables, was presented with a bouquet of yellow roses. "I'm going to let Mr. Gable do all the talking," she said graciously, adding, "I love you all." The motorcade into town was so exhilarating that Gable got into the mood and decided not to go into hiding, as he had planned. The fans were sincere, warm, and friendly. The population of Atlanta was three hundred thousand, but on this spectacular weekend, the city bulged with a million people.

Other than posing for group pictures with Selznick, Gable avoided the producer. Much of his bitterness had to do with the fact that Victor Fleming's name had been omitted from the premiere program. Even when Gable was informed that the omission was a mistake, he was still furious.

At the Grand Theater premiere, Carole was beautiful in a gold lamé evening gown and cape. Her rubies glistened in the spotlights as she clung to her husband when he stepped up to the microphones and said, "This is Margaret Mitchell's night and your night. Just let me be a spectator going to see *Gone With the Wind*."

Instead of watching the movie, however, Gable chose to have a long talk with Mitchell, who had persistently refused to reveal whether or not she had had Gable in mind when she created Rhett Butler. After all the guests were seated, Mitchell and Gable ducked into the ladies' room for complete privacy. Gable never revealed the entire conversation, but he told Lombard that Scarlett represented Mitchell during her restless and fiery youth, and that the author had patterned Rhett after her first husband, who, when she repeatedly rejected him, took her by force. Gable said that it was a relief to learn that the author had not had him in mind when she wrote the book, "because it was tough enough knowing that the readers saw me as Rhett."

At the Hollywood premiere, mobs of fans prevented Gable from viewing the film. He and Lombard stayed in the manager's office until everyone left the theater. When the phone rang, Lombard picked up and said there were no tickets left. "We're booked solid for a year," she said.

The story of an egotistic southern girl (Scarlett O'Hara) who survives the Civil War but finally loses the only man she cares for (Rhett Butler) is the basic theme of *Gone With the Wind*. After 225 minutes on the screen, Scarlett realizes she loves Rhett, her third husband, and begs him not to go away. When he opens the front door to leave, she sobs, "If you go, what shall I do?"

Rhett turns to her and says, "Frankly, my dear, I don't give a damn!" ("Frankly" was added by screenwriter Sidney Howard. The use of "damn" cost Selznick $5000 because profanity on the screen was a punishable offense. The other version was, "Frankly, my dear, I don't care.")

On February 29, 1940, the twelfth award ceremony of the Academy of Motion Picture Arts and Sciences was held at the Cocoanut Grove of the Ambassador Hotel in Los Angeles.

Gone With the Wind set an Academy record, winning ten Oscars. The Irving G. Thalberg Memorial Award for outstanding achievement by a producer went to David Selznick, who also accepted the best-picture Oscar. Master of ceremonies Bob Hope cracked, "What a wonderful thing, this benefit for David Selznick."

The other *Gone With the Wind* winners were Vivien Leigh (Best Actress), Hattie McDaniel (edging out Olivia de Havilland and three others to become the first black Oscar winner as Best Supporting Actress), Victor Fleming (Best Director), Hal Kern and James Newcom (Film Editing), Lyle Wheeler (Interior Decoration), Sidney Howard (Screenplay), and Ernest Haller and Ray Rennahan (Color Cinematography). William Cameron Menzies and Selznick International's Don Musgrave were given special awards for "outstanding achievement in the use of color" and "pioneering in the use of coordinated equipment," respectively.

The shock of the evening was Robert Donat taking Best Actor for *Goodbye, Mr. Chips*. Gable was crushed, and he blamed David Selznick, who he said had not campaigned on his behalf. Selznick admitted as much to his publicity director. But over the years we, the public, took it for granted Gable left with the Oscar.

For all the fame it has given him, Gable walked away from *Gone With the Wind* "empty-handed." No Oscar, no percentage of the profits, and no bonus. But *Gone With the Wind* granted Gable a reputation that has endured for over fifty years and will most likely last for years to come.

Gable was, however, happy for Victor Fleming, who did not show up at the Academy Award ceremonies.

The first Christmas in the Gables' new home was a festive one. Carole was thrilled with the ruby heart from Clark, who also bought her perfume and some clothes. "Pa isn't the most generous guy in the world, you know" was a famous saying of Lombard's, the ruby notwithstanding.

Carole gave him a robe and monogrammed pajamas—also sleeping bags and hunting and fishing equipment, without which Christmas wouldn't be complete.

When they were not filming, Lombard and Gable worked around the ranch. They always dressed in the evening; she had put a great deal of love into decorating the dining room, with its off-white beamed ceiling, natural pine walls, and oversize white brick fireplace, and dinner was a nightly ritual, with or without guests. The long, weathered refectory table, highly polished, was never covered with place mats or a tablecloth. Antique captain's chairs surrounded the table. Clark's was the largest.

In the sunny living room, the carpet and sofa were bright yellow; other furniture added splashes of red and green. Clark was very proud of his gun room, where he spent time alone. There was a secretarial suite and servants' quarters on the ground floor. Upstairs were two master bedrooms. His was brown and beige, with a tufted brown-leather headboard over the double bed. Carole's suite was a masterpiece of white and marble, with fur rugs, crystal chandeliers, floor-to-ceiling mirrors, and a four-poster bed. All together, there were eight rooms in the house—none for guests.

The household staff knew Gable's two quirks. Lombard didn't have to remind them that he did not like the color pink—"and for God's sake, never have his hats cleaned!" Gable was meticulous about the rest of his extensive and costly wardrobe and Lombard howled with laughter every time she saw the soiled hats lined up like museum pieces. "Pa's funny," she once said. "He wants his shoes shined before he feeds the chickens, and then he puts on a dirty hat."

Gable could be seen on his tractor early in the morning. Lombard romped with the dogs, cut fresh flowers for the house, and planned her husband's meat-and-potatoes dinners. Spareribs, baked beans, and apple pie were his favorites.

The year 1939 had got off to a rough start but turned out to be one of the happiest in either of their lives. It was the year that had brought Gable and Lombard an idyllic marriage, and a dream house. He had appeared in *Gone With the Wind*; she had made two successful films: *In Name Only* and, with Jimmy Stewart, *Made for Each Other*. On New Year's Eve 1940, they had drunk to having many children and another Oscar for Clark. But their champagne toasts were in vain.

The 1939 list of top-grossing movie stars contained a few new names. From one to ten: Mickey Rooney, Tyrone Power, Spencer Tracy, Clark Gable, Shirley Temple, Bette Davis, Alice Faye, Errol Flynn, James Cagney, and Sonja Henie.

Although Gable had slipped down two notches from the last year's list, he was nonetheless rewarded by MGM on January 25, 1940, with a new seven-year contract for seventy-five hundred dollars a week. The first three years, he was obligated to make three pictures a year; the next four, only two a year. MGM refused to omit the clause requiring Gable to be "available at all times in Los Angeles or any other place we may designate." He was granted the option to break the contract in five years, and the balance of his trust fund was turned over to him.

Few people knew that Carole Lombard wanted to win an Oscar of her own before having a baby. Gable led everyone to believe he wanted his wife to retire, but it was hard for him to overlook Lombard's earning $150,000 a picture, plus a piece of the profits. She had chosen to play a nurse in the tearjerker *Vigil in the Night*, hoping for an Oscar nomination. Lombard was superb, but the film got only middling reviews. *The New York Times* acknowledged "Lombard at her severest best." That was the problem. The public refused to accept Lombard in anything but a comedy. Lombard firmly believed that *Vigil in the Night* had been her last chance for an Oscar.

Lombard next got top billing over 1932/33 Oscar winner Charles Laughton in *They Knew What They Wanted*, from Sidney Howard's 1924 Pulitzer Prize-winning play. He played a grape farmer, and she was his mail-order bride, who becomes pregnant by the farm's foreman. For the second time, Lombard struck out. Her appeal at the box office was slipping and she admitted as much to the press: "I took the best roles that came along. But if my fans want me to play screwballs, I will. After all, they made me rich."

Lombard also talked about wanting a baby. She and Gable were forever having his sperm analyzed. She eventually claimed to be infertile, to spare Gable's masculine image. "I'd do anything to get pregnant," she said, "even fuck in a pile of manure if that would work."

In the spring of 1940, Gable costarred with Spencer Tracy in what was to be their last film together: *Boom Town*, a story of two wildcatters. Claudette Colbert played Gable's wife, Hedy Lamarr his mistress. Tracy had few chances to steal any scenes in *Boom Town* and was bored with both the film and his second billing.

Lombard was suspicious of Hedy Lamarr and showed up on location (the oil fields near Los Angeles) to see for herself if anything was amiss. But there was no chemistry between Lamarr and Gable, on or off the screen. Hedy Lamarr was one of the most stunning actresses ever to grace the screen, but studio photographers complained that she was static. They changed the lighting, but nothing changed in her face. There was no fire, and Gable liked plenty of fire in his women.

Boom Town was a winner with Gable fans and with the press. *The New York Times* said, "There hasn't been a picture in a long time to compare." The *New York Herald Tribune* called it "a good picture [with] a great cast . . . excellent entertainment."

MGM reteamed Gable and Lamarr in *Comrade X*, an implausibly perfect vehicle for Hedy, who played a dour Russian streetcar driver. Gable played a rowdy newspaperman smuggling stories out of Russia. Lamarr's father finds out Gable's identity and forces him to marry Hedy. The couple's escape to freedom fills out the plot of this fast and funny film.

The year 1940 did not bring an addition to the Gable household, but fans in buses, in cars, and on foot invaded the couple's privacy. Gable was forced to put a fence around the ranch and install an electric gate. Intruders still managed to get onto the grounds, but for fear of lawsuits, the servants were ordered not to touch them. The police were called to deal with trespassers, while Gable and Lombard hid behind locked doors. Day and night, admirers waited at the gate for a glimpse of the famous couple.

"We'll have to move," Gable said.

"I know, Pa."

"No fun anymore. Might as well be living on Hollywood and Vine."

But they never got around to seriously considering a move. Gable learned that he could not get the money he wanted for the property.

Having their home on the tourist map caused a great deal of tension in the Gable home, but Clark's romping with other women caused most of their marital conflicts. Carole was concerned because Joan Crawford was single again, but there was more that fueled her animosity towards Crawford than insecurity.

In 1926, Crawford had been a "Wampas Baby Star," one of a group of promising young movie actresses cited by the Western Association of Motion Picture Advertisers. Others that year were Mary Astor, Janet Gaynor, and Fay Wray. Crawford arranged weekly luncheons at the Montmartre Cafe in Hollywood, and gained the best table by charming the headwaiter. If her chosen table wasn't set up properly, the management heard about it.

One afternoon, when Lombard planted herself at the "royal table," Crawford told her to move.

"I prefer sitting here," Lombard said stubbornly.

"Who the hell are you?"

"The Charleston contests, remember?"

"Move your ass, kid. The first table near the palm is reserved."

"I recall your winning trophies, Miss Crawford, not the Montmartre."

Crawford screamed for the headwaiter and made a scene. Lombard stood up, adjusted her veiled hat, slowly put on her gloves, smiled at Joan politely, and exclaimed, "Fuck you!"

By 1940, Crawford's on-again, off-again affair with Gable

was common knowledge, of course, and Lombard's concern was perhaps justified. She had heard all the stories about him. One of the funniest (and his friends insisted it was true) took place in a hotel room, where a dowdy maid walked in and found Gable still in bed. He grinned sheepishly and said, "Why don't you join me?"

"How much?" she asked.

"I would think, my dear, just being with me is payment enough."

The maid didn't think so, and left the room.

Lombard could do little about her husband's harmless affairs, short of having the women—at least the ones who worked for Metro—fired. L. B. Mayer let it be known that there would be no more scandal where Gable was concerned; ensuring respectability was left to Howard Strickling and his staff. "Gable was a promiscuous man," they would admit, if only privately. Gable's buddies called him a rooster "cocks-man." Lombard, alluding to Gable's relationships with older women, claimed that her husband had been "sex starved" most of his life. Friends thought Clark and Carole would stay together *if* she learned to live with his infidelities, but most Hollywood insiders didn't give the marriage a chance.

Gable's leading lady in *They Met in Bombay* was his erstwhile costar Rosalind Russell, one of "Hollywood's Three Nuns." Who could be safer? Lombard wasn't so sure, however, as the other two "nuns" were Irene Dunne . . . and Loretta Young. But Russell was everyone's jovial friend, who arrived on the set with a smile and a few jokes, enjoyed her work, and went home without getting involved in love affairs and petty gossip. She had an "I don't give a damn" attitude towards Hollywood. "I played a career woman in twenty-three films," she later said. "I've been every kind of executive and I've owned everything—factories and advertising agencies and pharmaceutical houses. Except for different leading men and a switch in titles and pompadour, they were stamped out of the same Alice in Careerland. The scripts always called for a leading lady somewhere in her thirties, tall, brittle, and not too sexy. My wardrobe was a set pattern: a tan suit, a gray suit, a beige suit, and then a negligee for the seventh reel near the end, when I would admit to my best friend that what I really wanted was to become a dear little housewife."

Russell's one and only marriage was a happy one, which was unusual in Hollywood but suited Russell fine. She was aware from the minute she walked onto the *Bombay* set how Mrs. Gable felt about Mr. Gable's leading ladies. Russell told Lombard that Gable was a puppet during their love scenes. "He's easy to follow," she laughed. "One for the money, two for the show, three to get ready, and four to go! He does the same thing with Norma Shearer and Myrna Loy."

Lombard smiled. "Yes, but he's quite original with most of the others."

The Gables celebrated their second wedding anniversary on the set of *They Met in Bombay.* Hedda Hopper reported that they were happier than on the day they were married. At the party, arranged by Lombard and catered by the Brown Derby, Lombard told the press that she had no film commitments, in anticipation of becoming pregnant. "The doctor told me to give up horseback riding," she sighed, "because it bounces everything around inside." Lombard said that it was all right if anyone wanted to stop off and see the ranch, "but not on Sundays. That's the day Pa and I concentrate on making babies." This was not one of her gags.

Gable built a three-bedroom Cape Cod house for his father in North Hollywood, five miles from the ranch. Their relationship was still strained, but Lombard had a way of easing the tension. Gable was not close to his wife's brothers, Fred and Stuart, either. He was jealous of her attention and devotion to them. Her friendship with David and Myron Selznick annoyed him to no end, as well. Lombard said in an interview, "If I gave up acting, it would be great to produce films. If I had my choice of being anybody else, it would be David Selznick." Gable seethed; he had reason to believe that Lombard had had a fling with David Selznick some years before. Whenever Gable asked her about Selznick or other men in her life before him, Lombard let him think they were more than friends; she even compared their sexual prowess to his. Gable took these "admissions" very seriously. "How did you get away with it?" he once asked.

"Well," she said casually, "a woman can run faster with her dress up than a man can with his pants down."

After two years of marriage, Clark had yet to match Carole's energy and humor. He was able to play her game, however, win or lose. He made it clear that she was not to use raunchy language when others were present, but once, during a chichi dinner gathering at the ranch, Carole said to a guest, "Pass the fuckin' salt, please." All eyes were on Clark, who looked up from his plate and said, "Pass Ma the fuckin' salt."

Carole *was* able to behave; weeks could go by without a blue remark or an unbridled gag. She was certainly expected to be on her best behavior at a party thrown by Fred MacMurray and his wife; Lillian MacMurray did not approve of swearing, and Carole respected that. The evening was hot and humid, and the guests were seated around the pool when the Gables arrived. Carole was wearing a new and expensive white evening gown, but that didn't stop her from jumping into the pool. Clark doubled over with laughter. "Isn't she beautiful? She's fantastic. She's my girl!" Carole changed into a pair of her host's pajamas, which she wore for the rest of the evening. One of the guests asked whether her dress was ruined. "Yeah," she said, laughing. "But I'll get another."

"But you jumped in deliberately. Will Clark buy you a new one?"

"Of course not, but it was worth it to see him laugh."

Mr. and Mrs. Smith, starring Lombard and Robert Montgomery, opened at Radio City Music Hall on February 21, 1941. It was a silly comedy about a man and wife who find out that they're not really married. Director Alfred Hitchcock, who was known to make a brief appearance in each of his films, on this occasion chose to tip his hat to

Robert Montgomery. Lombard took charge. She said Hitchcock's walk wasn't right. He tipped his hat all wrong. He
wasn't on cue. She made a major project out of it, and
Hitchcock did as he was told, though he wasn't known for his
sense of humor.

Shortly after the Gables' second wedding anniversary,
Lombard signed for *To Be or Not to Be*, with Jack Benny,
and *He Kissed the Bride*. She said, "Maybe if I keep busy, I'll
get pregnant."

14.

King of Tragedy

arole and Clark had slipped off to Baltimore in December 1940. He wanted to see a specialist at Johns Hopkins about a painful shoulder injury sustained during the filming of *San Francisco*. Carole took this opportunity to consult gynecologists about her inability to conceive. Clark took a fertility test, also. Doctors concluded there was no reason why the couple couldn't have children.

On their way home, the Gables stopped off in Washington, D.C., for a visit with President Roosevelt, who, after a personal chat, expressed his concern that Hitler would overtake Europe. "We must give all our support to Great Britain," he said. Carole talked about little else when she returned to Hollywood.

This was not a happy time for Lombard. Feeling that her

agent, Myron Selznick, was not doing his job, she sued to break her contract with him. She won the court case, but it cost her $30,000. She also owed David Selznick a picture, but he chose to forget the obligation—he'd had enough of the Gables. Lombard's career was in a slump, fans and reporters continuously invaded the ranch, and her and Gable's attempts to have a baby failed. "The doctors told me that tension could make me barren," she said at the time, "that I should avoid stress if I wanted to get pregnant."

Gable was dissatisfied with both *Comrade X* and *They Met in Bombay*, neither of which was especially good. He liked a script he'd read, called *Honky Tonk*, about a ruthless gambler in the Old West. Lombard thought it was a lousy idea and L. B. Mayer agreed, but Gable was determined to do the film and asked his friend Jack Conway to direct. Conway had directed *Saratoga* and *Boom Town*. MGM offered to find something better, but Gable said he had more faith in a good director than in any script. Conway, a hearty drinker and womanizer, would ultimately work with Gable on five films.

"I know I'm stickin' my neck out on this one," Clark told Carole, "but I'm gonna fight for it." He remained adamant about *Honky Tonk* and wanted to begin production immediately. Mayer relented and cast Lana Turner, one of MGM's most beautiful blondes, as Gable's leading lady.

Lombard saw red when she heard the news. Turner's role in *Honky Tonk* of a sweet young Bostonian virgin did not reflect her reputation with her leading men. Turner denies to this day having had a teenage romance with Mickey Rooney; his comment: "If it didn't happen, it was the most beautiful dream I ever had!"

In 1941, Lana Turner was a lovely, wistful twenty-one-year-old divorcée—her ex was bandleader Artie Shaw—who had done well for herself in second-rate pictures. After *Ziegfeld Girl*, MGM decided to let her soar to the heavens with their other stars, and what better vehicle than Clark Gable?

Labeled "The Sweater Girl," Turner had been discovered, according to legend, by the publisher of the *Hollywood*

Reporter while sipping a Coke at the Top Hat Café, near Hollywood High School.

"Would you like to be in the movies?" he asked her.

"I'll have to ask my mother," she replied.

Turner made her movie debut at sixteen and signed a contract with MGM a year later for a hundred dollars a week. She had auburn hair until the studio chose her to be one of the blonde dancers in *Idiot's Delight*. Reluctantly, she submitted to a dye job, but instead of doing the movie, she reportedly ended up in a hospital, undergoing minor elective surgery. When she recovered, MGM gave her a bonus. This sequence of events has led to speculation that Turner was the chorus girl whom Carole Lombard had fired for flirting with Gable. Why would Turner have volunteered for surgery instead? The consensus is that she was not the chorus girl. The few who claim she was base their opinion on the fact that *Idiot's Delight* was her big chance.

Turner decided to remain a blonde, which apparently gave her an outgoing personality and upset Louis B. Mayer, who told her to "stop running around until all hours with men." She obliged by falling in love with attorney Greg Bautzer. Mayer didn't even get the chance to intercede in this romance, because Joan Crawford, who happened to be seeing Bautzer at the time, summoned Lana first. "I told her that Greg was in love with me," Crawford would recall, "that he liked to date and have a good time, but that occasionally he got overly dramatic about it, usually with girls who were young and gullible. Lana was stunned, poor dear, but it was best that she found out before getting hurt."

Clark Gable was Turner's first famous leading man, and after only a few days of filming *Honky Tonk*, rumors of a romance were so rampant that Carole Lombard threatened to confront the "lovers" on the set and "kick them both in the ass." Her fights with Gable were explosive. "I'll have her fired!"

"You can't do that," he argued.

"Then I'll have you fired!"

Lombard went directly to L. B. Mayer and threatened to keep Gable from reporting to work if Turner tried to "get her hands on him." A quiet alert was called on the set of *Honky Tonk* whenever Lombard drove through the MGM studio gates. Her visits ceased when Turner, rehearsing a love scene with Gable, spotted Lombard and ran to her dressing room in tears.

From then on, the set was off-limits to outsiders, including Mrs. Gable.

Turner later described how she looked over her shoulder and saw Lombard glaring at her. "I felt faint and went to my dressing room. Jack Conway asked me to come back, but I told him I couldn't do that. I had to get ahold of myself. My knees were shaking. Finally, someone knocked on my door and told me it was time to resume work. Carole Lombard was gone."

Turner apologized to Gable, who whispered, "I understand, honey."

Over the years, Lana Turner has denied there was ever anything between her and Gable. "Ours was a closeness without intimacy," she said. In 1982, while on tour to promote her autobiography, Turner said in a television interview that though she had a reputation for being a sexpot, she never was one, and that she had never had much feeling about sex at all.

A famous Hollywood columnist has written, "It has amused me to see how these ladies remember their pasts when interviewed on television—either too many men in their lives, or too few—mostly the latter. June Allyson and Lana Turner were shocked at the very suggestion that maybe they had succumbed to certain gentlemen of their acquaintance."

MGM finished *Honky Tonk* in record time to separate Turner and Gable, who were nevertheless so hot together on the screen that the studio could not overlook pairing them again as soon as possible. Lana was rushed into *Johnny Eager* with Robert Taylor, who later told a friend, "Lana wasn't very career-minded, and preferred men and jewelry over anything else. She wasn't as busty as her pinup pictures, but her face was delicate and beautiful. I've never seen lips like hers, and though I was not one to run after blondes, Lana was the exception. I couldn't take my eyes off her, and there were times during *Johnny Eager* that I thought I'd explode. She had a voice like a breathless child. I don't think she knew how to talk without being sexy. When she said, 'Good morning,' I melted. She was the kind of woman a guy would risk five years in jail for rape."

Working daily with Turner frustrated Taylor. He stood it as long as he could, but when he discovered she was making no effort to ignore his attentions and was, in fact, physically drawn to him, he decided he had to have her—"if only for one night."

Turner later admitted a very strong attraction to Taylor but denied any involvement. Taylor did, however, ask his wife, Barbara Stanwyck, for a divorce so that he could marry Turner. The Taylors separated for a few days, and when they reconciled, it was in name only. Stanwyck never spoke to Turner again.

Agent George Nichols told me that Turner did not want to be responsible for Taylor's getting a divorce. Furthermore, "MGM would not permit it," Nichols said. "But Taylor wasn't the type to take divorce in stride. He didn't want to be just another Hollywood statistic. So if he asked Barbara for his freedom, Bob knew what he was doing."

I asked Nichols if it was possible that Turner went from Gable to Taylor and back to Gable.

"Sure," he replied. "We used to say that Gable and Taylor shared the same girls. Bob was modest by saying he got Clark's leftovers. Gable once said he had them all at MGM, and I asked him if that included Norma Shearer. He lifted his eyebrows, that's all. From what I know, he didn't miss too many. Yes, Clark was nuts about Lana, but I honestly don't think she was a threat to his marriage."

Lombard didn't agree. She was angry; moreover, she was

deeply hurt, an emotion she rarely displayed. MGM officials kept their eyes on her because word was spreading around town that Lombard was "going in for the kill." Still, she rose above the occasion and accompanied Gable to the premiere of *Honky Tonk* in October 1941. They held hands during the entire movie. Reporters commented that it was unusual for Gable to attend a premiere or to display affection toward his wife in public. A few weeks later, Lombard went into another rage when she found out that Gable and Turner were going to costar in *Somewhere I'll Find You.*

The bickering and battling began all over again. Gable said that if his having affairs with other women meant nothing to him, then why should it mean anything to his wife? His argument added fire to Lombard's fury, but she knew she would have to put up with the situation because MGM's demands came first. *Honky Tonk* made Lana Turner a major star, and the public clamored for more of her in the arms of Clark Gable. That was business. But accepting another Gable–Turner picture with grace and poise wasn't in Carole Lombard. Her sense of humor and her faith in Gable had waned. Friends thought she was too quiet, sometimes sad and pensive, not bouncy and optmistic, as she usually was. She spoke more now than ever before about wanting a baby. She had finished *To Be or Not to Be* with Jack Benny and was preparing for *He Kissed the Bride* with Melvyn Douglas at Columbia. Gable professed no interest in her ongoing negotiations with Harry Cohn, whom he detested, a hangover from *It Happened One Night.* But Gable did not, as a rule, interfere with his wife's film career. George Nichols said, "He was only interested in the money. But that was Clark."

After December 7, 1941, Hollywood was just another town of Americans eager to volunteer for the war effort. The Gables sent a telegram to their friend President Roosevelt, asking how they could be of service. The reply was: "Entertainment. Stay where you are." They got involved with the Hollywood

Victory Committee, and Gable was appointed chairman of the Screen Actors Division.

The Gables sent Christmas cards to friends noting a donation to the Red Cross or enclosing a war bond. Clark gave Carole a pair of diamond-and-ruby clips that matched her wedding ring and the ruby heart he'd given her for their first married Christmas, and she presented him with an engraved cigarette case. It was not a holiday of celebration, however. Though Clark was almost forty-one, he wanted to get into the war and thought about applying for a commission. Carole was all for it, but she might have had an ulterior motive. If Clark went to Washington immediately, it would be a lengthy procedure. This would prevent him from starting *Somewhere I'll Find You* with Lana Turner, scheduled for mid-January 1942.

Henry Morgenthau, Jr., the secretary of the treasury, contacted MGM's New York publicity director, Howard Dietz, about enlisting movie celebrities to go on war-bond tours. Dietz called Gable and asked him whether Carole would go to her home state, Indiana, for a rally. Lombard accepted, and though she wanted Gable to go with her, MGM refused to postpone *Somewhere I'll Find You*. Lombard's mother would make the trip, though, along with Otto Winkler, Gable's public-relations man. As the wife of an MGM star, Lombard was entitled to the services of the studio's P.R. department.

It would be the first time since their marriage that the Gables would be separated. Lombard did not want to leave town, but patriotism, she felt, came first. She managed one last joke before leaving—a blonde dummy in Gable's bed, with a note: "So you won't be lonely." She gave her secretary five letters for Gable—one for each day she would be gone. Gable was in Washington, D.C., when Lombard left California by train on January 12, 1942. On the fifteenth, she arrived in Indianapolis, where she sold more than two million dollars' worth of war bonds.

"I'm anxious to get home to Pa," she said. "Let's fly back." Winkler didn't like the idea and tried to talk her out of it.

Lombard suggested flipping a coin, and she won. Bessie Peters hated planes and tried to convince her daughter to rest up on the train. "I don't like choo-choos," Lombard said, and made reservations on TWA flight 3. Bessie, a proficient numerologist, jotted down the flight data and came up with a fatal number. She showed it to Lombard, who despite her usual faith laughed it off. At 4:00 A.M., January 16, Lombard, Winkler, and Bessie Peters boarded the plane. Lombard sent Gable a telegram asking him to meet her at the airport that evening.

Gable had returned to Hollywood the day after Lombard's departure for Indiana. What was he doing while she was away? Accounts vary. All that is certain is that he was, as scheduled, filming *Somewhere I'll Find You* with Lana Turner.

Winkler and Bessie Peters had tried to dissuade Lombard from flying right up until they boarded the plane. Scheduled travel time was seventeen hours, including several stopovers. In Albuquerque, a number of servicemen were waiting to board flight 3. Because they had priority, some civilian passengers would have to disembark and take a train or another plane the next day. Lombard said that because she had been on a war-bond tour, she should be given special consideration. She was allowed to remain on board, as were her companions.

After an unscheduled stopover in Las Vegas, the plane took off for Los Angeles at around 6:50 P.M. Thirty-five miles west of Las Vegas, pilot Wayne Williams reported that he was slightly off-course, but there was no sign of distress in his voice at 7:07, the time of his last communication. Some witnesses claimed that the plane caught fire in the air. Others said it hit Table Rock Mountain and burst into flames.

Clark had planned a welcome-back dinner for Carole at the ranch, with a few close friends. The house was filled with fresh flowers, and the dining-room table was set elegantly. To get even with her little prank, Clark had put a male dummy with an erect penis in Carole's bed.

MGM publicist Larry Barbier was at the Burbank airport

waiting for Lombard. Informed that her plane had gone down, he called Howard Strickling who told Barbier to charter a plane for Las Vegas. Gable had not yet arrived at the ranch, but Strickling finally located him and arranged to meet him in Burbank. Lombard's brother Stuart, Otto Winkler's wife, and Gable barely spoke a word on the drive to the airport. With Strickling, the somber group flew to Las Vegas, hoping for a miracle.

Search parties were being organized to climb the snow-covered mountain. A Western Airlines pilot confirmed that he had seen Lombard's plane, engulfed in flames, hit Table Rock Mountain. Gable insisted on going with the rescue party, but halfway to the crash site, an MGM official said to him, "Carole wouldn't want you to see her in that plane wreckage, Clark." Gable thought for a moment and turned back. It was a blessing that he was spared the agony of seeing Lombard's charred, decapitated body—a script, a remnant of one of her diamond-and-ruby clips, and strands of blonde hair lying nearby.

Descending the mountain, the rescue party stopped at a way station and sent a telegram to Gable: "NO SURVIVORS. ALL KILLED INSTANTLY."

The next day, Gable was driven to within a few hundred feet of the crash site by a pilot, who explained: "There's no chance that Carole suffered for even a second. All twenty-two passengers didn't know what happened."

Gable accompanied the bodies of his wife, her mother, and his friend Otto Winkler back to California on the train. He wore Lombard's burned jeweled clip around his neck in a gold locket. Not wanting to go back to the ranch alone, he stayed with friends until after the funeral. Lombard had once requested to be clothed in white and interred in a modest crypt in Forest Lawn Memorial Park, in Glendale, California. Gable now bought three adjoining crypts—for Lombard, her mother, and himself.

Gable received thousands of telegrams, but the one he treasured most was from President Roosevelt, who expressed his sympathy over Lombard's death: "She gave unselfishly of her time and talent to serve her government in peace and in war. She loved her country."

The Defense Department offered a military funeral, but Gable declined. He followed Lombard's wishes, and on January 22, 1942, services were held at the Church of the Recessional in Forest Lawn. No prayers or hymns were heard, only the Twenty-third Psalm and a favorite poem of Lombard's. When it was over, friends took Gable back to the ranch.

Later that evening, his wife's secretary gave him the fifth and last letter Lombard had left behind. His sobs echoed through the house and into the valley.

Joan Crawford said that Gable came to her the night Carole Lombard was killed. "He was so drunk and he cried," she said. "There was nothing I could say because a stranger walked out my door that night and never returned—in the physical, maybe, but he was never the same. Clark was a walking corpse. He had every right to drink during that terrible ordeal, but he kept right on hitting the bottle. He was in another world and never came back to us." When I asked Crawford whether Gable was with her when he received the call from Howard Strickling, she ignored the question.

Gable took long drives alone, walked around the ranch with Lombard's dog, drove to Oregon by himself for some fishing, and avoided mutual friends whose presence reminded him of the woman he loved. He never complained. He didn't have to. His loss and grief and loneliness were etched on his face and set in his eyes. When liquor failed to drown his sorrow, Gable bought a motorcycle to "blow his mind." He almost succeeded in killing himself before MGM demanded that he stop the recklessness and forbade him (contractually, it's been alleged) from riding motorcycles again.

Lombard had left her entire estate to Gable. Her brothers never spoke to Clark again. It's possible that they resented Gable's rumored relationship with Lana Turner, which had resulted in their sister rushing home and, in turn, to her death. And they might also have heeded a rumor that Gable was with another woman the night Lombard was killed. Busy elsewhere, he *had* sent someone else to the airport to meet his wife.

It's possible that Gable had scheduled a last-minute quickie before his wife came home. If so, he had to live with the fact for the rest of his life. Regardless, Carole Lombard died for love, pure and simple.

Adela Rogers St. Johns came to see Gable at the ranch. He wanted to give her something of Lombard's, and they went together to the frilly, white, elegant bedroom that was so very typically Lombard. St. Johns was shocked to see that nothing had been touched. There were still traces of spilled face powder on Carole's vanity. But it was not a shrine, he insisted. It was simply the case that Lombard's will had yet to be probated. Still, he admitted, there was warmth in knowing that everything was as she had left it. Disconcerted, St. Johns looked through Lombard's books, finally choosing two: *The Cloud of Unknowing* and *Cosmic Consciousness*. Gable looked around the room and said to St. Johns, "They say in the midst of life we are in death, but I know now in the midst of death we are in life." They strolled outside, and Gable looked at St. Johns with a sad grin and recalled, "I told Ma we were very lucky, having each other and this beautiful place. Could she think of anything we didn't have? Well, she said, 'Yeah, I could do with another load of manure for the south forty.'"

St. Johns said, "Carole always made you laugh, didn't she?"

"Yes," Gable replied. "We liked to be alone. Just the two of us. She was the best companion."

Many people might find that last statement somewhat bland, but coming from Gable it was the supreme compliment. He could get sex anytime, anywhere, but a good companion was a rare entity, particularly in Hollywood.

Some of Gable's friends thought that his maintaining and

spending so much time in Lombard's room was morbid. To Gable, though, the room was a shrine—all he had left, really, except for a few strands of blonde hair and a charred piece of jewelry. Lombard's room was alive with the aroma of her favorite perfume, Chanel No. 5, and the powder puff that had touched her vital and beautiful face.

But it wasn't only her bedroom that made her live. It was the house and the stables and the fruit trees and the knickknacks. Everything represented Carole Gable. Clark searched for another house in Beverly Hills, but he didn't have the heart to leave Encino. He finally gave Lombard's possessions to friends but changed nothing in the house, including her bedroom suite.

This was their home.

On February 23, 1942, he reported for work on *Somewhere I'll Find You.* Louis B. Mayer had told everyone on the set to act as if nothing had happened. Above all, he commanded, no pity or tiptoeing around. In the MGM commissary, the King's chair had been tipped forward to lean against the table since the day Carole Lombard died. When Gable came in and sat down, everyone stood up, applauded, and cried.

Mayer had a private talk with Lana Turner and asked her to go along with Gable's moods. "If he wants to work, work. If he wants to leave, that's all right. If he wants to talk, talk. Go with the flow. I understand he doesn't like to eat alone, so if he asks you out, go."

Gable asked Turner to the ranch for dinner one evening, but he never mentioned Carole. . . .

Joan Crawford offered Gable an open invitation to her home for dinner. "He came almost every night until he finished filming," she said. "Clark could drink a quart of booze before dinner. He told me it was all wrong, and then he cried. There were times we talked until dawn."

Crawford volunteered to take Lombard's role in *He Kissed the Bride,* newly retitled *They All Kissed the Bride,* and she donated her $125,000 salary to the Red Cross. "My agent made the deal," Crawford recalled. "When he took ten percent, I fired the bastard." As for her relationship with Gable, it was developing into a deep and lasting friendship. "We made love," she said, "but I tried to lure him from the bedroom because there was so little satisfaction in it for me."

Gable finished *Somewhere I'll Find You* and spent time fishing the Rogue River. He told Howard Strickling, "I'm gonna enlist in the air corps, but I've gotta get my head together and sort things out." Mayer tried to talk him out of enlisting. "There's much to be done right here on the home front," he stressed.

MGM announced that Gable would appear in *Shadow of the Wing*. To entice him, they chose Victor Fleming to direct. Unbeknownst to Gable, the studio was doing its utmost to keep him out of the service and did not let him know that the War Department was processing his papers.

When his orders finally came through, Gable ignored pleas from MGM to reconsider. "I don't expect to come back," he said. "And I don't want to come back."

15.

Death Wish

While Gable was getting his business affairs in order, *Somewhere I'll Find You* was released in August. He and Turner play American war correspondents in the Far East who get caught up in World War II. The *New York Times* critic said that the plot was purposeless other than "to exploit the respective charms of its twin players."

Other reviews were favorable. Only *Photoplay* referred to Lombard's death: "The first picture made by Gable since his tragic bereavement comes out a honey. He proves himself a true hero in his adherence to duty; a duty that must have caused him suffering, what with the pertinent lines and situations all reminiscent of his sorrow."

Somewhere I'll Find You was Gable's only movie in 1942,

but at the box office he came in second for the year, just behind the comedy team of Abbott and Costello.

Clark kept a maid and caretaker on the ranch and asked his secretary, Jean Garceau, to oversee everything else while he was away. He made sure his trusty chef and valet had jobs to tide them over until his return. He wore the tiny gold locket containing Lombard's charred ruby-and-diamond pin, and he told Garceau to put the locks of blonde hair in a safe-deposit box. Of his own accord, Will Gable checked on the livestock and chickens several times a week.

Without advance notice, Gable went to the Federal Building in Los Angeles on August 12 and was sworn into the air force as a sixty-six-dollar-a-month buck private. He could have had a commission but chose instead to earn his rank at the Officers Candidate School in Miami Beach. He was one of the oldest enlistees; he wrote friends that he enjoyed the company of young men and didn't mind sleeping in a three-bunk room or getting up at five in the morning. He allowed a military photographer to take a picture of him shaving off his famous mustache, but he made it clear that he did not want any more publicity.

It wasn't easy for Clark Gable, movie star, to go through the rigors of calisthenics, marching, and inspection. The other men were aware of his age and rich life in Hollywood, so they expected he would get preferential treatment. Gable knew that he was being watched and tested, which made training all the more difficult for him.

The women in Miami Beach hung around the barracks to get a glimpse of their sex idol. But very few recognized the tall, thin, crew-cut man in baggy khakis. His eyes were weary-looking and his face was drawn. Some in his group didn't think he'd make it. One recruit said, "Gable was a mess. I thought he'd collapse, but he kept going."

Gable's letters to friends back home indicated his fear of failure. Long after lights-out at night, he sat in the bathroom studying the complex manuals. "I have to try harder than anyone else," he wrote, "because of who I am. Can you imagine the publicity if I flunk?"

But Gable graduated on October 9, volunteered for aerial gunnery duty, and was sent to Tyndall Field in Panama City, Florida. As a first lieutenant, he grew another mustache, ordered up custom-made uniforms, and sent home for his English shoes.

On December 18, Gable returned to the ranch for a few days. At a party in his honor, he was delighted to encounter Virginia Grey, whom he hadn't seen since she'd auditioned to be Jean Harlow's double in *Saratoga*. Though she hadn't got the part, Grey attracted Gable, and she became his protégée of sorts, appearing with him in *Test Pilot* and *Idiot's Delight*. Grey was one of Gable's favorites for many years, but he was not seen publicly with her until after the war.

Grey resembled Lombard. She was blonde, witty, and peppy, and she often played similar roles—the smirky, foulmouthed dame, the other woman. Grey was not as soft, lithe, or talented as Lombard, however, and her luck in films matched her luck in love. She always got supporting roles and remained single. In between Gable's marriages, it was Virginia Grey who strolled proudly on his arm, and after Lombard's death, she was expected to be the next Mrs. Gable.

In December 1942 Hollywood thought Virginia Grey the perfect substitute for Carole Lombard.

On January 7, 1943, Clark Gable received his gunnery officer's wings and was asked to make a training film about aerial gunners. He went to Spokane for special training in aerial photography.

At the end of January, Gable was assigned to the First Air Division, Eighth Air Force, 508th Squadron of the 351st Heavy Bombardment Group, in preparation for duty in Europe.

When the men in Gable's training group heard about his film assignment, they were disappointed. There was a war going on, and what was the King doing? He was using MGM to help with his film project, flying back and forth from Hollywood to his temporary quarters in New Mexico. This did not sit well with men who were in training for combat. Gable got the cold shoulder, and it hurt him.

In April, he was shipped overseas and stationed in Polebrook, about a hundred miles north of London. Trying to regain some respect, Gable chose to eat with the noncombat officers. He was offered special housing, but he preferred the officers' quarters. Still, Gable was ignored by the other men until May 14, when he and his film crew flew a mission in a B-17 over Belgium. He doubled as gunner and photographer on four more flights, over the Ruhr Valley, Gelsenkirchen, Nantes, and Villacoublay. On one flight, a German shell missed his head by a few inches, but Gable wasn't fazed—he was too drunk. It was common knowledge that Gable was virtually poured onto the plane before his missions.

Hitler put a five-thousand-dollar price tag on Captain Gable—dead or alive. "I'll never bail out," Gable said. "The Germans can have me dead or not at all." His biggest fear was being captured alive. What fun it would be, he said, for Hitler to parade him through the streets of Berlin like a caged lion. "I'll go down with the plane," Gable said, and he meant it, but on all of his missions, there were bomber escorts protecting his plane from German fighters. Gable later recalled coming so close to an enemy plane once that he could see the faces of its gunners. We'll never know how many Americans lost their lives protecting Gable from his own death wish.

Gable also had to be protected on the ground. He was mobbed by fans wherever he went. Women threw their arms around him and held on, despite his efforts to free himself. Without MGM's protection, Gable was fair game. Like all the male stars in the service, Gable thought the public should have respect for the uniform. It was one thing for a fan to pull a button off one of his civilian suits, but shredding his military garb, he thought, was unpatriotic. "I heard that some gal with no underclothes hopped on Gable's back," George

Nichols would recall. "Everything was hanging out, and he was shouting for help. John Lee Mahin [an MGM screenwriter] was with Clark in England helping with the aerial-gunner film. He said it was disgusting. Robert Taylor suffered, too. Leaving his quarters in dress uniform, girls mobbed him and cut off his tie and buttons with scissors. MGM had the power to keep Taylor from active duty, but they could do nothing about Clark, who figured if a five-foot-one blonde weighing a hundred and ten pounds could brave a seventeen-hour flight in bad weather, he'd made it up to her by facing death head on."

In the service, Gable apparently took more than his share of women and liquor. One of his fellow officers said, "I was compelled to ask Clark why he chose the dogs when so many pretty girls were drooling over him. He told me the ugly ones were really appreciative and didn't bother him later on. He was going out with one of the homeliest girls I've ever seen. She turned me off at first glance, so I asked him, 'Why her?' And Gable said, 'She's there.' I figured he must be pretty good. He had an insatiable appetite for liquor and homely women. There was something very lonely about him. He had a faraway look. He'd be listening to me and not be there somehow. I think he was punishing himself, but he rarely, if ever, talked about Carole Lombard. He wore a locket around his neck with his dog tags. Some guy asked him about it, and all Clark said was, 'That's all I have left of her.' I know he didn't want to go back home . . . back to Hollywood."

Frank Capra saw Gable in the lobby of the Grosvenor House in London and asked the commanding officer how Gable was doing. "How's he *doing*?" the general barked. "He's scaring the hell out of us, that's how he's doing. The damn fool insists on being a rear gunner on every bombing mission. He's a hot potato! And I'm pulling every string to get him out of my command. I'll tell you that! The guy gives me the willies. He wants to get killed so he can join his wife."

In October 1943 Gable completed the aerial gunner film and

was sent home. He and John Lee Mahin stopped off in Washington to see the general in charge of the film project; he'd forgotten all about it. Gable was dumbfounded. The general told him to proceed on his own.

Gable and Mahin went to Los Angeles and edited the training film at MGM. Meanwhile, though Gable expected to be shipped out again, this time to the Pacific, he negotiated a twelve-year contract with MGM at seventy-five hundred dollars a week, two films a year. Quitting time: five o'clock.

The Clark Gable who returned to Hollywood was handsomely gray at the temples, friendly but distant, smiling but forlorn, lonely and busy. The ranch had flourished while he was gone. His father and the servants wanted him to come home to fresh fruit and vegetables and fresh flowers. His home became his haven, and though Gable continued to hit the bottle, he no longer had a chip on his shoulder. Nor did he anymore feel sorry for himself, having seen the dead and wounded in England. His belief that he had been singled out by a capricious God to be the grieved widower of a vibrant and loving woman faded into a recognition of the blunt reality of life.

On January 15, 1944, L. B. Mayer was asked to preside over the launching of the ship *Carole Lombard*. Irene Dunne stood next to him, and Clark Gable, his fists clenched at his sides, gave a brief speech. When Dunne finally christened the ship, Gable could no longer control himself. He sobbed openly, tears streaming down his face. It made a heart-wrenching front-page picture.

Before Gable had left England, he had received an Air Medal for "exceptionally meritorious achievement," an American Campaign Medal, and a Europe–Africa–Middle-Eastern Campaign Medal. After D day, Gable put in a request to be discharged from the air force, and on June 12, he was relieved of duty with the rank of major. His report of separation was signed by Captain Ronald Reagan.

On a New York vacation, he spent time with society hostess Dolly O'Brien; then he attended a Christmas party at her

West Palm Beach home. O'Brien, a blue-eyed blonde, was a former Powers and Conover model whose picture had appeared on some seventy magazine covers. Her second husband, yeast millionaire Julius Fleischmann, had given her a five-million-dollar divorce settlement. (Fleischmann died a short time later, leaving an estate of sixty-six million dollars.) She had then married actress Mae Murray's former husband and dancing partner, Jay O'Brien, a friend of Clark Gable's. (Gable always felt comfortable with the ex-wives and widows of old friends.)

O'Brien was a bouncy society darling who liked the company of young men because they made her feel youthful and vibrant, she was six years older than Gable, but never showed her age. Gable relished spending time with Dolly and her socially prominent circle of friends, who were catered to at nightclubs, yacht clubs, and country clubs.

One of his frequent dates during this period was Kay Williams, a blonde divorcée under contract to MGM who got off to a Lombard-like start with Gable.

"Why don't you go upstairs and get undressed?" he suggested shortly after they'd first met.

"Why don't you go shit in your hat?" she replied.

Another cool lady in Gable's life was Anita Colby, occasional actress and consulting fashion coordinator for Selznick International. Thirty years old when she met Gable, she was another blonde former Conover model, and had once appeared on the covers of twelve magazines in a single month. Known as "The Face," Colby was outgoing, bright, and ambitious, and gave the impression that she danced from the party to the bedroom. She didn't, and this fascinated Gable. (Colby married for the first time in 1970, at the age of fifty-six.)

At this time, not many of Gable's former girlfriends were available to him. In 1943, Lana Turner had had a daughter, Cheryl, by her second husband, Stephen Crane. She had divorced Crane in 1944 and, though currently dating the handsome Turkish–Czech actor Turhan Bey, was about to begin a heated but ultimately tragic affair with Tyrone Power, the love of her life.

Joan Crawford, meanwhile, had taken husband number three. In July 1942, she married actor Philip Terry. "At last I'm in love," she cooed. John Wayne, Crawford's costar in *Reunion in France* said, "I knew what kind of marriage it was going to be when I saw her walk on the set. First came Joan, then her secretary, then her makeup man, then her wardrobe woman, then Phil Terry carrying her dog!" In 1943, after being overlooked for the roles she wanted, Crawford asked to be released from her MGM contract. Louis B. Mayer did not stand in her way.

Though he had been with countless women, Gable could not remember being single. His affair with Franz Dorfler had overlapped into his marriage to Josephine Dillon, which had overlapped into his affair with and marriage to Ria Langham, which had overlapped into his affair with and marriage to Carole Lombard. He had never experienced the freedom of bachelorhood, and women had changed during his two decades of wifely protection. Having survived the Great Depression, women were essentially running the country while American men were overseas fighting in the war. Women were wearing trousers, working in factories, driving taxicabs, tending bar, proving themselves valuable in big business, and leading the popularity polls in Hollywood.

Pinup girl Betty Grable was currently the moviegoer's delight. She danced, sang, and read her lines as if she didn't give a damn (she didn't). But Americans could identify with her hash-slinging style. Joan Crawford won the best-actress Oscar for *Mildred Pierce* in 1945. Mildred was a woman who baked pies so that her spoiled daughter could wear fine clothes. She was betrayed but still came out the winner. As Mrs. Miniver, Greer Garson portrayed a strong English woman who protected her family through World War II.

Protect and survive. If you want something said, ask a man. If you want something done, ask a woman. The women of America had not gained equality with men, but they had won recognition.

Americans also flocked to see John Wayne fighting on all

fronts, and they soothed their nerves with music, comedy, religion and romance: *Yankee Doodle Dandy*, *The Song of Bernadette*, *Going My Way*, Abbott and Costello, Bob Hope and Bing Crosby on the road to somewhere, all-American Van Johnson in his red socks, Peter Lawford's lovesick eyes, Cornel Wilde's dashing romantic passion. Marital plots were no longer frivolous. Wives and husbands were separated by war, and the other woman (or man) emerged as a fact of life.

Also in 1945, Ray Milland got the best-actor Oscar for his performance as an alcoholic in *The Lost Weekend*, the virtual story of Gable's life in those days. While Crawford was snuggling up to her Oscar (literally), Gable was driving recklessly up Sunset Boulevard, heading the wrong way in his Duesenberg. He tried to turn around and swerved into a tree. Fortunately, the accident occurred on property belonging to Harry Friedman, vice president of the Music Corporation of America. Friedman called Howard Strickling, who arrived at the accident site in minutes. Gable was taken to Cedars of Lebanon Hospital with cuts on his legs and face. The story released to the newspapers described a helpless Gable doing his best to avoid a head-on collision with another car. MGM took Gable's clothes away and told him to remain in the hospital for several days to evoke sympathy. (Drunk driving was nothing new for Gable. In 1935 MGM hushed up his involvement in an auto mishap causing the death of another driver.)

After three days in the hospital, Gable told his secretary to get him some clothes and demanded that the doctor prepare his release papers.

MGM decided to put him to work, and Adela Rogers St. Johns was assigned to find him a good property. Gable told St. Johns that he wanted to depict a man down on his luck. "A guy who has courage and principle, hope and confidence, regardless of the odds. He doesn't compromise. He doesn't give up."

St. Johns understood what Gable wanted, but she couldn't find the right story. Mayer took charge and cast him opposite Greer Garson in *Adventure*. Gable hated the film and disliked

Garson. Playing a philosophical sailor named Harry Patterson, Gable falls in love with Garson, a prissy librarian who helps the sailor find his soul. Victor Fleming, who directed, couldn't do much with either the spiritual theme or the corny plot.

The film was a comedown as well for Greer Garson, miserably miscast after a string of successes including *Goodbye, Mr. Chips*, *Blossoms in the Dust*, *Mrs. Miniver*, her Oscar winner, *Random Harvest*, and *Madame Curie*. L. B. Mayer, who had discovered Garson on the London stage, worshiped her. She was, he said, a great lady. But the pedestal he had built for her was so high that Garson was resented by the other members of Mayer's MGM "family." Gable put her in the same category as Vivien Leigh—Englishwomen taking away good parts from American actresses. "A good time to Miss Garson," Gable said, "is tea time."

Adventure may have been a bad film, but the public flocked anyway to see Gable after his three-year absence from the screen. And they loved Greer Garson, who was the third-highest box-office earner that year. Critics were kind to Gable. *Time* noted that he was a little chubbier around the jowls, but said that "in his bright eye is the same old wicked fire." *Photoplay* wrote, "What use for us to cite the flaws and bemoan the story, for it's Gable's first postwar picture. . . ." *The New York Times* had expected some sort of chemical reaction between Garson and Gable, and was disappointed: "Maybe he tries too hard . . . talks too loudly and persists in keeping his hat on to an irritating extreme."

Everything involving *Adventure* was irritating to Gable, and the most irritating was MGM's big promotion campaign: GABLE'S BACK AND GARSON'S GOT HIM. Gable was angry and embarrassed. The slogan would haunt him for years, and he could scarcely bear to pass a movie theater with *Adventure* emblazoned on its marquee.

Gable rushed off to the Rogue River and found another girlfriend, Carol Gibson, a pro at reeling in big salmon. Though Gable usually preferred blondes, he was smitten by the tall, slender, dark-haired sportswoman. He purchased some property near Grant's Pass, Oregon, and initially gave friends the impression that he was falling in love with Gibson. Ultimately, though, Gibson couldn't compete with the sophisticated beauties available to Gable in Hollywood.

Gable had had an enormous swimming pool built at the ranch, but he rarely used it. He preferred to swim late at night at the Bel-Air Hotel, where he had a suite with its own private entrance. According to the hotel staff, who provided him with absolute protection, the Bel-Air was Gable's secret hideaway. Apparently out of respect for Lombard (and, perhaps, his servants), Gable did not rendezvous with his women at the ranch. Nor would he risk being seen at the women's homes.

Aside from the swimming pool, Gable's home remained the same. He still showed Lombard's room to his dinner guests. It remained, four years after her death, just as she had left it. Friends respected his lingering love for his late wife, and did not gossip about Carole's toiletries, atomizers, and towels neatly displayed to her liking. The room was spotless, and one felt as if Lombard were about to return at any minute. Gable also bought prints of her films and viewed them when the mood struck.

Women who tried to emulate Lombard were usually put down. One of his dates, who never swore, once came out with a four-letter word, and Gable told her he didn't appreciate her profanity.

"How can you say that after being married to Lombard?" she asked.

"That's different," he said. "She could make 'shit' sound like 'sugar.'"

Gable often invited several of his girlfriends to the same party. Some were good friends. Marriage never came up, though. Gable's heart lay shattered on a mountain top near Las Vegas.

Kay Williams and Dolly O'Brien would remarry and divorce before Gable was able to put the pieces of his life back together. Joan Crawford left Philip Terry in 1946. She testified at her divorce hearing that Terry had kept her a virtual prisoner and criticized every script sent to her. She had lost twenty pounds from physical and mental anguish. "I'll never go through that again," she told reporters, who wanted to know if that meant she would never hear the Wedding March again.

She shrugged. "Maybe that's the trouble. I never had music at my weddings."

Crawford could see Gable in the open now, but they preferred to spend time together privately because of his never-ending feud with Mayer. Crawford was still very interested in handsome attorney Greg Bautzer, whom she'd pried loose from Lana Turner a few years back, but he was to remain a bachelor until he married the exquisite actress Dana Wynter, leaving behind many broken hearts. After a four-year courtship, Crawford might have become Mrs. Bautzer, but she did not appreciate his attentions to another woman at a dinner party one evening and let him know it. Driving home with Bautzer, Crawford pulled over several miles from Beverly Hills and asked him to get out and see whether one of the tires was going flat. He did, and she drove off, leaving him stranded. Some in Hollywood blamed Crawford's increasingly domineering behavior on her Oscar. *Nobody* was going to push Joan Crawford around any-more—no man, no producer, no director, and no son or daughter. She made the rounds of nightclubs with gay or unhappily married men in an attempt to show Hollywood who its best actress was. Meanwhile, Clark Gable was running around in circles, trying to forget who the best actor had been.

16.

Merry-Go-Round

"I hate heels, and this character is a heel!"

"Wakeman's novel about Madison Avenue is brilliant," Mayer argued. "You became a star playing a bastard. What's wrong with it now?"

"The book is filthy rotten."

"If you finished it, Clark, you obviously enjoyed it."

"Take your book, your script, your adulterous heroine, and shove it!"

"I had no idea you cleaned up your act," Mayer smiled. "I can always get Errol Flynn. He's no crybaby."

"That's right," Gable snarled. "He fucks them."

"I'm serious about Flynn. You've been bitching about *The Hucksters* too long. I want to start production."

"You forced me into *Adventure* with a goody goody, but I

went through with it, didn't I?"

"Not without a fight, but then you always face a new script by giving me a hard time. I don't know what the hell you're worried about. Do you remember what Sam Goldwyn said about you in the thirties?"

"What's the difference?"

"Sam said, 'When Robert Montgomery walks on the screen, you know he's got balls. When Clark Gable comes on, you can hear them clacking together. That's the difference.'"

"I've never done a film with my fly open."

Mayer laughed. "Don't give me that sanctimonious crap, Clark. I know about you and Louella."

"I don't give a shit!" Gable said, trying not to act surprised. "Besides, it was cheaper than buying her off. She wasn't very happy about not getting the scoop on Carole and me. . . ."

"I wasn't throwing dirt in your face. Just pointing out that you can't come in here with a halo over your head and expect me to see it. What is it you don't like about *The Hucksters?*"

"The female lead, for one thing. I won't tolerate acting an affair with a married woman."

"What else?"

"The guy I play is oversexed. He's a satyr."

"So? You should be able to do the part without looking at the script."

Gable clenched his fists. "Make her single and give my guy some character and you might have a deal."

"Might?" Mayer glared.

"In this story you've got a bastard who doesn't know how to fight another bastard. That doesn't make sense. I want to retaliate. I don't care how it's done."

"As I see it, you want to be a kinda bastard who kinda likes to fuck and kinda wants to get even with his boss. Is that it?"

"That's it!"

"You're castrating the novel, Clark. You're castrating the whole damn project, and you're trying to castrate me."

"No great loss on all three counts," Gable mumbled, walking out the door.

Mayer wanted Gable for *The Hucksters*, but he didn't want

to be seen giving in too easily to an actor's demands. He did, however, ask writer Luther Davis to revise the script. Gable stalled until he got more of what he wanted, and though still not entirely satisfied, he finally acquiesced. He tested with Deborah Kerr, a British actress hired by L. B. Mayer to teach the latterly temperamental Greer Garson a lesson. Kerr was another elegant redhead, but not as sugary as Garson.

The Hucksters would be Kerr's first American film. Ava Gardner, another MGM starlet, was chosen to play the sensuous singer who loses her man to the wholesome Kerr. Gardner, like Gable, didn't like *The Hucksters*. She resented being cast as the girl who's not good enough for the hero, a part she'd played once too often. She was willing to go on suspension, if it came to that, to get out of the film.

Gable phoned her.

"I hope you'll reconsider," he said.

"I'm fed up."

"Baby, when you've been around as long as I have, *then* you can say that."

"The only reason I have for doing the fuckin' movie is that you're in it."

"Best reason in the world," he laughed. "We'll have a good time. You'll see."

"I gotta tell you this," she said. "When I first came to Hollywood, I saw you driving down Sunset and I almost crashed into the car ahead of me."

"Then do the movie, Ava. You're only twenty-four years old. Plenty of time to find a really good script."

Deep sigh. "All right, you talked me into it."

Gable and Gardner were attracted to each other from the start. At the time, she was unhappily married to Artie Shaw, who wanted her to become a cultured lady. Never one to put on airs or pretend to be something she wasn't, she was bored with books, classical music, and Emily Post. No one in Hollywood was quite as direct and unpretentious as Ava Gardner, who had grown up in the tobacco fields of North Carolina. Her first marriage, to Mickey Rooney, had lasted only a few months, and now she was headed for her second divorce. By the time she met Gable, she was ready for him. She used profanity like Lombard, fought with Mayer, and wasn't sure she belonged in Hollywood.

Gable sensed Gardner's nervousness and remained by her side on the set of *The Hucksters*. She, in turn, saw the sadness in his eyes. Though she assumed his hands and head shook because he was suffering from hangovers, he told her that the tremors were caused by the Dexedrine he was taking to lose the weight he had gained from too much drinking. The camera could not do many close-ups of Gable, and this endeared him to Gardner. Both muffed their lines, but she took the blame. "I was terrified of our love scenes," she would recall. "I had to tilt my head the right way, take care that my lipstick didn't smear, and remember my dialogue. The worst was suddenly remembering it was Clark Gable kissing me, and everything went blank. I couldn't believe he apologized. Clark said he was so concerned about me, he blew it. Then he took me aside and whispered, 'I know you don't think you're an actress. Well, I'm not sure I'm an actor.'"

Gardner grew further devoted to Gable when she found herself shooting her nightclub scene after hours, singing to the cameraman. "It's not easy trying to be sexy and mouthing a torchy song to an empty studio," she said. "Then Clark came in carrying a wooden chair, straddled it, and smiled at me. He hung around to help me through it."

Gardner became one of Gable's favorites. He had his harem and she had her stable. He taught her about acting and the art of discretion. She found the latter rather difficult, but Gable was a perfectionist.

The gorgeous Ava Gardner later had an affair with Robert Taylor while they were doing *The Bribe*. On the verge of divorce, he saw her regularly. George Nichols said, "Bob seemed to follow in Gable's footsteps where women were concerned."

The Hucksters received very good reviews. It's safe to say this was considered the first of Gable's pictures after a long absence. *The New York Times* thought there was too much of Gable, however. When he wasn't on the screen, they noted, he was about to make an entrance. The *New York Herald Tribune* wrote, "The Gable–Kerr team-up is ideal." *Photoplay* said, "Here's a good picture with Clark Gable as an attractive 'Huckster.'" *Variety* agreed: "Love that picture!"

Despite the agony that preceded the film, Gable felt redeemed after the embarrassment of *Adventure*. Deborah Kerr and Ava Gardner were applauded by the critics, too, and went on to become two of MGM's most popular leading ladies.

Gable's occasional girlfriend Kay Williams married millionaire sugar heir Adolph Spreckels II, notorious for fighting with his wives. Gable wished her well and left for Phoenix, where he met the Jones Sausage heiress, Betty Chisholm, a thin, athletic blonde who was an excellent golfer. A classy widow with charm and wit, she became one of Gable's regulars. By this point, he had women in all parts of the country, except for New York City. Then he met Millicent Rogers, the Standard Oil heiress, there. This interesting brunette was as zany as she was rich. In her mid-forties, Rogers loved to shock society by wearing costumes instead of designer gowns to formal affairs. Would she arrive as a squaw or an Egyptian princess? Gable got a big kick out of her clowning, but she had a serious side, too. Rogers fell in love with Gable.

Then the fabulous socialite Dolly O'Brien married for the fourth time. Only Gable's most intimate friends knew that she had turned down his marriage proposal, hurting him deeply. One acquaintance of Gable's later asserted, "Maybe he did and maybe he didn't propose to Dolly. Clark wasn't possessive, and yet there were times he acted like a sheikh. God forbid if a girl left him for another man. He drank so much, and loneliness caught up to him. If the setting was right, he might have proposed marriage. When Dolly married someone else, he made a funny remark that maybe he didn't satisfy her in bed."

After a four-month vacation on the Rogue River and a trip to Phoenix for some golf with Betty Chisholm, Gable came back to the ranch, Anita Colby, and Virginia Grey.

Gable next began *Homecoming* with Lana Turner, who was, at the time, planning to wed Tyrone Power. But while she was in Gable's arms on the movie set, Power was in the arms of actress Linda Christian, whom he would marry. To spite Power, Turner became the wife of millionaire Bob Topping.

Homecoming was a touching movie about a married society doctor (Gable) who becomes a major in the medical corps during the war. He tangles with his nurse (Turner) but learns humility in the process and falls in love with her. Soon afterward, the nurse is killed and the doctor returns home to his wife (Anne Baxter), dedicating himself to helping the needy.

Some critics and many moviegoers liked *Homecoming* and its bittersweet story of a rich man and a poor girl caught up in war, reaching out to each other. *The New York Times*, however, tore the movie to shreds. "It's nothing more than a cheap, synthetic chunk of romance designed to exploit two gaudy stars. . . . Talk about insincerity! *Homecoming* is one great big blob. . . ."

But MGM's theory of combining Gable and Turner on movie marquees was, as usual, a sure winner in 1948. For two years, Gable had come in seventh in the box-office polls. Bing Crosby and Betty Grable were the favorites from 1943 to 1950, during which time the only MGM stars in the top ten were Gable and Spencer Tracy.

Metro was faring better than the other Hollywood studios in 1948, but their profit was below five million dollars. Mayer, looking for another Irving Thalberg, hired producer, screenwriter, and director Dore Schary as chief of production. Mayer never doubted his ability to dominate Schary, but L.B. was gradually losing control over MGM, knowingly or not.

Gable still cursed him: "I can't wait for the day I throw my dentures in Mayer's face!"

Gable's friends saw very little of him from 1947 through 1949. He was fair game for such beauties as Paulette Goddard, whom he dated on and off. She was divorcing her third husband, Burgess Meredith, and was one of Hollywood's most determined go-getters. Gable was at the top of her list of conquests. If Goddard didn't get her man, she'd at least get a car or a diamond ring from him before the affair ended. Gable was the exception, though. Goddard was unexpectedly dismissed one day when he saw her off at the airport. Reporters were on hand when she asked him to kiss her good-bye. He refused. She laughed it off: "Well, that's that. So long, sugar!" After Goddard boarded the plane, reporters asked Gable whether he was planning to marry her. "No," he replied. "We're longtime friends and that's all." Unofficially, he told friends that Goddard came on too strong and that he had to go out of his way to avoid her.

One of the reasons Gable wasn't seen in his usual haunts in those days was his latter-day relationship with Errol Flynn, whose house was a haven for pretty girls, liquor, and dope. Mickey Rooney wrote in his memoirs about showing up for a 1938 Flynn dinner party with Wallace Beery. "When we knocked on the door," Rooney recalled, "it was opened by a pair of exquisitely beautiful twins, and they were absolutely nude! Some of the other dinner guests were Clark Gable, Robert Taylor and Spencer Tracy." At age eighteen, Rooney had been around, but this little episode caught him off guard.

Actress Ann Sheridan once said that the powder room at Flynn's house was secretly bugged. "We didn't know who would end up with whom most of the time," she recalled, "so we'd discuss it in the ladies' room. We really raked over some of the guys—demeaned their manhood. Looking back, it was very embarrassing. In the late forties, it was a coincidence that so many of us were going through divorces. We were adjusting

from the war, and feeling the fall of the star system. We clung to each other. Errol was the kind of guy who could make everyone forget their problems. He and Clark smoked, drank, and played to excess. David Niven said to me, 'Take a look at those two handsome legends, because they're about to fall apart. It's a bloody shame!'

"I remembered the first time I saw Errol Flynn. He was the most beautiful man I had ever seen. Flawless. But he didn't have the startling effect that Gable did. I have yet to figure it out. Errol made my heart beat faster, but the first time I saw Gable, my heart stopped beating. My eyes were glued on him. This was one of the discussions in the powder room at Errol's house—What the hell was it about Clark that stopped the world?"

For a time, Gable dated the energetic and ambitious starlet Nancy Davis. Davis, of course, would eventually make it to the White House when her actor husband, Ronald Reagan, became president. But in 1947–48, Nancy used every contact she had to further her career in Hollywood. Spencer Tracy fixed her up with Clark Gable, who took her out at least three times in New York. Davis's dates with the King paved her path to MGM.

Millicent Rogers came to Hollywood to wage an elaborate campaign to marry Gable. She bought a monkey and "wore" it on her shoulder wherever she went. She gave Gable expensive jewelry (he gave her nothing), wooed his friends, servants, and secretary, followed him on the nights he wasn't with her, and, ultimately, dropped her campaign when she found him with another woman. Having lost Gable, Rogers became a recluse for the rest of her life.

Dolly O'Brien's fourth marriage, meanwhile, was over almost before it began. A week after her divorce, she was being squired about Hollywood by Gable, and the two seemed to be taking up where they left off. But she was wiser than Millicent Rogers had been. Before she would consider Gable for her fifth husband, she made it clear that he would have to live in the East—New York, Palm Beach, or Newport. From there, she said, it would be faster to hop a ship to Europe. That was very nice, he said, but not an easy drive to the MGM studios.

Before leaving on a Continental vacation with O'Brien, Gable went up to Oregon to see Carol Gibson, who wanted no part of his glamorous life in Hollywood. Their favorite pastime was getting a group together, taking a boat down the river, and camping overnight along the way. Carol's father, "Rainbow" Gibson, owned an inn on the Rogue; Gable stayed there frequently over the years while on his fishing trips. He felt at home with the Gibsons and often considered building a cabin in their area. Maybe there was a future for him with Carol. . . .

On July 12, 1948, Gable sailed for France, where Dolly O'Brien was waiting for him. He attended parties given by Elsa Maxwell, golfed with the duke of Windsor, spent leisure hours at the casino playing baccarat, drove to Switzerland in an open car, and thoroughly enjoyed O'Brien's company. "She's a funny and witty woman," he said. Candid pictures of the couple proved they were happy together—always laughing and too busy for posing. O'Brien wasn't one for intimate romantic dinners. No sir! She adored a distinguished crowd of pleasure-seeking thoroughbreds and was not a lady to fawn over a man. It was Gable who pursued her from the beginning.

It was a splendid vacation, perhaps the best of Clark's life, but it was cut short when Will Gable died of a heart attack. Clark left for home immediately. His father's third wife had died a few months previously (Clark did not attend her funeral), and the house built for them was sold at a loss—Clark hated bargaining. Money was something he kept in a safe-deposit box or in his pocket. No one could convince him to invest, nor did he have a financial adviser. Clark Gable was a very frugal man.

His secretary, Jean Garceau, nagged him until he eventually allowed her to buy blue-chip stocks in his name. Gable never carried his own checkbook. "He couldn't be bothered," Garceau said. Gable was very fond of Garceau and promised to buy her a Paris original when he was in Europe. Rushing home for his father's funeral, he couldn't keep his promise, but he did finally get her a very expensive Paris gown from a shop in Beverly Hills.

Gable never introduced his more casual affairs to Garceau, but she was acquainted with the regulars—Anita Colby, for instance. Colby was Gable's best pal, and though she loved him, she wasn't *in* love with him. Gable often enlisted her assistance when planning important parties. When she decided to further her career and settle in New York City, Clark felt a surge of panic. Colby was different from his others. Her life did not revolve around him, nor did she share his bed, but their bond was strong.

A short time before Anita Colby was to leave Los Angeles, Gable proposed to her. His speech, warm and genuine, was apparently thought out carefully. Colby was stunned. She had assumed, since their relationship was chaste, that Gable understood how she felt about him. As he described their future together, Colby was not as aware of his sincere words as she was his apparent loneliness. She worried about leaving him in the clutches of so many women who were in love only with the movie star, not with the man. Colby said she wasn't ready for marriage and didn't think being a wife was in her future; she was a businesswoman foremost. But she hoped he would visit her in New York, she told him, and continue their friendship. Gable was gloomily silent. Colby added bluntly that she thought he drank too much.

"That's because I'm so lonely," he said.

Her heart went out to him. "Don't rush off and do something you'll regret," she warned. "I worry about that."

Oddly, the two women he considered marrying preferred life on the East Coast to life with him.

Gable soon overcame his disappointment and gave a birthday party for Joan Crawford at the ranch. They were seen in public, too, but nothing came of it. As Crawford later said, "We understood each other. That was the problem. We understood each other too well."

In 1948, Gable made *Command Decision*, taken from the novel and play by William Wister Haines. Also included in the movie's all-male cast were Walter Pidgeon and Van Johnson. Critics commended Gable's performance as an air-force brigadier general, especially in a tense and effective scene, original to the film, in which he unsuccessfully tries to talk down a warplane being piloted by an inexperienced bombardier.

Command Decision was not aimed at Gable's romance-oriented fans, but the vitality of the story and the fine performances of the cast made the film a hit.

Dore Schary spoke at MGM's Silver Anniversary luncheon in February 1949, and he promised bigger and better films. Referring to *Command Decision*, he said, "If we can't make money with this one, fellows, we all better go back to vaudeville!"

But Gable wasn't in the mood to celebrate. Victor Fleming had died of a sudden heart attack on January 6, 1949. Life without Fleming was almost as inconceivable as life without Lombard.

17.

Sylvia

n July 1948, Dore Schary had signed a seven-year contract with MGM for $6,000 a week, and though he had subsequently brought Metro out of its slump, he was not popular with many contract players, including Gable, who turned down the lead in the multi-million-dollar production *Quo Vadis*.

When Gable flatly refused to do the film, Schary threatened to put him on suspension. That was fine with Gable. "I'm not going to be seen in a Roman toga with my bloody knees sticking out," he stated firmly. "It's not my thing and I won't do it."

"*Quo Vadis* will be our most expensive film to date," Schary explained. "But you may have a point about the garb. I think Bob Taylor would make a better Roman officer."

"Why the hell can't you find something that's right for me?"

"I'm looking. In the meantime, how about *Any Number Can Play*, with Alexis Smith?"

"Another reformed gambler? Jesus Christ!"

"Until I can find what you want, Clark. Deal?"

"Yeah. . . ."

In *Any Number Can Play*, Gable is the owner of a legitimate casino. His wife (Alexis Smith) and son (Darryl Hickman) have little respect for his profession until he stands up to crooked gamblers and almost gets killed. In the end, Gable deliberately loses his casino in a card game. Critics agreed that Gable handled his role with ease; supporting players Frank Morgan and Wendell Corey got their share of praise, too.

While Gable waited for that Oscar-winning script, Schary asked him to film *Key to the City* with Loretta Young. Gable wasn't thrilled about this one, either, but he was fond of Young and wanted to work with her again. During production, Loretta, pregnant by her second husband, Thomas Lewis, suffered a miscarriage. She recovered quickly, though, and was soon back on the set. The shoot was uncharacteristically upbeat. Gable fell off the edge of a park bench in one scene when Young edged too close to him, and disappeared into a cloud of artificial fog. The two stars took their time, utterly unconcerned how long it took to finish the movie. Even though her contract did not contain a no-overtime clause like Gable's, Young demanded the right to leave with her costar at five. "I don't like working when he's not here," she said. "When someone else feeds me his lines, it's not the same. . . . I don't react the same."

In *Key to the City*, Gable and Young meet at a mayors' convention in San Francisco. Playing an ex-longshoreman, Gable had the chance to show off his manliness. Critics said the role was tailor-made for him, and his fans, agreeing, lined up at box offices.

When the movie was finished, Loretta Young and her husband threw a celebratory party. Gable came alone.

In September 1949, Gable's good friend Frank Morgan died

at age fifty-nine. Coming only nine months after Victor
Fleming's fatal heart attack, Morgan's death left Gable
distraught. He went into another deep depression, smoked
and drank more heavily than usual, and raced his Jaguar XK-
120 sports roadster in the desert. He was growing increasingly
discouraged as an actor—and as a lover. Fascinating scripts
were as hard to come by as fascinating women. He was bored
and tired and lonelier than he thought possible. The girl most
likely to reach the altar with Gable was patient Virginia Grey,
now thirty-two. Gable had been a widower seven years. It was
time to stop running. It was time to make peace with himself.
It was time for marriage. Gable began seeing Virginia Grey on
a steady basis. There was no announcement or formal
engagement. Only an "understanding." Gable's close friends
believed he would never come nearer to finding another
Carole—Virginia looked like her, talked like her, and dressed
like her. Gossip columnists expected to hear about an
elopement any day.

But Gable still managed golf outings with Betty Chisholm
and fishing trips with Carol Gibson. He also took up with
Joan Harrison, a beautiful British writer–producer associated
with Alfred Hitchcock.

Shelley Winters, still a relative unknown in 1949, met Gable
when Yvonne De Carlo invited her to an intimate dinner at
Errol Flynn's. When Winters pulled up to the house, Gable
opened the car door for her; Winters fell out. He caught her
just in time, got his wristwatch entangled in her wool shawl,
and had to be disentangled by Flynn, who asked Winters if
she'd managed this on purpose.

"I knew Mr. Gable would catch me," she said.

Gable grinned. "I would catch her anywhere, anytime,
under any circumstamces."

"After three double martinis, I'm surprised you were so
alert," Flynn quipped.

De Carlo managed to get Winters alone and asked, "Which
guy do you want?"

"Do I have a choice?"

"I think Errol likes you, so I'll make the big sacrifice and take Gable."

The two couples sat at opposite ends of a long couch to watch a movie. When it was over, Gable left with De Carlo. Winters said in her memoirs that she spent a long and beautiful weekend with Flynn, who wanted to give a party in her honor for the Hollywood press. "I'll get Gable to be your escort," he said. "Then I'll get jealous and have a make-believe fight with him. The press will have a field day."

On the night of the big party, Gable picked up Winters in a navy Rolls-Royce. They went to Romanoff's, where a restless and very nervous Winters asked, "When are we going to Errol's house, Mr. Gable?"

"Am I boring you?" he replied.

"No, you paralyze me. I'm sure if we wait too long, the Rolls is going to turn into a pumpkin."

He pinched her on the fanny and said, "Shelley, that feeling of unreality is an occupational hazard. After every movie, I feel I'll never be hired for another one. And please call me Clark."

When they arrived at the party, Gable asked Winters to dance and held her very close. He kissed her and whispered into her ear. Then Flynn cut in. He and Winters danced until Gable in turn cut in. Flynn pretended to be very angry, Gable mumbled obscenities, and the two men got into a heated argument. Before they could exchange blows, the police arrived, handcuffed Winters, and drove off. She cried all the way to the Hollywood Canteen, where, the officers said, she would have to entertain for an hour.

It had all been arranged. All a joke. Winters was furious, upset, and confused, but she sang at the policemen's benefit for the U.S.O. When she returned to the party, she found Flynn's house in a shambles, but her host and Gable were drunk and happy. "Hey, as long as they spell your name right!" they told her, howling with laughter.

The next day, Shelley Winters's name appeared on the front page of all the newspapers. Scripts were delivered to her house before she even had a chance to have a cup of coffee. A star was born.

In the summer of 1949, Gable attended a dinner party given by Minna Wallis, his former agent. One of the guests was Lady Sylvia Ashley, whom Gable had known casually as the third Mrs. Douglas Fairbanks, Sr. Ashley was yet another Lombard look-alike, without Lombard's softness. She was three years younger than Gable, divorced twice and widowed once by Fairbanks. Her jewels were astounding; once, when asked how much they were worth, she said she thought "about half a million," maybe more. Ashley was something of a combination of Gable's women: Carole Lombard, Dolly O'Brien, Anita Colby, Millicent Rogers, and Ria Langham. She had class, money, beauty, wit, intellect, charm, and guts.

Born Sylvia Hawkes in England, she was the daughter of a footman. She made her debut on the London stage in *Midnight Follies*. Partnered with Dorothy Field—they were billed as "Silly and Dotty"—she sang ballads and played the ukulele. In 1925, Sylvia appeared in *Tell Me More!* at London's Winter Garden and, to make ends meet, modeled lingerie. She was a very ambitious and determined young woman. The theater was grand and applause was very appealing, but they could not compare to nobility to which Sylvia aspired. She was blonde, thin, and shapely, and she carried herself well. In 1927, at age 23, the footman's daughter married Lord Anthony Ashley, heir to the ninth duke of Shaftesbury.

Being Lady Sylvia Ashley might have been enough for any eager young woman, but four years later, Sylvia fell in love with forty-eight-year old Douglas Fairbanks, Sr., who was still married to, albeit separated from, Mary Pickford. Quite an affair, insiders said. What a shock, outsiders gasped. But Sylvia had never been married to a world-renowned movie star before. Sylvia had her title; now she wanted fame. Fairbanks left for England "on business," and called Pickford in June 1933 to tell her he was not returning to Pickfair. She was consoled by actor Charles "Buddy" Rogers, who had been secretly in love with her for a long time.

To avoid a scandal, Pickford spoke to her friend Louella Parsons. "My marriage to Douglas is over," she confessed. Parsons tried to play the rift down, but reporters, hungry for the sordid details, followed Pickford everywhere. Trying to maintain her dignity, she told them, "Where there had been only heartbreak"—she wept—"and hope, a full-size scandal stares me in the face." When Pickford fell in love with Buddy Rogers, Fairbanks was free.

Lord Ashley accused his wife of adultery in 1934, and two years of scandal on two continents followed. Finally, in March 1936, Sylvia married Douglas Fairbanks, and Mary Pickford became Mrs. Buddy Rogers in June 1937. Everyone settled down happily except for poor Sylvia, who hated giving up her title. Making sacrifices was not her style. In 1939, Fairbanks died of a heart attack. Five years later, Sylvia married Edward John, Lord Stanley of Alderly. Within months, however, he charged her with adultery and began divorce proceedings that were to last four years. In 1948, "Lady Ashley" settled down in the fifty-thousand-dollar Malibu beach house left to her by Fairbanks.

Less than a year later, she set her sights again. This time the target was Clark Gable.

Following the dinner party given by Minna Wallis, Gable took Sylvia Ashley out occasionally, but not more often than he dated others. He and Sylvia weren't even mentioned in the gossip columns. Gable was just as attentive to Joan Harrison and Betty Chisholm and Carol Gibson and, of course, Virginia Grey, who was still waiting for him to name the day.

On December 17, 1949, Gable's biggest alcoholic binge to date began at a party given by agent Charles Feldman. Other guests said that Sylvia Ashley's behavior was shocking. "She was practically on top of Clark," one said, "and he was responding. They were acting like horny teenagers, and Sylvia was the aggressor. We knew he was plastered, but we had never seen him like this before. Clark wasn't himself. He

wasn't in control. It was really something to see a woman
taking advantage of him! But I felt very uneasy about it."

The next day, Gable called Howard Strickling. "I'm going
to marry Lady Ashley," he slurred.

"Who?" Howard asked.

"Sylvia! Lady . . . Sylvia . . . Ashley! I want you to make
the arrangements, and tomorrow won't be too soon."

Gable called close friends to invite them to the wedding.
"I'm marryin' Syl," he said.

Their reaction was, unanimously, the same as Strickling's:
"*Who?*"

MGM's publicity staff hoped to talk Gable out of it.
Everyone tried to convince him to wait a few days, to think it
over. Sylvia, however, was with Gable every second, and to
everyone's invariable "Are you sure?" she responded urgently,
"Sure he is."

On December 20, 1949, three days after Feldman's party,
Clark Gable married Lady Sylvia Ashley at the home of a
friend. Sylvia wore a navy wool dress, and Gable wore a navy
suit. They sliced a four-tiered cake with a Spanish sword. The
newlyweds spent their wedding night at the ranch and
boarded the *Lurline* for Honolulu three days later. Mobs of
fans were waiting everywhere the couple went to get a glimpse
of the new Mrs. Gable. MGM was so concerned about the
continually drunken groom that they sent Strickling to Hawaii
as chaperon to make sure the honeymoon went smoothly.

Virginia Grey received a telephone call on December 20.
"Gable just got married" was the message.

"This is a joke!" she laughed.

"No."

"Who?"

"Lady Ashley."

"Who?"

"Sylvia Hawkes Ashley Fairbanks Stanley."

Virginia Grey was devastated. And angry. Her telephone
rang constantly, and when she chose to answer, she said,
"Yes, yes, I know! Clark married Lady Ashcan!"

The honeymoon proved that Clark and Sylvia had little in common. While he sat in the sun, she sat in the shade wearing a hat and gloves to protect her white skin. He played a little golf and drank a lot of booze. When Clark wasn't sure what had happened, Howard Strickling was there to remind him. Sylvia, meanwhile, looked after Sylvia. That was the difference between the two blonde Mrs. Gables. Carole Lombard devoted her life to Clark, but Sylvia Ashley would fit him in as she liked. Two weeks later, the newlyweds sailed home.

As soon as Gable had a minute alone, he called Virginia Grey, who asked him, simply, "Why?"

"I was drunk," he replied. "Can you forgive me?"

"Don't ever call me again," she said.

"But I didn't know what I was doing."

"Don't ever call me again!" Grey repeated. He did, of course, so often that she was forced to change her phone number. He approached her on the street and in restaurants when "Syl" wasn't around, but Grey refused to have anything to do with him. Several days later, she got a call from a friend who asked whether it was all right to give Robert Taylor her new telephone number, and she agreed. Taylor called and suggested that he might come over with some steaks, wine, and phonograph records. Grey knew that Taylor did not want to be seen in public with a date until his divorce from Barbara Stanwyck was final. So they spent their evenings at her place.

"Bob was a big mystery to me," Grey would recall. "After our first evening together I left the room for a minute, and when I returned, he had disappeared. He simply decided it was time to go home. He reminded me of Clark. You could get to know them so far, and then the wall."

Grey wasn't the only one who decided not to see Gable. Many of his old friends were not comfortable with him these days, and they were annoyed with Sylvia, who wanted them out of his life, anyway. She also made up her mind to bury the late Mrs. Gable once and for all. She had no intention of being identified with anyone, especially Carole Lombard.

Sylvia set out to erase her husband's past life and all memories connected with it. She made it obvious to Gable's old chums that they weren't her type, and she did not even make the effort to remember their names. There was too much talk about hunting and fishing, she complained. Too many laughs about "roughing it." She wanted Gable to begin again—new friends, new hobbies, and a new outlook.

Joan Crawford had little to say on the subject except "If I were still married to Douglas junior, Clark would be my father-in-law."

Maybe Crawford thought Gable's marriage was a big joke, but his servants didn't laugh as they watched Sylvia putting Carole Lombard's mementos in storage. To the amazement of everyone, Gable had given his new wife complete charge of the house. There was nothing left of Lombard except the dining room, which was a bit too informal for Sylvia, God knows, but she left it alone. Naturally, she took over the white bedroom—and painted it pink! Gable *hated* pink. Even Lombard had been allowed only her collection of pink Staffordshire—which was removed by Sylvia. Everything "Lombard" was replaced. The servants expected Gable to protest when Sylvia suggested building another dining room more to her liking, but he compromised, and they built an extension.

The biggest surprise of all was Sylvia's taking over Gable's gun room for her paintings. "I don't know how that happened," Howard Strickling said. "I wasn't the only one who almost passed out. She made it look like a French drawing room. If she was going to leave anything for last, it should have been Clark's gun room. I don't think she did anything without his prior knowledge, though, even Carole's horrid pink bedroom. But I'll give Sylvia credit for the English rosebushes she planted all over the place. They were lovely. Gable looked great, though. I'll say that for him."

Another friend said, "When Clark came back from Hawaii, he stopped fighting the world. I don't know if he'd made up his mind that this was it—with Sylvia, I mean. Or maybe he felt guilty about marrying her in the first place. She had very expensive taste. Her furniture was the best you could buy, but when she had the brightly colored living room redone with her antiques, it lost its charm. The whole house did, except for the old dining room, which was rarely used. She had her own, which was done elegantly—more to her liking. Sylvia was very uneasy with anything of Carole's around. I can understand that. She married a guy who was obsessed with a butterfly that didn't fly high enough and collided with a mountain. We all talked about it often, about how Sylvia could never get rid of Carole. She could take Clark to Tibet and Lombard would be there. I, frankly, did not see the resemblance, but he did. Sylvia was hard-looking to me. She wasn't delicate or tender or pliable. Well, as I said, her putting Clark's guns in the shed, or wherever, was the epitome."

Sylvia had a guesthouse built despite Gable's distaste for anyone spending the night on his grounds other than the servants. She also tried to get rid of secretary Jean Garceau by suggesting that Garceau work at her own place. The office was made into a sitting room. It took Gable a while to realize that the new arrangement was all wrong, that he needed Garceau close by; she agreed to work in the guesthouse.

The dinner menu changed, too. No more meat and potatoes, baked beans, or spareribs. Instead, Sylvia served gourmet French or English dishes. The food was Continental, and so were the guests—the Ronald Colmans, the David Nivens, the Charles Boyers, the Tyrone Powers, Clifton Webb and Joan Fontaine—all European or so inclined.

But the most offensive sight was Gable carrying Sylvia's little diamond-collared terrier while his wife spent lavishly on evening wear. It was not long before he reminded her, "You're richer than I am, right, Syl?"

"Why bring that up, Bird?" She'd taken to calling him by this odd nickname.

"I want you to feel free to spend your millions," he said seriously.

She gasped. "You'd ask me to sell my jewels? My securities? My beach house?"

"Something like that."

"I'm somewhat taken aback."

"So am I when I see the bills, my dear."

"I'll see what I can do, Bird."

"I'll drink to that."

Gable felt much better about his career when MGM put him in *To Please a Lady* with Barbara Stanwyck. He played a racing driver and she a newspaperwoman. With these two pros, the film was a success before it was even in the can. As he had done in *Night Nurse* almost twenty years earlier, Gable let Stanwyck have it.

"You'd better listen to what I'm saying or I'll knock that smile off your face," he said in one scene.

She smirked. "Knock it off."

He did, with one swift swing of his right arm, and she went spinning. Moviegoers loved it. *Motion Picture Exhibitor* wrote, "Gable is his charming best." The other reviews were also good.

As soon as the picture was finished and Sylvia was sure there was no romance between her husband and the recently divorced Stanwyck, the fourth Mrs. Gable left for Europe to disentangle some of her assets. Gable spent the three weeks she was gone with friends and conferring with Mayer and Schary. "I liked doing *To Please a Lady*," he told them. "Haven't enjoyed myself so much in years."

"We have a better one," Mayer smiled. "What we have in mind is a role you can get your teeth into—a rugged trapper hunting for pelts in Indian country. Here's the script."

"On location," Schary added. "In Colorado, where there's plenty of good hunting and fishing."

"I like it. If you can get Ava . . ."

Mayer smiled. "If she's not filming, Ava's screwing around with Sinatra."

"Who's the girl in *Across the Wide Missouri*?" Gable asked.

"Maria Elena Marques. She's new," Schary replied.

"Fine with me, I guess, but give me Ava next time."

"Give my regards to your charming wife," Mayer said.

"Yeah."

Sylvia returned in time to accompany Gable to Durango, Colorado, where *Across the Wide Missouri* was to begin filming in July. Despite the rough terrain, he was eager to drive, but she felt ill at the very thought. "I'd prefer taking the train," she said.

"The train? With all that goddamn baggage? We're only staying two months."

"That's a long time," she said. "Must you drive, Bird?"

"I was looking forward to it, yes."

"In that case, I can take along a few more things."

"I'm not hiring a private train for you, Syl. Just a private compartment."

She laughed. He could be *so* witty. "I know, I know," she chirped. "Do you mind taking Minnie with you in the car?"

"Take that dog on the train, for Christ's sake!"

"But she's so attached to you, darling."

The car was so overloaded with trunks and suitcases that Gable could barely see through the back window. "Are you sure this is everything?" he asked, holding the terrier.

"Well, I have some shopping to do, but I'll manage somehow on the train. Somehow, someway, I'll manage."

"Yeah," he groaned, trying to fit himself into the front seat. "You don't need much where we're goin', Syl. All you need, really, are some britches, sweaters, and boots."

Sylvia was more interested in kissing little Minnie good-bye. And then her husband. "Safe trip, my darling!" After he had gone, Sylvia went on a shopping spree in Beverly Hills for a complete western wardrobe. With an exorbitant amount of excess luggage, she boarded the train, which would be the last of her luxuries for a while.

"Jesus, Syl, we're not movin' here," he said when she arrived.

"Aren't you silly, Bird. How could I come to beautiful Colorado without my easel and oils?"

"Yeah," he said, waving to some husky men to help him unpack. Meanwhile, Sylvia reached for the smelling salts when she saw the rustic cabin assigned to them.

Gable, busy filming, scarcely paid attention to anything else. The frilly lace curtains came first. Then the landscaping. Sylvia had sod put in and trees planted, and she supervised the garden herself. It all came together one morning when Gable peeked through the window and saw trees that hadn't been there when he went to sleep. Beautiful green trees, too, nicer than he had at home. The flowers were blooming, but he couldn't remember anyone's putting seeds in the ground.

Then came breakfast, and Sylvia's best china, silverware, silk napkins and tablecloth, candelabra, and finger bowls. He had a drink, gulped down some black coffee, and left for the day in a quiet huff.

It got worse. Sylvia served him cocktails in her best crystal.

"We're having dinner with the others," he announced. "It's ranch style."

"Is that the name of the restaurant?" she asked.

"No, my dear. We sit at a long table with the crew and eat what's served on big platters and in big bowls. We serve ourselves."

"That might be fun once in a while," she smiled.

"Every night," Gable said. "Each and every night."

At least this gave Sylvia a chance to wear her new western outfits—a different one every night. Gable put up with this, but bringing the dog to the table was too embarrassing for him to take. Sylvia took a nibble and then Minnie took a bite. The crew kidded him about this unmercifully, but no one dared mention the frilly cabin that did not blend into the rugged territory. Gable tried to escape with his fishing gear, but Sylvia tagged along. She hated the sport, so she sat under a tree wearing her hat and gloves. Sometimes, she brought along her needlework.

It never occurred to her that Gable was doing what he

enjoyed most of all—hunting and fishing—and getting paid for it. It didn't occur to her that he resented living differently from the others working on the film, not to mention the added expense of redecorating the cabin and landscaping the grounds.

One of the technicians tried to make Gable feel at ease about Sylvia's fussing. "I told him it was very nice that his wife tried to make a dreary place look more comfortable," the technician later recalled. "She really went to a lotta trouble."

"Yeah," Gable had replied. "There goes the profit."

He endured it for two months, and it's up for grabs who was happier to get back to the Encino ranch, he or Sylvia. She considered the eight weeks in Colorado a disaster. Gable considered it the end of his marriage. But Sylvia did not grasp what was happening. He drank beer when she and her friends sipped champagne. At one of her catered pool parties, Gable rode his horse into the sunset. One of the British guests said, "All we could see was the horse's ass. I do believe he was trying to tell us something."

Gable told his wife that her personal servants had to go. They were an unnecessary expense, he said, and he had managed with his staff very nicely over the years. She gave in reluctantly. When Sylvia said she was inviting her family for a visit—they'd scarcely left from their last—Gable said, "The guesthouse isn't a guesthouse anymore. It's Jean's office." From the day they had returned from Hawaii, Gable had had no privacy. Sylvia's family came to the ranch and lingered for an eternity. As they were going *out* the front door, her friends from England were carrying their luggage in the back door.

If Hollywood snickered at Gable's carrying little Minnie, they guffawed when he fell asleep one evening at the opera while Sylvia dug her elbow into his ribs. She pretended to be amused when the incident made the gossip columns—Clark Gable in white tie and tails, snoring as some diva sang. Sylvia thought that Gable should at least pretend to be interested in the arts, but he wasn't pretending any longer. Maybe this was a sign that he was bored with Sylvia's way of life, but his change in attitude became very apparent when a fishing buddy asked him, "Are you thinking of building on your Rogue River property?"

Yes, he was.

"Do you think your wife will like it there?"

"That won't matter at all," Gable answered.

Across the Wide Missouri is a colorful film with a colorful supporting cast: Ricardo Montalban, John Hodiak, Adolphe Menjou, and Jack Holt. William Wellman, who had last worked with Gable during *Call of the Wild*, directed. Playing a trapper in the Northwest Territory, Gable marries an Indian girl to ensure his expedition's safety. She is killed, and he returns with his son to live in the Indian village. In between, there's a good deal of action and humor, all in beautiful Technicolor.

Dore Schary's idea that MGM should make lavish productions was paying off. Whether it was Gable crossing the Missouri or Gene Kelly dancing in Paris, the public was turning off their TV sets to enjoy the magnificence of the big screen. In 1950–51, MGM released such extravaganzas as *Quo Vadis*, *Show Boat*, *An American in Paris*, and *King Solomon's Mines*. In production were *Singin' in the Rain*, *Ivanhoe*, and *The Merry Widow*. In the battle with television, the studios were fighting back with the biggest weapons they had.

When a friend of Sylvia's offered her and Gable a villa in Nassau for a Christmas 1950 holiday, he agreed to go, but the couple came home barely speaking. The servants heard loud bickering about what he should wear to dinner parties. Gable told his wife he was perfectly capable of dressing himself properly for any occasion. Sylvia wanted him to change the cut of his clothes, but he refused. When she didn't take the hint, Gable told her never to approach the subject again. She had yet to recognize the seriousness of his protests.

For Gable's fiftieth birthday, Sylvia decided to give him a party with *his* friends instead of *hers*. She'd surprise him with one of his favorite dishes, chicken and dumplings. Maybe the guests and menu weren't the crème de la crème, but the table setting was. She might have given in just this once with less formality, considering the simple meal being served. Not Sylvia.

She had just hired a new cook, and Gable suggested it might *not* be a good idea to have a party under the circumstances. But Sylvia wasn't the least bit concerned. Who the devil worried about chicken and dumplings?

The house was filled with fresh flowers, the fireplace flickered during the cocktail hour, and Gable seemed more relaxed and content than he had been in a while. Then Sylvia announced that dinner was served, and the guests took their places in the new dining room. The serving platter was put in the middle of the table. *Voilà!* Or was it *merde?* A foul odor filled everyone's nostrils. The ladies felt sick and put down their forks, though the gents, including Gable, dove in. But no one could pretend politeness for long. There was gagging and coughing. The women covered their noses with the lace napkins, and the men wiped their foreheads. One of the servants apologized, explaining that the new cook had prepared the meal a day ahead of time and had not refrigerated it overnight.

Gable left the room and did not return until much later in the evening. He was not amused. What hurt him most was Sylvia's carefree attitude toward his friends, as if they weren't important. As if chicken and dumplings didn't matter. This would not have happened at one of her own dinner parties. He made up his mind that night that he needed to work—to get his mind off the formality of life that presented itself day after day with Sylvia.

Two months after the disastrous dinner party, Gable began filming *Lone Star* with Ava Gardner. He had no intention of having Sylvia around to distract him, and in April 1951, he came home one night, told her he wanted a divorce, and locked himself in his room. Once Gable had made up his mind, there was no turning back, no discussion, no argument. Sylvia turned to his friends for advice. It was all wrong, they said, to turn Gable's life around so drastically—to change the ranch he loved, to crate Lombard's knickknacks, to keep him from the woods and streams, to remove his guns, to allow her relatives to invade his treasured privacy. She was reminded that Lombard had changed for Gable without losing her identity.

Sylvia hoped it wasn't too late, but Gable refused to discuss it with her or anyone else. He wanted her out of the ranch as soon as possible. She left for Nassau, hoping he would change his mind. When she returned, all the locks had been changed and the servants had instructions not to allow her inside. On May 31, 1951, she filed for divorce in Santa Monica and left for Hawaii the next day with the George Vanderbilts on their yacht.

Ava Gardner and Clark Gable resumed their close relationship while shooting *Lone Star*. He had aged considerably and was drinking heavily throughout the filming. His head shook uncontrollably, and a rumor sprang up that he was in the first stages of Parkinson's disease. Because he was still taking diet pills to control his weight, it seems likely that the amphetamines and his continual hangovers were the cause of his tremors. Again Gardner's heart went out to Gable, and she handled him gently and calmly.

Spencer Tracy dropped by the set for lunch one afternoon, and the three discussed their never-ending career dilemmas. Gardner told Tracy about a scene in the film where she walked happily down the street after spending the night with Gable. "Schary cut it out," she complained.

Tracy said, "Yeah, since Dore took over, nobody gets laid at MGM."

Gable laughed all through lunch and confided, "You two guys are good for my soul."

On June 22, 1951, midway through *Lone Star*, L. B. Mayer resigned. Gable felt like the other old-timers at MGM. Confused. If Mayer could be forced out of the studio that he symbolized as much as Leo the Lion did, what about the contract players, the "family"? Gable didn't think that

Mayer's perennial chicken soup in the commissary was so corny anymore. He had never liked the man, but he scarcely respected Schary. There was an aura of fear on the MGM lot, and Gable was not immune. During the filming of *Lone Star*, the makeup people said, "Gable doesn't look like Gable anymore." Gardner didn't agree. Gable would always be Gable, she said. The gray at his temples, the sheepish grin, and the twinkle in his eyes. "Ava makes me feel like a man," Gable said.

Lone Star is the story of a nineteenth-century adventurer (Gable) who tries to persuade Sam Houston to renege on an agreement with Mexico. Gardner is Gable's lady love, but it is his long and bloody fistfight with Broderick Crawford at the end of the film that one remembers. The critics loved it!

After he finished *Lone Star*, Gable prepared for battle with Schary by signing with the most powerful talent agency in the country—M.C.A. Then he called Sylvia to pick up her things at the ranch, but she stalled. He knew what that meant. She was holding out for a reconciliation or a huge settlement, so he took the situation into his own hands. After drawing out all his money and throwing it into a suitcase, he left for Lake Tahoe, Nevada, and checked into the exclusive Glenbrook Lodge to set up residence and file his own divorce suit in October.

18.

Ba and Grace

By law, Gable could not leave the state of Nevada for more than twenty-four hours while pursuing his divorce. Friends drove down for a visit with his guns and fishing equipment. When the Glenbrook Lodge closed for the winter, Gable moved to the Flying M.E. Ranch in Carson City, had his license plates changed, and settled down for the required six weeks. A young brunette socialite, Natalie Thompson, helped Gable pass the time. Thinking he had outsmarted Sylvia, Gable was feeling pretty good until he received word that her attorney, Jerry Geisler, had obtained an injunction against his Nevada divorce action. Gable was advised to return home and wait it out until the trial. Thompson followed him to Beverly Hills, where her mother lived, but he wasn't interested in a steady affair. One-nighters

were more Gable's style. He was eager to get his divorce over
with and to restore the ranch to its original décor.

It was a brighter day when Gable looked into his gun room
with pride. Sylvia's antiques were crated and Carole's
possessions were back in their proper places. This was home
to Gable, and no one would change it again. The servants and
Jean Garceau were more comfortable, too, when the ranch
was restored. Gable was back on the plow, playing with the
dogs and caring for the other animals.

Joan Crawford wanted Gable for *Sudden Fear*, but RKO
told her Gable was too expensive. She went into a rage when
Jack Palance got the part, but the film still came out good
enough to earn Crawford a third Oscar nomination. She
blamed her loss on not having had Gable as her leading man.

Gable's fifty-first birthday was a quiet one. Jean Garceau
baked him a coconut cake and, laughingly, they agreed it was
better than the chicken and dumplings the year before.

Sylvia's attorneys notified Gable that she had broken an
ankle and was in New York City at Doctors Hospital. She was,
however, willing to discuss the terms of the divorce. At first,
Gable refused to see her; then he changed his mind. When he
walked into Sylvia's hospital room, they were all over each
other, his lawyer said. "Clark and Sylvia were like two kids,"
he explained, "laughing, joking, gabbing. I wanted to get the
matter of the settlement over with. It got to a point I thought
they were going to call the whole thing off. They were having a
great time and calling each other by their silly affectionate
nicknames. They didn't want to talk business. After an hour
of this, I reminded Clark we had a dinner appointment. He
told me to go back to the hotel and he'd be there shortly. I
had to call him several times, and when he finally showed up,
Clark was all smiles. He said everything would be all right
. . . that Sylvia wouldn't make trouble. She wanted to be
fair."

On April 21, 1952, Clark met his wife in Santa Monica
Court, where she received an uncontested interlocutory
divorce decree and a $150,000 settlement, to be paid over a

five-year period. Sylvia could have got much more, but she still wanted Gable back. But when Gable walked out of court, he refused to discuss Lady Ashley—as if their marriage never existed. Sylvia married Prince Dimitri Djordjadze when her divorce from Gable was final. She was always more satisfied when she had a title, and this time around, she scored big.

Actor Stewart Granger approached Dore Schary about *Mogambo*, the forthcoming remake of *Red Dust*. Following his success in *King Solomon's Mines*, Granger was eager to do another film on location in Africa. Schary went ahead with the script, but he told Granger, "I'm putting Gable in *Mogambo*. His career has been in a slump, and he needs all the help he can get right now."

Schary asked Gable, "Do you want the good or the bad news first?"

Gable shrugged.

"How would you like to go to Africa and do *Mogambo* with Ava Gardner?"

"I'd love it, but what's the catch?"

"The Mau Maus are about to rebel, so there'll be a delay."

"Why don't we get started *before* they go on the warpath?"

"We haven't found the right location yet, and we still haven't cast the part of Linda."

"Then I'll go up the Rogue. You can reach me through Strickling."

"No, you'll go to London and make *Never Let Me Go*."

"Gone are the days when I do two pictures in a row, my friend."

"Do you want *Mogambo*?"

"Sure. But I have to pay the price, is that it?"

"From England, you'll have time for a vacation before going to Africa. Twenty months out of the country will give you a tax break. I'm sure the extra money will come in handy, in light of your divorce. . . ."

"Yeah. *She* should have paid *me* alimony," Gable spat out.

On May 6, 1952, he sailed for Europe on the *Liberté*. In

Paris, he met a tall and beautiful Schiaparelli model, Suzanne Dadolle, who offered to show him around. She was blonde, twenty-seven years old, and, perhaps inevitably, resembled Carole Lombard. Gable felt that his life was finally turning around. He loved Paris, he was falling in love with Dadolle, and he was elated with the *Mogambo* script. His *Never Let Me Go* leading lady, Gene Tierney, was waiting for him in London, and Ava Gardner was preparing to leave the United States for Africa.

Gable's friends were shocked when he wrote home that he had given Dadolle a huge topaz ring. He was captivated, but how many French girls did he have in his long list of conquests? Maybe that's why she fascinated him. The reason wasn't important. That he was considering marriage was.

In mid-June, Gable left Dadolle in Paris and checked into the Dorchester in London to prepare for *Never Let Me Go*. Gene Tierney, who was to play Gable's Russian ballerina wife, had recently divorced designer Oleg Cassini and was traveling with her mother, who was a very observant woman. On the movie set, Tierney's mother commented, "You could have Gable if you set your mind to it." Tierney wasn't interested at the time, having recently been introduced to the one man on earth who was arguably more charming than Clark Gable: Prince Aly Khan.

"I knew Clark was vulnerable," Tierney would recall. "We had dinner one evening and he told me how much he loved and missed Carole Lombard. I found him to be tough on the outside and gentle on the inside. He had a quality that was hard to resist, but my mother was too anxious. I don't think she realized that Clark always romanced his leading ladies. He and I laughed about our beginnings in Hollywood. We both had physical drawbacks that might have kept us off the screen—my protruding teeth and his protruding ears. We had a good laugh about that. He was a thoughtful man. My feet were blistered from extensive ballet lessons, and he remembered to bring back some salve from Paris that helped a lot."

Gable hated the damp weather in London and preferred to

lounge in front of the fireplace in his Dorchester suite when he wasn't filming, often in the company of Spencer Tracy, who needed a drinking companion while he waited for Katharine Hepburn to arrive in England. On weekends, Gable joined Suzanne Dadolle in Paris.

He ordered a custom Jaguar, which was delivered to him while he was filming an outdoor scene on the outskirts of London. With the camera still rolling, he grinned and rushed into the rain for a ride in his new car. It was MGM policy that stars did not drive themselves to and from the studios, but the look on Gable's face convinced director Delmer Daves to go around the block a few times. "It was such a relief to see Gable happy again," Daves said. "It took me a while to recover from that short spin in his new Jaguar, but I knew he was more concerned about the car than my life."

In *Never Let Me Go*, Gable plays an American newsman in Moscow trying to smuggle Tierney out of the Soviet Union. *The New Yorker* said that Gable's dimples were "like craters of the moon." *The New York Times* wrote that Gable was "a little older, a little fatter, a little shrewder." But even as the star system was fading in Hollywood, critics hailed the love team of Tierney and Gable.

When *Never Let Me Go* was finished, Tierney apologized to Gable for turning down the part of Linda in *Mogambo*. "I can't bear to be away from my baby, as much as I'd like to see Africa," she explained. "Six months is too long." They discussed the actress who would do the old Mary Astor part. She was newcomer Grace Kelly, who had appeared in only two films, *Fourteen Hours* and *High Noon*.

In London, Gable occasionally had dinner with Joan Harrison. He also disappeared for a few days with Betty Chisholm, who had also crossed the Atlantic to be with him. On September 20, he flew to Paris. He had the Jaguar sent along, picked up Suzanne Dadolle, and drove with her to the Villa D'Este on Lake Como, where the couple stayed for three weeks. He promised Dadolle he'd let her know when he was coming back, stored his car in Rome, and flew to Nairobi on November 2, 1952.

Gable and director John Ford were waiting at the Nairobi airport when Ava Gardner, accompanied by her husband, Frank Sinatra, and Grace Kelly arrived. On the drive to the New Stanley Hotel, Gardner invited everyone to her anniversary party. "Hey, this is the first time I've been married for a whole year," she said, laughing.

"Aren't you tired?" Gable asked.

"The only cure for that, honey, is a party!"

Kelly checked into her room, and within minutes she could hear Gardner's phonograph blasting and people laughing. Still a bit shy and not sure if she belonged with this close-knit group, Kelly hesitated in the doorway of Gardner's room. Gable asked her to sit down. "Bumpy trip?" he asked.

"Quite."

"Yeah, I flew into a storm. The hailstones were as big as my fist. The damn plane had dents all over. Scared the hell out of me."

One of the technicians sat down next to Kelly and told her that Gable had got off the plane as white as a ghost.

"But you were in graver danger during the war," she said.

"I almost turned down this picture because I don't like to fly," Gable said.

Kelly smiled. "I was so anxious to get here, nothing else mattered. This is such a charming hotel."

"Yes, but you won't see much of it. We shoot the film at Mount Kenya, sixty miles from here."

She watched Gable pour himself another glass of scotch.

"I didn't mean to frighten you," he said. "The compound is very impressive. It ain't the Stanley, but it's pretty fancy camping."

"I must confess, I can't believe I'm in Africa!" Grace exclaimed. "After I got my shots, Actors Equity wouldn't grant me a permit to work here because this movie is an MGM British film, and aside from the director and the three principal players, the entire cast and crew have to be British.

I was devastated because the only reason I signed a contract with MGM was to work with you in this movie."

"But good ol' MGM came through," Gable said sarcastically.

The technician tapped Gable on the shoulder and pointed to Sinatra, who was giving Gardner a mink coat for their anniversary. When she tossed it aside, Gable's teeth almost fell out. "I'd never let a woman treat me like that," he said, loud enough for her to hear.

"You would if she paid for it, honey," Gardner cracked.

At dinner that evening, Kelly spoke to the waiter in Swahili. Gable pretended to be impressed, but he considered the performance rather juvenile. The English-speaking waiter yawned, and Gable puckered his lips quizzically. This tall, slim blonde had class underneath that Swahili act, he said to himself, but no way is she Philadelphia Main Line. If anyone could tell the difference between the blue bloods and the nouveau riche, it was Gable.

The main topic of conversation was the Mau Mau infiltration. "Women carry pistols in their pocketbooks," he said. "The white residents can't trust their servants these days."

Kelly was blasé about all that. She wanted to know why he had accepted the role of a man having an affair with a married woman. He had, after all, turned down such parts previously.

"Because, my dear, the relationship between Linda and Victor does not go beyond infatuation."

"I didn't get that impression," she said, peeling a banana.

"Victor is a white hunter who plays by the rules on and off safari."

"In the script, he's described as a two-legged boa constrictor, Mr. Gable."

"Clark. . . ."

"May I call you 'Ba'?"

He grinned. "Did you say 'Pa'?"

"*B-A.* 'Ba.' Swahili for 'father.'"

"I'm old enough to be."

" 'Ba' has nothing to do with age, necessarily," she explained. "It refers to one who is admired and respected. Would you like my 'ndizi'?"

"I've never turned down an offer like that in my life."

She handed him half of her banana.

"Thanks," he said, trying not to laugh.

"Do you plan any hunting while you're here?" she asked.

"I'm looking forward to it."

"Might I tag along?"

"This is dangerous territory, Grace."

"That's all right," she smiled. "I don't frighten easily."

Gable looked into her aqua eyes. She didn't blink. Very interesting girl, he concluded. . . . Smooth tawny skin, perky lips, sculptured nose with sensuous nostrils, and soft yellow hair pulled back from her square jawline.

Gable asked, "Where did you learn to speak Swahili?"

"On my own. Do you know what 'mogambo' means in English?"

"Tell me."

"It means 'passion.' "

"Does it?" he said, lifting his drink for a toast.

"So you see," she said, avoiding his eyes, "there *is* more between Linda and Victor."

"That depends on one's interpretation of passion."

"You're rather old-fashioned about not playing a man who makes love to a married woman on the screen."

"Maybe little girls from Philadelphia who have never been away from home before think it's old-fashioned, but I call it professional ethics. When you've done as many films as I have, you'll be as holy as I am."

Gable saw many facets to Grace. She was corny, innocent, brazen, flirty, childish, and seductive. Like a baby cobra, he told his technician friend.

Grace Patricia Kelly had lived eighteen sheltered years in Philadelphia. Before leaving home to attend the American

Academy of Dramatic Arts in New York, she had a secret rendezvous with a friend's husband for the sole purpose of "getting rid" of her virginity. Kelly dated the Shah of Iran, who gave her expensive jewelry, as did Prince Aly Khan. She had affairs with a teacher at the Academy and with actor Gene Lyons. Kelly mesmerized director Fred Zinnemann, who cast her in *High Noon*. Costar Gary Cooper was also taken with Kelly, who sat on his lap when they weren't filming. He said, "She looked like she could be a cold dish with a man until you got her pants down, and then she'd explode."

Director John Ford said, "I was looking for Kelly's type for the part of Linda. You know, the frigid dame that's really a pip between the sheets."

Despite her reluctance to be tied down, Kelly was forced to sign a seven-year contract with MGM (for $750 a week) if she wanted *Mogambo*.

Flying over the MGM location setttlement near Mount Kenya, Gable told Grace, "This landing strip is eighteen hundred yards long. It was literally hacked out of the jungle. Those tents down there are on the banks of the Kagera River. Thirteen of them are dining rooms. Over there is the movie theater, an entertainment section with pool tables, and a hospital."

After they landed, he made sure she was settled in her tent, complete with hot and cold running water. "Around the back are two large oil drums," he explained. "The one propped over the wood fire is the hot water."

"A fire so near to my tent?"

"The flames will keep the lions away at night."

"Are you serious?" she asked.

"Nothing to fear. Roaming around someplace are a hundred and seventy-five whites and three hundred and fifty natives at your service. All part of the film unit. There's also a great guy by the name of Bunny Allen, a true-to-life white hunter. You'll like him." Then he pointed to a truck coming into camp. "Natives wives who stay home and do the menial work.

Earning a few shillings by just standing around is quite a treat for them, and better than working in the fields. They're even allowed to speak in this film, and that's quite an accomplishment."

Kelly looked around the compound as she and Gable walked to his tent. "Signing my life away to MGM was worth it," she sighed.

Gable was silent for a minute; then he blurted out, "I've been under contract for more than twenty years, and now they're planning to dump me after one more film." He was in a talkative but pensive mood. "They want to give me a two-year extension," he said, "but I'm getting out on my own terms."

"You aren't giving me much to look forward to," she said, forcing a smile. "Any advice?"

"Be on time, know your lines, and don't stumble over anything."

John Ford, however, expected more than that. He was a rough, gruff, and abusive bull who once told John Wayne what he could do with his horse. Ford liked Grace, but he wanted to make sure she knew who was boss. "Don't you have any instinct, Kelly?" he bellowed on the set. "We're doing a movie, not a script!" He was also unsympathetic to the palsied trembling of Gable's head and hands, particularly during one love scene with Ava Gardner. Gable knew his timing was off and asked for a retake. Ford turned him down, commenting bluntly on the actor's affliction.

But Ford had it in for Gardner particularly. He swore at her and called her a terrible actress, ranting in front of the assembled cast and crew. Gable put his arm around Ava and walked her off the set. Ford waited a few days before taking Gardner aside and telling her, "You're damn good. Just take it easy."

When Frank Sinatra returned home to test for the part of Angelo Maggio in *From Here to Eternity*, Gardner told Ford she was pregnant and wanted an abortion. He gave her permission to fly to London.

Grace had complained to Gable about the Sinatras. "They

fight all the time," she said. "I wish their tent weren't so close to mine."

"I bet they have a great time making up," Gable said, smiling.

"I hear that, too."

"They can't live together and they can't live without each other. That's gotta be hell," Gable said.

British officials complained about Gardner's walking around nude in front of the native boys who prepared her bath. Ford tried to keep the complaint from her, but when Ava found out about it, she took off her clothes and ran through camp in front of everybody.

Grace was mildly shocked, but she said nothing; Gable didn't give her the chance. "Do you remember that mama hippo charging our canoe in the river the other day?"

"How could I forget it?"

"Ava was alone in another boat. She might have been killed. And how about the rhinos that charged the truck? Ava didn't scream or panic or complain. Those are the things that are important. Ava's a brave girl, but right now she's a bewildered girl."

"I'm not sure I agree with your reasoning, Ba."

"I'm not so sure I care," he said sternly.

Kelly found out that Gardner—the sophisticate, the happy-go-lucky girl—wept inwardly but never gave up. Alone and unchaperoned for the first time in her life, Grace grew up fast in Africa. If Gable would not respond to her femininity, she'd approach him differently. She got up early to be with him even when she wasn't needed for the morning's shoot. "Why do you do it?" he asked. "It's hard to bounce around in a jeep with nothing but heat and humidity and mosquitoes."

"I don't want to miss anything," she said. "I want to have stories to tell my grandchildren. That's why I want to go hunting with you and Bunny."

"We'll see," he muttered.

"What more can I ask?" Kelly said, taking Gable's hand. They strolled along the banks of the Kagera River and did not try to hide their growing attraction to each other. One afternoon, Gable returned from location and couldn't find her. Told that she had gone for a walk, Gable demanded to know why someone hadn't stopped her. Fuming and concerned, he hurried off and found Grace by the water. She was sitting on a rock reading Ernest Hemingway's *The Snows of Kilimanjaro*. He wanted to shake the life out of her, but then he noticed the tears in her eyes. "It's so beautiful," she sighed. "Hemingway's leopard in the snow, and then I saw a lion walking along the—"

"A lion!"

"Yes, a beautiful lion—"

"And you weren't afraid?" he asked, sitting next to her.

"No. It was so moving. I had no fear at all."

They sat together until dark. Observers said that this was to become a common occurrence. She read to him, and he recited poetry to her. Gable's technician friend said, "Grace was very plain. She wore frumpy clothes and her glasses and no makeup. She and Clark often had their meals alone, or they'd sit together in the lobby of the New Stanley Hotel. Grace followed him around. He'd get up from a chair and she'd get up from hers. She was more attracted to him than he was to her. This was fairly obvious. Clark was flattered, I think, that Grace was crazy about him. He always held her hand when they took long walks, and she'd lean against him."

It was taken for granted that they were practically living together. Louella Parsons wired Gable that she'd heard about the romance, and he replied, "This is the greatest compliment I've ever had. I'm old enough to be her father."

Sinatra returned in time for the holidays. He had gotten the part in *From Here to Eternity*, which eased the tension between him and Gardner and was cause for celebration. He surprised her with noodles and all the ingredients for her homemade spaghetti sauce. Ava and Grace borrowed evening gowns from the wardrobe tent for Christmas Eve. "The generator broke down," Gable later recalled, "so we ate by candlelight. On Christmas Day, I found one of my socks hanging on the tent. Grace had stuffed it. MGM flew in a holiday dinner of turkey, Christmas puddings, and champagne. We were a family and it was a nice feeling."

At a party John Ford threw for Sir Andrew Cohan, the British governor of Uganda, the director attempted to get a laugh at Ava's expense. "Why don't you tell the governor what you see in that hundred-twenty-pound runt you're married to?" he goaded her.

"Well," Gardner replied, "there's ten pounds of Frank and one hundred and ten pounds of cock!"

Everyone, including the governor and his wife, thought her retort hilarious. Gable cherished Ava at times like this. He laughed the loudest at her description of him. "Clark?" she once said. "He's the sort of guy if you say 'Hiya, Clark, how are ya?' he's stuck for an answer."

Soon after the holidays, filming at Kagera was completed. While the new location was being set up, Gable, Kelly, and the Sinatras spent a weekend in Malindi, a seaport town on the Indian Ocean. They were forced to take an old plane that Gable later described as "being held together by baling wire. I spoke to the pilot, who assured me there was nothing to worry about. But I kept thinking about the four of us—maybe the hottest properties in Hollywood—taking a chance like this. MGM would not have been happy."

Grace and Clark swam together in the sea, walked along the beach, and watched the sun rise from their veranda. To her, this was not an idle affair—a fact that Gable was forced to face and think over very seriously. At the outset, he hadn't been especially interested in Kelly, but she had livened up. She remembered his raunchy jokes and repeated them, went on safari and proved to be pretty good with a rifle. But she stopped trying to keep up with his whiskey drinking, having sickened and passed out during a romantic dinner for two in his tent. John Ford may have made an actress out of her, but Gable made a woman out of her.

Leaving the cool breezes of the beach resort, the two couples settled into the Isoila desert country in Uganda, where the waterholes were safe for swimming and the camel transportation proved to be great fun.

Wrapping up filming in Africa, the cast and crew traveled to London to finish the picture. Gable checked into the Connaught Hotel, where he thought he might avoid reporters and the British MGM publicists, who had booked Grace into the luxurious Savoy. Gable was eager to see Suzanne Dadolle, but his helping Ford edit *Mogambo* prevented him from flying to Paris.

Gable dated Grace frequently, and for her, the end of their collaboration had come too quickly. "Can we fly back to New York together?" she asked.

"I'm doing a movie in Holland. And I'd like to see more of France and Switzerland."

"Why didn't you tell me?" she asked, fighting back tears.

"Grace, this might be my last chance to see Europe. When I was your age, I didn't know the Riviera existed. A strange-sounding name to me was 'Oregon.' I didn't know what it was to live in a house, and now that I have one, it's full of emptiness. So you tell me, why should I rush back?"

"I could stay in London for a while. . . ."

"MGM has plans for you, honey. Enjoy it."

On April 15, 1953, Gable drove Kelly to Heathrow Airport. Reporters were everywhere, but he ignored them as he led Grace to the gate and gave her a fond hug and kiss. She burst into tears. He whispered something to her; she hesitated, kissed him again, and rushed to the plane. Many accounts of this farewell were printed at the time, but they all agreed that Grace Kelly was very much in love with Clark Gable.

19.

MGM Farewell

few weeks after Grace's departure, Gable was in Paris with Suzanne Dadolle. In May he received word that his divorce from Sylvia was final, and friends held their breath. If he had sent Grace Kelly home and rushed to Dadolle's side, was the French girl going to be wife number five? She told the press, "*Oui.*"

And that was the end of Gable's affair with Dadolle!

Gable traveled for a while, then reported to the Netherlands for work in *Betrayed*, with Lana Turner, who was honeymooning with husband number four, actor Lex Barker. "It seemed whenever I worked with Clark," she said, "he was going through a major crisis. First, it was Carole's death, and then his sad homecoming from the war. Now his days were numbered at MGM. It was just a matter of time with me, too. The studios could no longer afford us. We were all a little frightened."

Gable quit MGM when they would not agree to his terms. He had demanded a salary increase and a percentage of the profits on every picture. They turned him down. *Betrayed* was filmed on a one-picture deal. Gable played a Dutch intelligence officer during World War II. Turner, a brunette for this film, was a former spy, and Victor Mature played a traitor. *Betrayed* is a forgettable film except for an effective finale in which Turner, whom Gable has presumed dead, reappears, dazed in trench coat and military boots, with a troop of returning servicemen. Reviewers complained about the complicated, draggy plot.

Gable returned to the ranch just before Christmas 1953, an unhappy and angry man. *Betrayed* summed up his feelings about his relationship with the studio he had served for twenty-three years. Their final insult: he had asked MGM for a print of *Gone With the Wind*; they had demanded over $3000 for it.

Waiting for Gable at the ranch was a burro named Ba, a gift from Grace Kelly. Gable was still bubbling about Africa, and had taken to wearing safari outfits on hunting trips. His household staff recalled the day a rattlesnake was discovered curled up and hissing on the grounds. Gable quickly changed into his African wardrobe, grabbed a rifle, and killed the rattler with one shot. He was quite proud of himself.

Clark surrounded himself with mementos from the Dark Continent. He had a jeep upholstered in zebra skin he had brought back with him. His friends got quite a chuckle when they saw him tearing up the roads and flying over bumps in his new toy.

Spending almost two years in Europe and Africa had been good therapy for Gable. It helped him face the day he packed up his belongings at MGM, put them into his Jaguar, and exited through the studio gates for the last time. Dore Schary and Howard Strickling wanted to have a farewell party, but Gable declined. He lunched with a few lower-echelon studio friends, and the drinks and laughter flowed. "Strange how it all happened," he said. "I never should have gotten this far. Here I am, though. *Mogambo* will be a hit, and I don't have a job." When someone reminded him of his enduring popularity, he said, "Yeah, figure it out. I don't know how to begin again, because I really can't say how it all started. But I feel free. This much I know. I'd like to produce my own stuff and I want Grace Kelly for my leading lady. You know, I have a good feeling about her. I'm proud of Ava, too. Who could have predicted these gals would be nominated for Oscars for *Mogambo*, huh? Two great kids, but they'll never know the Golden Era. The MGM family was like any other family, always bitching and complaining. It was tough, but looking back, we were the exceptions . . . Lionel, the Baby, Joanie, Myrna. Well, it's over . . . nobody to tell me what to do, how to do it, and when to do it. . . ."

Gable released a statement to the press about the end of his long association with MGM, adding that he wanted to freelance. He finished with "I wish to pay tribute to friends and associates who are no longer alive whose help and guidance over the years meant so much to me." Surely, this indirect reference to Irving Thalberg was a jab at Dore Schary and Louis B. Mayer.

Now that Gable was no longer under the protective wing of MGM, he was fair game for less-than-charitable members of the press. Columnist Dorothy Manners wrote that the studio had fired Gable and let him go without the usual farewell party. *Confidential* magazine described him as an opportunist with no heart or guilt or gratitude to his first wife, Josephine, who was now, it had come out, living in poverty. Hedda Hopper publicly defended Gable, saying that he hadn't seen Josephine in twenty-five years and wasn't aware of her living conditions. Hopper also claimed to have convinced Gable to help Josephine. It's doubtful that he did so in life, but in his will, Gable included an order to retire the mortgage on Josephine's property.

Josephine was featured in articles trumpeting the vivid contrast between the tanned, robust, and rich King of

Hollywood and the old wrinkled face of his poor drama coach, whom he deserted for a wealthy socialite.

At this time, Gable was seeing Grace Kelly regularly at the Bel-Air Hotel. They discussed marriage, but Gable pointed out that he'd be retiring in a few years, while she was on the brink of a brilliant career. He said, "When you're thirty, I'll be ready for Social Security." Grace told reporters that the age difference between her and Gable was insurmountable. They appeared at the Academy Awards together, and the press went wild. Nominated for best supporting actress, Kelly lost to Donna Reed in *From Here to Eternity*, which took a number of Oscars, including best picture. Frank Sinatra got his Oscar for best supporting actor, but Gardner lost to Audrey Hepburn in *Roman Holiday*. Ava did not attend the awards because the Sinatras were getting a divorce.

Clark Gable and Robert Taylor were both bachelors playing the field in the early fifties. Their hunting trips together usually included dames as well as games. A close friend of Taylor's recalled, "Six or eight of us would pile into several cars and take off late in the afternoon. There was nothing fancy about these trips. We wore old clothes, drove station wagons, and didn't bother shaving. One of our favorite spots was high pheasant country in Idaho. Bob and Clark were fast drivers and usually in the lead cars, sometimes an hour ahead of the rest of us. By the time I reached a town along the way, there were no girls or booze left. Picking up waitresses was an old habit, and no one was recognized. Taylor had a problem because he was exceptionally good-looking. He pulled his hat down to his eyebrows. So did Gable. Since we traveled after dark to make better time, it was more conducive to picking up girls without being recognized. Once, I had a flat tire. When I got it fixed, I stopped at the first roadside inn and asked a girl behind the counter if my hunting buddies had been there. She glared at me and asked, 'Two bums with mustaches and one with a beard?' "

Taylor's friend said that Gable never got bored trying to

pick up girls in bars. "Bob did, though. He'd find a back booth, pull his hat down, and go to sleep. Sometimes I got restless and tried getting Clark to leave. He said as long as a girl was breathing, it was a challenge to him. But make no mistake about it, we did more hunting and fishing than chasing girls."

At this time, Gable also saw a good deal of Betty Chisholm. She stayed with him at the Encino ranch, and he enjoyed visiting her in Phoenix. The weather influenced him—the hotter the better. He hinted that one of the reasons he did not follow Dolly O'Brien or Anita Colby was due to the cold weather in the East. It depressed him. The dry heat of Arizona appealed to Gable and was in Betty's favor.

Virginia Grey never forgave Gable for marrying "Lady Ashcan," but she allowed him back into her life. Adela Rogers St. Johns remained close to Gable, too. Joan Crawford's door was open to him, but in 1956 she married the chairman of the board of Pepsi-Cola, Alfred Steele, and settled in New York City.

Gable's harem was thinning out, and there were no contenders for wife number five. Gable's loneliness waned with age. Romance, time, and money were no longer so important. If he couldn't find a good script (in the fifties, they were rare), he had many hobbies to keep him busy. Gable's greatest accomplishment in 1955 was getting Dore Schary to beg him to come back to MGM. Each time Gable turned the studio down, they raised the ante. "Rub it in and see how high you can get those sons of bitches to go," he told his agent. "And when you get their very best offer, tell them to shove it up their ass." Schary had come through with a five-hundred-thousand-dollar offer that was flatly and colorfully refused.

Twentieth Century-Fox wanted Gable to appear in *Soldier of Fortune*, and he eventually signed a contract for two Fox films at $400,000 up front and 10 percent of the profits. Gable wanted Grace Kelly for his leading lady in *Soldier*, which was to be filmed on location in Hong Kong, but Grace was going to the Riviera to shoot *To Catch a Thief*. Fox told Gable that they had signed Susan Hayward. "Who?" he asked. But when they met, Clark remembered her well. "I used to stare you down at parties and never got a nod," he said on meeting Hayward.

"I'm as blind as a bat," she replied. "Why didn't you come over and say something?"

"Not without some kinda look. Know what I mean?"

"You bastard!" she said, laughing. "Friends said you couldn't keep your eyes off me, but I didn't believe them."

When Susan was scheduled for *Soldier of Fortune*, she was involved in a child-custody battle with her estranged husband, Jess Barker, and could not leave the country. Gable did go to Hong Kong, but his scenes with Hayward were filmed in Hollywood.

The movie received middling reviews, but the CinemaScope and Deluxe Color views of the Asian scenery made it worth seeing. Gable, of course, played the title role. He rescues Hayward's husband (Gene Barry) from behind the Bamboo Curtain and wins her in the end.

When Gable heard that Kay Williams, now Kay Spreckels, had divorced her millionaire husband and moved to Bel-Air, he called her up. Knowing his passion for golf and hot sun, she invited him to her Palm Springs house. Kay was now a very wealthy woman. Her two children, Adolph III, age five, and Joanie, age three, had million-dollar trust funds, and her divorce settlement had included half a million dollars. Her oil wells weren't doing badly, either.

Kay's marriage to Adolph Spreckels had not made sense to those who knew her as a well-adjusted, witty woman. Spreckels had a reputation that rivaled Bluebeard's. He had been accused of beating his first wife, and each subsequent wife (Kay was his fifth) had taken him to court for assaulting her. Kay had endured her share of pain for three years, until he beat her unconscious with the heel of her own shoe.

Kay was thirty-nine when she came back into Gable's life. They began to date before his trip to the Orient, and she was

waiting for him at the airport when he returned, just before
Christmas 1954. They saw each other every day until he left
for Durango, Mexico, in March 1955 to film *The Tall
Men*—the story of a post-Civil War drive of Texas longhorns
from San Antonio to Montana—with Jane Russell, Robert
Ryan, and Cameron Mitchell.

Gable liked Jane Russell immensely. In the movie, he called
her "Grandma," and the name stuck. She reminded him of
Ava Gardner. "They both had [acting] potential," he would
recall, "but never the chance to prove it because of their
enormous sex appeal."

Knowing that Russell had recently reconciled with her
husband, Robert Waterfield, Gable teased her about John
Payne, whom she had dated in the early days of her career.
"Clark was a big kidder," she said. "He'd wait until Bob was
nearby and then he'd talk about John. It was all in fun, but if
Clark thought he was gettin' to ya, he kept it up. I'm glad we
worked together when he was finally at peace with himself.
Kay Spreckels came to Mexico to visit him, and they were so
happy. He told me they were engaged."

Russell wanted Gable for her next movie, *The King and
Four Queens*. He read the script in Mexico and said, "I'll do
it, Grandma!"

Kathleen Williams was born in Erie, Pennsylvania, on August
7, 1916, on her parents' farm. After marrying a local boy, she
traveled to New York City to try her hand at a modeling
career. Kay enjoyed the company of the supper-club set and
soon outgrew Erie and her husband. She married Argentine
playboy Alzago "Macoco" Unzue and left him ten days later.
Kay then moved to Hollywood and took up acting. Gable
dated her for a time until she married Adolph Spreckels,
whom she separated from and reconciled with many times.
Spreckels once accused Kay of committing adultery with
Clark Gable, but the suit was dropped after one of the
couple's reunions.

If Kay reminded Gable of Carole Lombard, it was perhaps

with good reason: in Hong Kong, he was asked about his relationship with Kay and he replied, "Just friends." She called him long-distance and exclaimed, "Listen to me, you son of a bitch! Don't do me any favors. It'll be a long, long time before I'll marry you!"

On July 11, 1955, Clark and Kay drove across the California border to Minden, Nevada, and were married by a justice of the peace. The bride wore a navy-blue suit. The groom did, too, as usual. He sometimes called her Kathleen; often, in a replay of the Gable–Lombard pattern, they called each other "Ma" and "Pa." Her children, Joanie and Adolph, known as "Bunker," were very fond of their stepfather, who spent as much time with them as possible. They lived in the guesthouse with a governess. Otherwise, nothing was changed at the ranch. "Clark offered to buy a new house," Kay later said, "but I had my fill of mansions and palatial homes. I was comfortable at his ranch."

Thinking of the children, Gable put his rifles away and converted the gun room into a den. The Gables settled down to a routine life that delighted Clark—planting, plowing, and painting fences. Late in the afternoon, he and Kay spent time with the children, but they dined alone after cocktails. Their social life was as active as they wanted it to be. Clark's boozing subsided, but he and Kay enjoyed perhaps more than their share of liquor.

Howard Strickling had helped Gable plan his elopement, and he released the news in much the same way he had done when Carole Lombard was Clark's bride. "The contract players were lost without MGM," Strickling explained. "Everything was arranged for them. I remember Lana Turner's telling me how she felt rushing out of a restaurant to avoid a mob and there was no limousine waiting for her. They took these things for granted . . . didn't know how to make an airline reservation. They didn't have to worry about a thing. Bob Taylor lasted the longest at MGM, twenty-five years, but he said he waited too long. One of the reasons was that some stars were getting a percentage of the profits. Taylor left in

1958 with a million dollars and a pension, however. He never said an unkind word about MGM. Like Gable, Bob found the right woman in Ursula Thiess and had two beautiful kids. He said Clark wouldn't have lived as long as he did without Kay."

Strickling was right about Kay. She tried to make up for what she considered "lack of attention and care" that MGM had provided. It was a joyous day when Kay told Clark she was going to have a baby, three months after they were married. Several weeks later, she became ill with a viral infection and had a miscarriage. Clark was close to tears, but finding out that he could, in fact, father a child was a revelation—and meant that another chance was possible. Doctors said that Kay, despite a minor heart ailment, could attempt another pregnancy.

The holidays helped the couple forget their loss, and Clark discovered the fun of having children around on Christmas. He told Joanie and Bunker his childhood memories of searching out a tree, chopping it down, and lugging it home. No fancy trimmings. A string of popcorn, some candles, and homemade paper decorations. His stocking would be filled with fruit and candy, and he'd receive one gift each year. "If it hadn't been for my stepmother, I doubt that I would have gotten anything," he said.

It had been almost a year since Gable had filmed *The Tall Men*. It had turned out so well that he'd decided to form a production company with Jane Russell and her husband to make *The King and Four Queens*. While details were being worked out, Clark and Kay accepted an invitation to take a cruise on the magnificent yacht owned by shipping magnate D. K. Ludwig. At the end of January 1956, they sailed down the West Coast to Acapulco. "The weather was bad," Gable later said. "All I did was eat and sleep." He knew that his excess weight would have to come off before he started another picture. Putting on and losing weight had taken its toll on Gable. Though he told everyone how great he felt, Kay knew better. Twice while driving, he had suffered chest pains severe enough to force him to stop his car and lie on the grass until the pressure subsided. This cured him of speeding. He thought it was a big joke when police gave him a ticket for driving too slowly.

Joan Crawford, who hadn't seen Gable in a while, commented after his death that she couldn't understand why he usually got a clean bill of health after a physical examination. "I heard that he was trembling something fierce," she said. "His complexion was gray, and when he didn't have to stand, he sat down. Clark did not want to give in, and that was one reason he continued to drink. He wasn't a closet drinker, but he'd slug down a few if no one was looking. I also heard he had Parkinson's disease, but I never got any confirmation on that one. He didn't look good, but he was happy as hell. Who said attitude wasn't important?"

In the spring, Clark Gable, Jane Russell, and Bob Waterfield formed Gabco-Russfield Productions. Gable was disappointed that Russell was not ultimately able to costar with him in *The King and Four Queens*, but he was pleased with replacement Eleanor Parker, who joined him in this western about a suave desperado who seeks refuge with four women in a ghost town.

One member of the production crew that worked on the film said that Gable "was a mess. He was puffy and flabby, and his eyes were dull. There was very little kidding around because, as he put it, his money was involved. He even worked overtime."

Gable eventually decided that *The King and Four Queens* left a lot to be desired, and Bosley Crowther, critic for *The New York Times*, agreed with him: "Clark Gable may still be regarded as the 'king' of Hollywood, but he won't be for long if he continues to appear in pictures like this. It certainly represents a dreary comedown for Hollywood royalty."

When the Gables returned home from location filming of *The King and Four Queens*, Kay went into the hospital with chest pains. Clark stayed in an adjoining room for three weeks. The doctor permitted Kay to continue her convalescence at the ranch, provided she did not attempt to climb any stairs. A bedroom was set up for Kay on the main floor, and Clark stayed with her until she was well enough for him to go on a long-overdue hunting and fishing trip.

Gone With the Wind was re-released, and Gable was voted the most popular actor in the United States. "If it hadn't been for that damn picture," he said, "nobody would want me anymore. In fact, they wouldn't even remember who I was." Having his face before the public and his name on marquees across the country didn't hurt his next film for Warner Bros., *Band of Angels*, about a slave trader (Gable) in the Old South who falls in love with a woman (Yvonne De Carlo) who is secretly a mulatto.

De Carlo recalled, "I purposely acted like a saint in his company but lost my composure when some fans got out of hand and I blurted out some four-letter words. That eased the tension and we were friends again. His wife, Kay, was good fun. She'd be very quiet and ladylike and then come out with something raw. She loved to tell Clark to get off his ass, and he'd grin and do it. He loved dirty jokes. That was one way of getting his attention."

In January 1957, Representative Wayne L. Hays of Ohio paid tribute to Gable's twenty-fifth anniversary as a screen star, calling him a "hometown boy who made good in Hollywood." The tribute was read into the *Congressional Record*: "Mr. Gable still reigns unchallenged as one of the world's most popular and best-known movie personalities. Time cannot wither nor custom stale his infinite appeal." The congressman cited Gable's rise from obscurity as an example of "how a young American can advance himself and become famous."

Gable had found out the hard way how *not* to advance himself. He gave up the idea of producing his own films. In truth, he was not a fast study, and it was all he could do to learn his lines on time. Worrying about production costs and film distribution and profits and losses was almost as tiresome as balancing his own checkbook, and he couldn't even do that. He told Kay, "Hell, I'm an actor, not a businessman."

"That's not true," she said.

"Are you kidding?"

"I think you do very well figuring ten percent of the profits, Pa."

Paramount Pictures wanted Gable for *Teacher's Pet*, a comedy with Doris Day. He was cast as a cynical newspaperman, and Day was a small-town journalism teacher who mistakes him for a student. Gable apparently liked Doris well enough to accept an invitation to an alcohol-free barbecue she was throwing for the cast, though he did bring along a flask of bourbon.

Kay was so impressed with Day's house that she hired the actress's decorator to "brighten up the ranch." While the work was being done, the Gables went to the Del Monte Lodge at Pebble Beach near Carmel, California, where they celebrated their second wedding anniversary.

Teacher's Pet did not turn out well. Gable and Day were miscast, and he looked dreadful. Gig Young, in a supporting role, stole the picture. Critics no longer pampered Gable. *Films in Review* said that they would not have bothered noting *Teacher's Pet* at all but for the sad fact that "Clark Gable is feeling and showing his age. The masculine self-confidence has gone." And they predicted the imminent end of his film career.

Gable had put on twenty-five pounds, but he told a reporter he felt good about himself and about life. "I'm a very happy man. What can I say about Kay? She's a wonderful woman and the perfect companion. I worry about her health, though. She has angina pectoris. It's not serious, but very painful. Sometimes it's indigestion, but I worry anyway."

Kay walked into the room during the interview. She laughed and said, "When I do the cooking, it's indigestion."

The reporter wanted to know if she prepared many meals.

"When we're on location," she replied. "We usually rent a house, and it's more relaxing to stay home and have a cozy dinner after a hard day's work. We love to camp out, and I cook then, too. It's more fun to rough it than get all dressed up and go to a restaurant."

Did she hunt and fish with her husband?

"Yes. At least I try. Clark is a good teacher," she said. "Very patient. We've taken to golf. He plays very well and I'm not bad. We don't get a chance to do all the things we'd like to. Clark is busier now than he ever was. After he makes a movie, we travel across the country to promote it. We had a marvelous time during *The King and Four Queens*, filmed in Louisiana. Southern hospitality is very much alive. Clark was mobbed wherever we went. It was fun and very gratifying."

The Gables were happy. They were busy. They talked about selling the ranch, and they went house hunting. On his penny-pinching days, Clark reminded Kay that he had bought the property with the idea that it would pay for itself. That hadn't happened. "He'd bitch and moan," Kay later told friends. "Ursula said Bob [Taylor] was the same way. Something was always breaking down on the ranch. Clark would grab some tools and fix whatever it was. The place was too big; the fruit trees blossomed but didn't bear fruit; sometimes the chickens laid eggs, but more often they didn't. Clark would moan about the expenses, but I knew he didn't have the heart to sell. If he didn't have something to worry about, he'd go out and find something."

Gable bought a new Mercedes-Benz 300 SC two-door coupe and ordered custom luggage to match the car's light-tan upholstery.

In September 1957, Gable costarred with Burt Lancaster in *Run Silent, Run Deep*, an adventure film about underwater warfare, for United Artists. On location in San Diego, Gable insisted on taking a submarine ride so that he'd know what it was like. This time around, Gable and the movie got good reviews. *The New York Times*'s Bosley Crowther noted the "superior acting on the part of Mr. Gable."

Howard Strickling said that the Golden Era matinée idols shied away from lover parts in their later years. "Clark made a few mistakes, but he was thinking of the money, not his image," Strickling said. "Taylor was a real stickler. He automatically turned down scripts if the leading man was under fifty. Producers found out and changed the age to 'over fifty,' and Bob accepted."

In 1958, Gable filmed *But Not for Me* with twenty-seven-year-old Carroll Baker (playing his young girlfriend) and forty-four-year-old Lilli Palmer (playing his ex-wife). Gable played an aging Broadway producer who almost makes the mistake of marrying Baker, but returns instead to Palmer.

Again, *The New York Times* called attention to Gable's age, albeit positively: "He is willing to act his age. What's more, he's willing to make jokes about it. That's refreshing." The critical consensus was that Gable was charming, Palmer was charming, and Baker was *young* and charming.

"I'd like to make two or three more films," Gable said, "and then retire. But when a man has a family to support, it's hard to say." Though Gable had cut back on drinking when he married Kay, he had gradually gone back to his old habits. He joked about doctors' orders to slow down, to give up excessive drinking and smoking, but Gable's philosophy was "What's the point of living if you can't enjoy it?" He considered himself lucky. Spencer Tracy had misbehaved once too often and been fired by MGM. "He sat down on a rock and cried like a baby," Gable said at the time. "Mayer died not long ago, and his last words to Howard Strickling were 'Don't let them worry you. Nothing matters.' But that's not the way he lived, by God."

Joan Crawford had recently asked everyone in the movie colony not to appear on television. But Loretta Young, Ann Sothern, Donna Reed, Robert Young, Dick Powell, and Robert Taylor, among others, got good properties and the money they wanted.

Gable told Taylor, "A weekly show's gotta be tough to do,

but you've got ten years on me. Besides, I don't think I'm cut out for it."

"That's what you said about appearing on Jack Benny's radio show."

"I was scared of doing that kind of comedy. But if I were you, I'd be more scared of Crawford picketing your TV show."

"I wish she would," Taylor said, laughing. "Think of all the publicity I'd get. Hell, I don't even own a television set."

"I do because of the kids."

"Any good scripts come your way lately?"

"Thought you'd never ask, babe. I'm going to Italy to make a film with Sophia Loren. Kay and I would like to see Europe with the kids."

"Sophia Loren, huh?" Bob smiled.

"Yeah. Wish I were ten years younger, babe. But I gotta be satisfied holding and kissing them and getting paid for it. Take Jane Russell. She was there. *All* of her. Now Sophia Loren."

"When you get back from Rome, we'll do some trout fishing."

"That's a deal, babe!"

Gable surprised the world when he agreed to present an Oscar with Doris Day at the 1958 Academy Awards. They were introduced by Bob Hope as "two of the most popular stars in Hollywood." Gable's dignity and carriage were extraordinary. Any rumors that he was ill were dispelled that night. Except for the gray hair and the excess weight, he looked the same as ever. Gable was "nervous as hell," he said, but his awed peers gave him a standing ovation.

20.

Sundown

*I*n June 1959, Clark and Kay
sailed for Europe with the children. After a vacation in
Austria, they left for Rome, where Gable filmed *It Happened
in Naples* with Sophia Loren. He played an American lawyer
who discovers that his late brother had a child, born out of
wedlock, who now lived with a fun-loving aunt (Loren) in
Naples. Gable finally gets custody of the boy, but decides to
marry the aunt and live in Italy.

It Happened in Naples was Loren's picture. Gable knew it,
most likely, and wasn't disturbed a bit. The *New York Herald
Tribune* said, "Gable and Miss Loren are a surprisingly
effective and compatible comedy pair."

Clark and Kay lived in a villa outside of Rome and stayed
through November. (The children returned in September for
school.) They talked about building a house at Bermuda

Dunes near Palm Beach. Golf was taking up more of Clark's time now, and Bermuda Dunes would be the perfect site for a vacation house. In his spare time, Gable browsed through a script by Arthur Miller called *The Misfits*. "I don't get the story and I don't understand my character," he told Kay, putting the script aside.

Gable arrived back in the United States weighing 230 pounds. "It was the delicious pasta," he said. "I ate it every day—sometimes three times a day." Having put on so much weight, Gable had no intention of working for a while. Then his agent called. "Have you read the Arthur Miller script yet?"

"Since when is he doing screenplays?" Gable asked.

"What's the difference?"

"I'd like to know before I get involved, that's all."

"He wrote it for his wife. Do me a favor and read it, Clark. Miller's in town, and he wants to talk to you."

"I'm going to Palm Springs for the holidays. We'll discuss it when I get back."

Gable was dead set against *The Misfits*. He liked the part of the aging, drifting cowboy who makes a few bucks rounding up mustangs for a dog-food factory, but Gay Langland was a complicated role. "A little too heavy for me," he told Kay. "Let's face facts. The public comes to see Gable as Gable. They don't like me getting serious on 'em."

Howard Strickling was opposed to Gable's doing *The Misfits*, too. "Forget about it," Strickling said. "It's not for you. Marilyn Monroe and Montgomery Clift are Method actors hooked on drugs. She's got problems and she's never on time. They're not in your league."

Miller and Gable met to discuss the screenplay. Miller later said that he had had no one actor in mind when he conceived the part of Gay Langland, but that after meeting Gable, he realized they were one and the same.

Gable held out until Seven Arts, the company behind *The Misfits*, offered him $750,000, 10 percent of the gross, $48,000 a week for overtime, and complete control of the script. The

King was going to show them all that he was the actor who got more money than anyone else—his way of retiring with dignity.

Meanwhile, Marilyn Monroe was giving her soon-to-be ex-husband, Arthur Miller, a bad time about *The Misfits*. She argued with his wanting to do the film in black-and-white instead of color, she argued with him about the depressing theme, and she argued with him about money. They were splitting a salary of half a million dollars; she wanted more.

But Monroe relented when she heard about Gable. "My mother gave me a picture of him when I was a kid," she once said, "and told me he was my father." Monroe believed this to be true for a long time, and her dream of "incest" might have become a reality had Gable been younger.

In January 1960, Gable went on a crash diet to lose thirty-five pounds before beginning *The Misfits* in March. Director John Huston hoped to finish the film before the onset of unbearable summer heat in Reno, Nevada, but an actors' strike held up production of Monroe's current film, *Let's Make Love*. The new starting date was July 18.

Gable drove his Mercedes to Minden, Nevada, where he and Kay celebrated their fifth wedding anniversary before settling into their living quarters in Reno. The one-story house had a swimming pool and adjoined the golf course.

Producer Frank Taylor gave a dinner party for the cast, but Gable wasn't eager to attend. "I know it's gonna bug the hell out of me to work with those Method actors," he told Kay, "but I don't have to socialize with them."

She convinced him to go anyway. "Do you want them to think you're a snob, Pa?"

"No. . . ."

"It might ease the situation if you met them on common ground instead of before the camera."

"Yeah, I suppose so. . . ."

Montgomery Clift and Kevin McCarthy assumed that Gable was over the hill. They had no respect for his acting because, they said, "it had no range." He had made millions by playing himself, and that, in their eyes, was not talent. Instead of meditating before a scene, like any self-respecting Method actor would, old man Gable simply looked at himself in the mirror, and that was the character he portrayed.

When Clark and Kay walked into the Taylors' living room, however, the entire group, including Clift and McCarthy, stood up instinctively. They had had no idea he possessed such a magnetic and powerful aura. When he sat down, they gathered around him on the floor like children. Gable listened to Clift talk about getting into the mood to act and living his character, and then, when he was asked how *he* planned to approach his role, Clark said casually, "I gather up everything I was, everything I am and hope to be. That's about it. . . ."

Gable's stand-in, Lew Smith, had known the King for many years. "He didn't have to explain a damn thing to those kids," Smith said. "He won the battle the minute those amateurs saw him. Clark never lost that presence. He was taller and more broad-shouldered than most people expected, and he never slouched. If there was any doubt who the King was, Clark proved it that night by just being himself."

Gable and Clift had one thing in common. Neither could pass the insurance physical for *The Misfits*. Gable had to remain in bed for a week before the doctor would sign the necessary papers. Clift leveled off on booze and pills in order to pass the examination.

Gable warned Monty only once about the younger actor's getting too deep into his role: in one scene, Clift had punched Gable black-and-blue. Finally, Clark hissed, "If you do that again, you little bastard, I'm gonna hang one on ya!" Clift burst into tears.

But Gable never turned on Marilyn, the tortured, unstable girl whose career-long role as sex goddess had done nothing for her self-esteem. Her affair with Yves Montand while filming *Let's Make Love* had nearly killed her. She would never have done *The Misfits* had it not been for Gable, but she was terrified of the thought of working with him. She might have attended Taylor's get-acquainted party had Miller been willing to go with her, but he was busy at the typewriter and she was afraid to go alone.

On the night before her first scene with Gable, she tossed and turned alone in bed, gulping down Nembutals until she fell into a sound sleep. In the morning, no one could get her out of bed. For two hours, Miller and her masseur and her secretary tried to rouse Monroe. After she finally opened her eyes—and having taken some uppers—she still couldn't face Gable, knowing she was two hours late. "What will he say?" she cried. "How could I have done this to him?"

Shaking, nauseous, and weak, Monroe reported for work with an entourage of fourteen. She took one look at Gable and rushed to the honey wagon to throw up. When at last she pulled herself together—another hour had passed—Monroe approached her idol.

"I'm so sorry for being late," she purred.

"You're not late, honey," he said, smiling and putting his arm around her, whispering into her ear. They walked away from the others. He talked to her softly, and she giggled. "I was in heaven," she told Clift afterward. "He told me I was worth the wait . . . that I was beautiful, sexy, and all he expected. He said it would be fun working together . . . if only he were younger, you know . . . that kind of thing. I wanted to tell him he was perfect just the way he was. I loved him at first sight. I adore him."

Clift, who had switched to grape juice laced with liquor, was interested in his own well-being, not in Monroe's crushes. He was unsure of himself, and bothered by the heat and the sick perfection of director John Huston. And so the pathetic show began. Gable looked after Monroe, and Monroe looked after Clift. Gable tried to resist Monroe, and Clift yearned for his boyfriend back in New York.

Lew Smith said *The Misfits* was a circus. "Maybe Marilyn idolized Gable like a father," he said, "but she was in there pitching for more. She wanted him, and he was a big flirt. He loved to pinch her fanny, knowing she wasn't wearing anything underneath. Or he'd hug her and whisper something. The whole thing was a sideshow."

Carefully selected reporters were allowed onto the movie set. They were interested in Monroe, but she avoided them, much to the distress of producer Taylor. Gable offered to fill in for her. "I'm a poor substitute, I know," he said, "but maybe it will pacify them."

One article described the fifty-nine-year-old King of Hollywood as "robust, weather-beaten, a heavy smoker who never puts a Kent in his mouth without a Dunhill filter. He also likes Cuban cigars with his own labels. He inhales over ten of these a day."

Reporters noted that the beautiful Kay Gable always looked at her husband as if to say, "Let's go to bed." And that he grinned back as if he were thinking the same thing.

Gable made excuses to the press for Monroe, explaining that the heat took its toll on everyone, and that after a day's work in the blazing sun, they were all exhausted.

Monroe asked him one day, "How do you take it? The mobs of people? The press? I hate it."

"When things get tough, I take out my teeth, like this, and do my Gabby Hayes impersonation."

She giggled and looked at him lovingly. Teeth or no teeth, he was the best thing that ever happened to her. He was known to have affairs with his leading ladies, but not since his marriage to Kay. Maybe this time it would be different. He drove sixty miles to and from work every day, and his wife wasn't always around. If she couldn't seduce Clark Gable, she might never sleep again. She made her first move while they were shooting the bedroom scene showing the morning after hers and Gable's characters have spent their first night together. He comes in and finds her wrapped only in a sheet. The scene, with Gable kissing her good morning, had to be repeated several times. "I was so thrilled when his lips touched mine. I wanted to do it over and over," she sighed to her staff. "Then the sheets dropped and he put his hand on my breast. It was an accident, but I got goosebumps all over. Everything he did made me shiver. That night I didn't need a sleeping pill, but I dreamed of seducing him. Whenever he was near me, I wanted him to kiss me, kiss me, kiss me. His wife caught us smooching once. I don't think she likes me, but she's got him. I don't."

Gable was frustrated because Reno was a wild town, and everyone in it seemed to be having more fun than he was—picking up girls, gambling, drinking. He saw himself as he'd been a few years before and wanted to go back in time, do some carousing, spend one wild night with Monroe, be the envy of the other men, wake up with empty liquor bottles and blurred memories of the blonde who had slipped back to her own room before dawn.

He envied John Huston's wild binges and orgies, recounted in vivid detail every morning. He had done all those things—with style—not too many years ago, but he didn't brag about it. "In my day," he said, "I used to take off on Fridays and show up on Monday morning for work in my tux. That told the whole lovely story. . . ."

Though Monroe raved about Gable, she ranted at Miller— often in front of the entire cast. She and her husband came and went in separate cars and slept in separate suites. The tension mounted.

On August 26, seated with Monroe in a station wagon, Gable delivered the lines: "Honey, we all got to go sometime. . .Man who's afraid to die is too afraid to live."

That night, Monroe took an overdose of sleeping pills. After her stomach was pumped, she was wrapped in a wet sheet, carried to a plane, and flown to the Westside Hospital in Los Angeles for ten days. She tried to reach Yves Montand, who was in Hollywood at the time, but he refused to take her calls.

Bored and restless, Gable began to drink heavily in the 115-degree heat. Dressed in his western garb, he sat and waited, waited and sat, with his script open, chain-smoking, gulping whatever was around—bourbon, scotch, or brandy. He had spent so much time observing the cowboys working with the wild horses that he was convinced he could do most of his own stunts. The amazing thing is that no one tried to stop him, including John Huston. While Gable's stand-in and the other stuntmen watched helplessly on the sidelines, the aging star balanced himself on the hood of a car, rolled across it, and fell to the pavement. In another scene, he was dragged by a truck traveling twenty-five miles an hour. He wrestled with a wild stallion, got snarled in a lariat, and was dragged facedown until a wrangler could stop the horse.

Kay knew nothing about this until one night when she saw him coming out of the shower. "He was bruised and bloody on one side. When I asked him what happened, he said he was dragged on a rope by accident. I told him he was out of his mind!"

Whatever pain he suffered was soon forgotten when Kay told him she was pregnant. They wanted to keep it a secret until she had carried beyond the four-month danger period. He called Joan Crawford, who found the news "exhilarating" but also noticed that his voice was despondent. "Spit it out," she said. "What's wrong?"

"This fucking film," he replied. "They're all nuts. Monroe's never on time—if she shows up at all—so *no one else* gets here on time. We don't start shooting until afternoon, but goddamn it, I leave at five and that's it. The title pretty much sums up this group."

Monroe returned to the shoot, and Gable greeted her with, "Get to work, beautiful!" Her tardiness continued, but he quipped, "Why are sexy women always late?" When she did not forget her lines, he kissed her on the lips and said, "Thanks, honey." To get a smile out of her, he called her "Chubby" or "Fatso" and pinched her fanny.

Monroe got flustered easily and often ran to the honey wagon to throw up, which meant more delays while she changed her clothes and had her hair and makeup redone. Gable knew she was upset, and he would lead Monroe away from the others and talk to her. "Take it easy. . . ."

"I have problems, you know. . . . I'm sorry. . . ."

"You don't have to apologize to me, honey. I'd like to do another picture with you."

"Are you serious?" she exclaimed.

"Yes, I am. After *Diamond Head*, let's get together and discuss it."

Monroe threw her arms around him. "You won't forget?"

"I'm the kinda guy who keeps his promises," he said with a grin.

Kay was upset about two things—Monroe's chasing after her husband and his doing his own stunt work. She did not mention Monroe, but she ripped into him about his overexerting himself. He later explained to her, "I thought it would be easy. Day after day, I watched the same stunts. The horses were so tired, I figured by the time it was my turn, they'd be too pooped to give me any trouble. But no one stopped me, by God. We were never allowed to take chances when the studio had us under contract. Huston was actually cheering me on. Clift did his own thing and is one bloody guy, but he's self-destructing like Marilyn. They don't care if they live or die. I don't understand this generation."

"You'd better understand the next one, Pa. Our son will be part of it."

"It's gonna be a good life from now on. The *Diamond Head* deal is for the same money I'm getting now—good enough for me to retire. So, Kathleen, while I'm finishing up this picture, why don't you make a sketch of the nursery?"

"I've already done that, Pa. There's room for another wing, and I thought it would be nice if the children were all together. What do you think?"

"As soon as we get home, the job's done, Ma."

On October 18, 1960, the entire cast flew back to Los Angeles. Gable argued with Miller about script revisions. "As far as I'm concerned, we're finished," he said. "All I'm interested in now is seeing what's on film."

Gable viewed *The Misfits* with producer Frank Taylor. When it was over, Gable said, "I want to shake your hand. I now have two things to be proud of in my career—*Gone With the Wind* and this."

On Friday, November 4, he said good-bye to the cast but did not stay for the farewell party. He felt achy and thought he might be coming down with the flu. The next day, at the ranch, Gable was changing a tire on his jeep when he got a chest pain so severe that he collapsed. He lay down until the pain subsided. When he came into the house, Kay said, "He was ashen and looked very tired. We had an early dinner and went to bed." During the night, Gable complained of indigestion; the following morning, he was too weak to get dressed. Kay called the doctor, despite Gable's protests. The Encino Fire Department came to administer oxygen. "Clark was so embarrassed," Kay said, "but we made him get into the ambulance. Through it all, he was concerned because I was pregnant, and he kept apologizing to me."

Joan Crawford, however, told this author a different version: "Clark should have been rushed to the hospital on Saturday. A good friend of mine was passing by the ranch and noticed the abandoned jeep and tire. He stopped to see if anything was wrong, and there was Clark lying down in the house, gasping for breath. Kay had had a few cocktails and didn't realize the seriousness of his condition."

Others were also told this story by Crawford's friend, who also said that he returned to the ranch the following morning and saw to it that Gable was taken to the hospital.

Doctors at Presbyterian Hospital told Kay that her husband had suffered a coronary thrombosis and was in critical condition. The back of his heart muscle was badly damaged, they said, and if he recovered at all, he would still not be out of danger for two weeks. Kay sat by his bedside during the day and slept on a cot next to him at night.

In forty-eight hours, Gable was sitting up in bed. The only visitors allowed were Kay and Howard Strickling, who made regular reports to Gable's friends. A week later, the exterior pacemaker was removed from Gable's room. Kay left to spend an hour or two at the ranch, but when she returned to the hospital, Gable asked her never to leave him again.

On the morning of Wednesday, November 16, Gable requested that Kay bring him some good books to read. He asked her to stand sideways against the light so that he could see her blooming silhouette. Beaming with pride, he used a stethoscope to hear the heartbeat of the baby he had wanted for such a long time.

That night, around ten o'clock, Kay kissed her husband good night and went to her adjoining room to rest. The doctor said, "Around eleven, Clark turned the page of a magazine he was reading, put his head back, took a deep sigh, and died."

Kay held her husband in her arms for two hours. . . .

The King of Hollywood was buried with full military honors by the United States Air Force on November 19. Private services were held at the Church of the Recessional at Forest Lawn. Among the pallbearers were Spencer Tracy, Jimmy Stewart, Howard Strickling, and Robert Taylor. Chaplain Johnson E. West read from the 46th and 121st Psalms. There was no eulogy.

The coffin was blanketed by red roses, atop which rested a small crown of miniature darker red roses. The Episcopalian service was preceded by a medley of Strauss waltzes and concluded with "Taps."

After the services, the coffin was opened for Kay's final farewell.

The following week, Clark Gable was laid to rest, next to Carole Lombard, in a crypt in the Sanctuary of Trust at Forest Lawn in Glendale, California.

Aftermath

I n November 1960, Arthur Miller packed his bags and moved out of 444 East Fifty-seventh Street in New York. He said nothing to Marilyn Monroe and took nothing that reminded him of their marriage.

On November 17, Monroe learned that Clark Gable was dead. "I loved him," Marilyn told the press. "We were planning another movie together."

Kay Gable didn't think that was true. In an interview given days after her husband's death she said, "It wasn't the physical exertion that did it. It was the horrible tension, that eternal waiting, waiting, waiting. He waited around forever, for everybody. He'd get so angry waiting that he'd just go ahead and do anything to keep occupied. That's why he did those awful horse scenes where they dragged him behind a truck. He had a stand-in and a stuntman, but he did them himself. I told him he was crazy, but he wouldn't listen."

Reporters embellished Kay's account, and put the blame for Gable's death directly on Marilyn Monroe's tardiness and absence during the shooting of *The Misfits*. They lauded Gable's patience, kindness, and self-control, which, they said, eventually erupted in the heart and took his life. Some witnesses spoke candidly about Monroe's lack of concern for her co-workers—Gable, in particular.

Marilyn denied the accusations, telling anyone who would listen, "Why didn't he tell me? Why didn't he say something? I'd have done anything for him. Anything! All he had to do was ask me to be on time. That's all. He always said, 'That's all right, honey'—like he understood."

Monroe locked herself in her apartment, pulled down the shades in her bedroom, and remained in the dark for days, until she had thoroughly convinced herself that if it hadn't been for her problems, Gable might still be alive. She had killed him—the father figure she adored and respected. The guilt mounted until there was nothing else to do but end her own life. In mid-December, Monroe was about to jump out of her bedroom window when a maid pulled her back, just in time. A few weeks later, she was admitted to the Payne Whitney Clinic by her psychiatrist.

John Clark Gable was born on March 20, 1961. Marilyn Monroe was invited to his christening. Kay apologized for any misunderstanding and said, "Clark never said an unkind word about you."

If there was any lingering belief in Monroe's mind that she had contributed to Gable's death, perhaps it was erased that day, as she held his son in her arms with pride and affection.

Sixteen months later, Marilyn Monroe was dead at the age of thirty-six.

Critics had mixed feelings about *The Misfits*. *The New York Daily News* thought Gable was at his best. *The New York*

Times said that the characters and theme did not congeal, but that "Clark Gable was as certain as the sunrise. He was consistently and stubbornly all man."

In the fifties and sixties, movie fans lost their male legends who were "stubbornly all man": Humphrey Bogart in 1957, age fifty-eight; Tyrone Power in 1958, age forty-five; Errol Flynn in 1959, age fifty; Clark Gable in 1960, age fifty-nine; Gary Cooper in 1961, age sixty; Dick Powell in 1963, age fifty-nine; Alan Ladd in 1964, age fifty-one; Spencer Tracy in 1967, age sixty-seven.

Shortly before Robert Taylor died in 1969, at age fifty-seven, he was approached by a young girl who asked, "Haven't I seen you on television?"

"More off than on," he replied.

"You'll have to get with it," she giggled.

"An old book is better than a blank page," he said.

In the last five years of his life, Clark Gable made more than seven million dollars. The common stock he held amounted to very little, but his twenty-acre ranch in Encino and the house in Palm Springs were very valuable.

Clark Gable's last will was dated September 19, 1955, two months after he married Kay, who was appointed executrix and beneficiary of the bulk of his estate. Gable bequeathed a house and property in North Hollywood to Josephine Dillon.

When Kay died of heart disease in Houston in 1983—her tomb adjoins Gable's crypt—John Clark, then twenty-two, became very wealthy. He had gone to private schools—Buckley in Los Angeles, Brooks in North Andover, Massachusetts, and Aiglon College in Villars, Switzerland—before attending Santa Monica College, a public institution. He developed a Clark Gable-like passion for fast cars and half-ton trucks, which he raced in organized competitions.

John had two children—a daughter, Kayley, and a son, Clark James—by Tracy LaRue Yarrow, whom he married in 1985. The couple divorced in 1991. In 1989, John filmed *Big*

Jim, a low-budget western that never made it to movie theaters. He receives $22,000 a month and an additional $500,000 every five years from the Gable estate.

"My name definitely helped me get my foot in the door," John said, "but I am my own person." He has blond hair, green eyes, and small ears, but he does have his father's cocky look when he raises his eyebrows.

The once isolated farmhouse that Clark Gable bought for Carole Lombard with her fifty thousand dollars still stands in what is now the fashionable and overcrowded San Fernando Valley. The property has been subdivided into an expensive housing development called Clark Gable Estates. Some tracts have been sold for more than a million dollars each. The streets bear such names as Tara Drive and Ashley Oakes.

And in Cadiz, Ohio, the Clark Gable Foundation is reconstructing the town's favorite son's birthplace, adding a gift shop and a theater-museum. John Gable and Joan Spreckels are on hand each year to celebrate the King's birthday.

After Gable's death, Adela Rogers St. Johns wrote, "The King is dead. Long live the King. There has been no successor, nor will there be. The title died with him. It is strange that from the man who was an 'exaggeration of life,' I learned that death is a door life opens. . . ."

Epilogue

Gable was America's dream of itself, a symbol of courage against all odds. He was a man's man, daring and dashing—the guy who gave dames a hard time but got hooked in the end. The villain with a heart of gold. It was easy for the public to lionize Gable, but not easy for the King to live up to his crown.

He once told Robert Taylor, "There are plenty of Gable types selling shoes because they couldn't stand the constant rejection an actor faces. Part of being a star is having the guts to hang in there and refuse to take no for an answer."

Gable used some unorthodox methods to crash the studio gates, but he succeeded and proved himself the true Hollywood star he remains to this day. Had he lived an uncomplicated life—sober citizen, faithful husband, complacent contract player—his star would not be quite as luminous.

E p i l o g u e

Adela Rogers St. Johns once referred to Clark Gable as the Great Common Denominator of Hollywood. I think that says it all.

CHRONOLOGY OF CLARK GABLE'S FILMS*

Forbidden Paradise (Paramount, 1924). **Director:** Ernst Lubitsch. **Cast:** Pola Negri, Rod La Rocque, Adolphe Menjou. (Gable was an extra.)

The Pacemakers (F.B.O., 1925). **Director:** Wesley Ruggles. **Cast:** William Haines, Alberta Vaughn, George O'Hara. (Gable was an extra.)

The Merry Widow (MGM, 1925). **Director:** Erich von Stroheim. **Screenplay:** Erich von Stroheim and Benjamin Glazer. **Cast:** Mae Murray, John Gilbert, Tully Marshall. (Gable was an extra.)

The Plastic Age (F.B.O., 1925). **Director:** Wesley Ruggles. **Cast:** Clara Bow, Donald Keith, Gilbert Roland. (Gable was an extra.)

* Year indicates U.S. release date.

North Star (Associated Exhibitors, 1926). **Director:** Paul Powell. **Cast:** Strongheart, Virginia Lee, Stuart Holmes. (Gable was an extra.)

The Painted Desert (Pathé, 1931). **Director:** Howard Higgin. **Cast:** William Boyd, Helen Twelvetrees, William Farnum, Jr., Farrell MacDonald, Clark Gable. 80 minutes.

The Easiest Way (MGM, 1931). **Director:** Jack Conway. **Screenplay:** Edith Ellis, from the play by Eugene Walter. **Cast:** Constance Bennett, Adolphe Menjou, Robert Montgomery, Anita Page, Clara Blandick, Clark Gable. 86 minutes.

Dance, Fools, Dance (MGM, 1931). **Director:** Harry Beaumont. **Screenplay:** Richard Schayer, Aurania Rouverol. **Cast:** Joan Crawford, Lester Vail, William Bakewell, William Holden*, Clark Gable. 82 minutes.

The Secret Six (MGM, 1931). **Director:** George Hill. **Screenplay:** Frances Marion. **Cast:** Wallace Beery, Lewis Stone, John Mack Brown, Jean Harlow, Clark Gable, Ralph Bellamy. 83 minutes.

The Finger Points (First National, 1931). **Director:** John Francis Dillon. **Screenplay:** Robert Lord. **Cast:** Richard Barthelmess, Fay Wray, Regis Toomey, Robert Elliott, Clark Gable. 90 minutes.

Laughing Sinners (MGM, 1931). **Director:** Harry Beaumont. **Screenplay:** Bess Meredyth and Martin Flavin, from *Torch Song*, a play by Flavin. **Cast:** Joan Crawford, Neil Hamilton, Clark Gable, Marjorie Rambeau, Guy Kibbee. 71 minutes.

A Free Soul (MGM, 1931). **Director:** Clarence Brown. **Screenplay:** John Meehan, based on a novel by Adela Rogers St. Johns. **Cast:** Norma Shearer, Leslie Howard, Lionel Barrymore, Clark Gable, James Gleason, Lucy Beaumont. 91 minutes.

Night Nurse (Warner Bros., 1931). **Director:** William Wellman. **Screenplay:** Oliver H. P. Garrett, based on the

---

* Not the later star.

novel by Dora Macy. **Cast:** Barbara Stanwyck, Ben Lyon, Joan Blondell, Clark Gable, Charles Winninger, Vera Lewis. 72 minutes.

Sporting Blood (MGM, 1931). **Director:** Charles Brabin. **Screenplay:** Willard Mack and Wanda Tuchock, from the novel *Horseflesh*, by Frederick Hazlitt. **Photography:** Harold Rosson. **Film Editor:** William Gray. **Cast:** Clark Gable, Ernest Torrence, Madge Evans, Marie Prevost, Lew Cody. 82 minutes.

Susan Lenox—Her Fall and Rise (MGM, 1931). **Director:** Robert Z. Leonard. **Screenplay:** Wanda Tuchock, Zelda Sears, and Edith Fitzgerald, from the novel by David G. Philips. **Photography:** William Daniels. **Film Editor:** Margaret Booth. **Cast:** Greta Garbo, Clark Gable, Jean Hersholt, Alan Hale. 76 minutes.

Possessed (MGM, 1931). **Director:** Clarence Brown. **Screenplay:** Lenore Coffee, from the play *The Mirage*, by Edgar Selwyn. **Photography:** Oliver T. Marsh. **Cast:** Joan Crawford, Clark Gable, Wallace Ford, Skeets Gallagher. 76 minutes.

Hell Divers (MGM, 1931). **Director:** George Hill. **Screenplay:** Harvey Gates and Malcolm S. Boylan, based on a story by Frank Wead. **Photography:** Harold Wenstrom. **Film Editor:** Blanche Sewell. **Cast:** Wallace Beery, Clark Gable, Conrad Nagel, Dorothy Jordan, Marjorie Rambeau, Marie Prevost. 100 minutes.

Polly of the Circus (MGM, 1932). **Director:** Alfred Santell. **Screenplay:** Carey Wilson and Laurence Johnson, based on the play by Margaret Mayo. **Photography:** George Barnes. **Film Editor:** George Hively. **Cast:** Marion Davies, Clark Gable, C. Aubrey Smith, Raymond Hatton, Ray Milland. 72 minutes.

Red Dust (MGM, 1932). **Director:** Victor Fleming. **Screenplay:** John Lee Mahin. **Photography:** Harold Rosson. **Film Editor:** Blanche Sewell. **Cast:** Clark Gable, Jean Harlow, Gene Raymond, Mary Astor, Donald Crisp, Tully Marshall, Willie Fung. 83 minutes.

Strange Interlude (MGM, 1932). **Director:** Robert Z. Leonard. **Screenplay:** Bess Meredyth and C. Gardner Sullivan, based on the play by Eugene O'Neill. **Photography:** Lee Garmes. **Film Editor:** Margaret Booth. **Cast:** Norma Shearer, Clark Gable, Alexander Kirkland, Ralph Morgan, Robert Young, May Robson, Maureen O'Sullivan. 110 minutes.

No Man of Her Own (Paramount, 1932). **Director:** Wesley Ruggles. **Screenplay:** Maurine Watkins and Milton H. Gropper, based on a story by Edmund Goulding and Benjamin Glazer. **Photography:** Leo Tover. **Cast:** Clark Gable, Carole Lombard, Dorothy Mackaill, Grant Mitchell, George Barbier, Elizabeth Patterson. 85 minutes.

The White Sister (MGM, 1933). **Director:** Victor Fleming. **Screenplay:** Donald Ogden Stewart, based on the novel by F. Marion Crawford and Walter Hackett. **Photography:** William Daniels. **Film Editor:** Margaret Booth. **Cast:** Helen Hayes, Clark Gable, Lewis Stone, May Robson, Edward Arnold. 110 minutes.

Hold Your Man (MGM, 1933). **Producer and director:** Sam Wood. **Screenplay:** Anita Loos and Howard Emmett Rogers, from Loos's original story. **Photography:** Harold Rosson. **Film editor:** Frank Sullivan. **Cast:** Jean Harlow, Clark Gable, Stuart Erwin, Dorothy Burgess, Muriel Kirkland, Gary Owen. 89 minutes.

Night Flight (MGM, 1933). **Producer:** David O. Selznick. **Director:** Clarence Brown. **Screenplay:** Oliver H. P. Garrett, based on the novel by Antoine de Saint-Exupéry. **Photography:** Oliver T. Marsh, Elmar Dyer, and Charles Marshall. **Cast:** John Barrymore, Helen Hayes, Clark Gable, Lionel Barrymore, Robert Montgomery, Myrna Loy, William Gargan. 84 minutes.

Dancing Lady (MGM, 1933). **Producer:** David O. Selznick. **Director:** Robert Z. Leonard. **Screenplay:** Allen Rivkin, Zelda Sears, and P. J. Wolfson, based on the novel by James Warner Bellah. **Photography:** Oliver T. Marsh. **Film Editor:** Margaret Booth. **Cast:** Joan Crawford, Clark Gable, Franchot Tone, May Robson, Fred Astaire, Robert Benchley, Ted

Healy and his 3 Stooges, Nelson Eddy, Sterling Holloway. 94
minutes.

It Happened One Night (Columbia, 1934). **Director:** Frank
Capra. **Screenplay:** Robert Riskin, based on "Night Bus," a
story by Samuel H. Adams. **Photography:** Joe Walker. **Film
Editor:** Gene Havlick. **Cast:** Clark Gable, Claudette Colbert,
Walter Connolly, Alan Hale, Ward Bond. 105 minutes.

Men in White (MGM, 1934). **Producer:** Monta Bell. **Director:**
Richard Boleslawski. **Screenplay:** Waldemar Young, based on
the play by Sidney Kingsley. **Photography:** George Folsey.
Film Editor: Frank Sullivan. **Cast:** Clark Gable, Myrna Loy,
Jean Hersholt, Elizabeth Allan, Otto Kruger, Wallace Ford.
80 minutes.

Manhattan Melodrama (MGM, 1934). **Producer:** David O.
Selznick. **Director:** W. S. Van Dyke. **Screenplay:** Oliver T.
Marsh, Oliver H. P. Garrett, Joseph L. Mankiewicz, based on
an original story by Arthur Caesar. **Photography:** James
Wong Howe. **Film Editor:** Ben Lewis. **Cast:** Clark Gable,
William Powell, Myrna Loy, Mickey Rooney. 93 minutes.

Chained (MGM, 1934). **Producer:** Hunt Stromberg. **Director:** Clarence Brown. **Screenplay:** John Lee Mahin, based on
an original story by Edgar Selwyn. **Photography:** George
Folsey. **Film Editor:** Robert Kern. **Cast:** Joan Crawford,
Clark Gable, Otto Kruger, Stuart Erwin, Una O'Connor,
Akim Tamiroff. 74 minutes.

Forsaking All Others (MGM, 1934). **Producer:** Bernard
Hyman. **Director:** W. S. Van Dyke. **Screenplay:** Joseph L.
Mankiewicz, based on the play by Edward Barry Roberts and
Frank Morgan Cavett. **Photography:** Gregg Toland and
George Folsey. **Film Editor:** Tom Held. **Cast:** Joan Crawford,
Clark Gable, Robert Montgomery, Charles Butterworth, Billie
Burke, Rosalind Russell. 82 minutes.

After Office Hours (MGM, 1935). **Producer:** Bernard
Hyman. **Director:** Robert Z. Leonard. **Screenplay:** Herman
J. Mankiewicz, based on a story by Laurence Stallings and
Dale Van Every. **Photography:** Charles Rosher. **Film Editor:**
Tom Held. **Cast:** Constance Bennett, Clark Gable, Stuart
Erwin, Billie Burke. 75 minutes.

Call of the Wild (Twentieth Century-Fox, 1935). **Producer:** Darryl F. Zanuck. **Director:** William Wellman. **Screenplay:** Gene Fowler and Leonard Praskins, based on the novel by Jack London. **Photography:** Charles Rosher. **Film Editor:** Hanson Fritch. **Cast:** Clark Gable, Loretta Young, Jack Oakie, Reginald Owen, Frank Conroy, Katherine De Mille, Sidney Toler. 95 minutes.

China Seas (MGM, 1935). **Producer:** Albert Lewin. **Director:** Tay Garnett. **Screenplay:** Jules Furthman and James K. McGuinness, based on the novel by Crosbie Garstin. **Photography:** Ray June. **Film Editor:** William Levanway. **Cast:** Clark Gable, Jean Harlow, Wallace Beery, Lewis Stone, Rosalind Russell, C. Aubrey Smith, Robert Benchley, Akim Tamiroff. 90 minutes.

Mutiny on the Bounty (MGM, 1935). **Producer:** Irving Thalberg. **Director:** Frank Lloyd. **Screenplay:** Talbot Jennings, Jules Furthman, and Carey Wilson, based on the book by Charles Nordhoff and James N. Hall. **Photography:** Arthur Edeson. **Film Editor:** Margaret Booth. **Cast:** Charles Laughton, Clark Gable, Franchot Tone, Herbert Mundin, Eddie Quillan, Dudley Digges, Spring Byington, Movita. 132 minutes.

Wife Versus Secretary (MGM, 1936). **Producer:** Hunt Stromberg. **Director:** Clarence Brown. **Screenplay:** Norman Krasna, Alice Duer Miller, and John Lee Mahin, based on the novel by Faith Baldwin. **Photography:** Ray June. **Film Editor:** Frank E. Hull. **Cast:** Clark Gable, Jean Harlow, Myrna Loy, May Robson, James Stewart. 88 minutes.

San Francisco (MGM, 1936). **Producers:** John Emerson, Bernard Hyman. **Director:** W. S. Van Dyke. **Screenplay:** Anita Loos, based on a story by Robert Hopkins. **Photography:** Oliver T. Marsh. **Film Editor:** Tom Held. **Cast:** Clark Gable, Jeanette MacDonald, Spencer Tracy, Jack Holt, Ted Healy, Shirley Ross, Margaret Irving, Al Shean. 115 minutes.

Cain and Mabel (Warner Bros., 1936). A Cosmopolitan Production. **Director:** Lloyd Bacon. **Screenplay:** Laird Doyle, based on a short story by H. C. Witwer. **Photography:**

George Barnes. **Film Editor:** William Holmes. **Cast:** Marion
Davies, Clark Gable, Allen Jenkins, Roscoe Karns, Ruth
Donnelly. 90 minutes.
Love on the Run (MGM, 1936). **Producer:** Joseph L.
Mankiewicz. **Director:** W. S. Van Dyke. **Screenplay:** John
Lee Mahin, Manuel Seff, and Gladys Hurlbut, from the story
by Alan Green and Julian Brodie. **Photography:** Oliver T.
Marsh. **Film Editor:** Frank Sullivan. **Cast:** Joan Crawford,
Clark Gable, Franchot Tone, Reginald Owen, Mona Barrie,
William Demarest. 81 minutes.
Parnell (MGM, 1937). **Producer and director:** John M.
Stahl. **Screenplay:** John van Druten and S. N. Behrman,
based on the play by Elsie T. Schauffler. **Photography:** Karl
Freund. **Film Editor:** Frederick Y. Smith. **Cast:** Clark Gable,
Myrna Loy, Edna May Oliver, Edmund Gwenn, Alan
Marshal, Donald Crisp, Billie Burke. 96 minutes.
Saratoga (MGM, 1937). **Producer:** Bernard Hyman. **Direct-
or:** Jack Conway. **Screenplay:** Anita Loos and Robert
Hopkins. **Photography:** Ray June. **Film Editor:** Elmo
Vernon. **Cast:** Clark Gable, Jean Harlow, Lionel Barrymore,
Frank Morgan, Walter Pidgeon, Una Merkel, Hattie McDaniel.
102 minutes.
Test Pilot (MGM, 1938). **Producer:** Louis D. Lighton.
Director: Victor Fleming. **Screenplay:** Vincent Lawrence and
Waldemar Young, based on a story by Frank Wead.
Photography: Ray June. **Film Editor:** Tom Held. **Cast:** Clark
Gable, Myrna Loy, Spencer Tracy, Lionel Barrymore,
Marjorie Main, Virginia Grey. 118 minutes.
Too Hot to Handle (MGM, 1938). **Producer:** Lawrence
Weingarten. **Director:** Jack Conway. **Screenplay:** Laurence
Stallings and John Lee Mahin, based on a story by Len
Hammond. **Photography:** Harold Rosson. **Film Editor:**
Frank Sullivan. **Cast:** Clark Gable, Myrna Loy, Walter
Connolly, Walter Pidgeon, Marjorie Main. 105 minutes.
Idiot's Delight (MGM, 1939). **Producer:** Hunt Stromberg.
Director: Clarence Brown. **Screenplay:** Robert E. Sherwood,
based on his play. **Photography:** William Daniels. **Film**

Editor: Robert J. Kern. **Cast:** Norma Shearer, Clark Gable, Edward Arnold, Charles Coburn, Burgess Meredith, Skeets Gallegher. 105 minutes.

Gone With the Wind (MGM, 1939). **Producer:** David O. Selznick. **Director:** Victor Fleming. **Screenplay:** Sidney Howard, based on the novel by Margaret Mitchell. **Photography:** Ernest Haller. **Film Editors:** Hal Kern and James Newcom. **Cast:** Clark Gable, Leslie Howard, Olivia de Havilland, Vivien Leigh, Hattie McDaniel, Thomas Mitchell, Evelyn Keyes, Ann Rutherford, Butterfly McQueen. 225 minutes.

Strange Cargo (MGM, 1940). **Producer:** Joseph L. Mankiewicz. **Director:** Frank Borzage. **Screenplay:** Lawrence Hazard, based on the novel *Not Too Narrow, Not Too Deep*, by Richard Sale. **Photography:** Robert Plank. **Film Editor:** Robert J. Kern. **Cast:** Clark Gable, Joan Crawford, Ian Hunter, Peter Lorre, Paul Lukas, Albert Dekker. 105 minutes.

Boom Town (MGM, 1940). **Producer:** Sam Zimbalist. **Director:** Jack Conway. **Screenplay:** John Lee Mahin, based on a short story by James Edward Grant. **Photography:** Harold Rosson. **Film Editor:** Blanche Sewell. **Cast:** Clark Gable, Spencer Tracy, Claudette Colbert, Hedy Lamarr, Frank Morgan, Chill Wills. 116 minutes.

Comrade X (MGM, 1940). **Producer:** Gottfried Reinhardt. **Director:** King Vidor. **Screenplay:** Ben Hecht and Charles Lederer, based on a story by Walter Reisch. **Photography:** Joseph Ruttenberg. **Film Editor:** Harold F. Kress. **Cast:** Clark Gable, Hedy Lamarr, Oscar Homolka, Felix Bressart, Eve Arden. 90 minutes.

They Met in Bombay (MGM, 1941). **Producer:** Hunt Stromberg. **Director:** Clarence Brown. **Screenplay:** Edwin Justus Mayer, Anita Loos, and Leon Gordon, based on the story by John Kafka. **Photography:** William Daniels. **Film Editor:** Blanche Sewell. **Cast:** Clark Gable, Rosalind Russell, Peter Lorre, Reginald Owen. 86 minutes.

Honky Tonk (MGM, 1941). **Producer:** Pandro S. Berman.

Director: Jack Conway. **Screenplay**: Marguerite Roberts and John Sanford. **Photography**: Harold Rosson. **Film Editor**: Blanche Sewell. **Cast**: Clark Gable, Lana Turner, Frank Morgan, Claire Trevor, Marjorie Main, Albert Dekker, Chill Wills. 105 minutes.

Somewhere I'll Find You (MGM, 1942). **Producer**: Pandro S. Berman. **Director**: Wesley Ruggles. **Screenplay**: Marguerite Roberts, based on a story by Charles Hoffman. **Photography**: Harold Rosson. **Cast**: Clark Gable, Lana Turner, Robert Sterling, Patricia Dane, Reginald Owen, Lee Patrick. 108 minutes.

Adventure (MGM, 1945). **Producer**: Sam Zimbalist. **Director**: Victor Fleming. **Screenplay**: Frederick Hazlitt Brennan, Anthony Veillar, William Wright, and Vincent Lawrence, based on a novel by Clyde Brion Davis. **Photography**: Joseph Ruttenberg. **Film Editor**: Frank Sullivan. **Cast**: Clark Gable, Greer Garson, Joan Blondell, Thomas Mitchell, Tom Tully, Harry Davenport. 125 minutes.

The Hucksters (MGM, 1947). **Producer**: Arthur Hornblow, Jr. **Director**: Jack Conway. **Screenplay**: Luther Davis, based on the novel by Frederick Wakeman. **Photography**: Harold Rosson. **Film Editor**: Frank Sullivan. **Cast**: Clark Gable, Deborah Kerr, Sydney Greenstreet, Adolphe Menjou, Ava Gardner, Keenan Wynn, Edward Arnold. 115 minutes.

Homecoming (MGM, 1948). **Producer**: Sidney Franklin. **Director**: Mervyn LeRoy. **Screenplay**: Paul Osborn, based on the original story by Sidney Kingsley. **Photography**: Harold Rosson. **Film Editor**: John Dunning. **Cast**: Clark Gable, Lana Turner, Anne Baxter, John Hodiak, Cameron Mitchell. 113 minutes.

Command Decision (MGM, 1948). **Producer**: Sidney Franklin. **Director**: Sam Wood. **Screenplay**: William Laidlaw and George Froeschel, based on the play by William Wister Haines. **Photography**: Harold Rosson. **Film Editor**: Harold Kress. **Cast**: Clark Gable, Walter Pidgeon, Van Johnson, Brian Donlevy, Charles Bickford, John Hodiak, Edward Arnold. 112 minutes.

Any Number Can Play (MGM, 1949). **Producer:** Arthur Freed. **Director:** Mervyn LeRoy. **Screenplay:** Richard Brooks, based on the novel by Edward Harris Heth. **Photography:** Harold Rosson. **Film Editor:** Ralph Winters. **Cast:** Clark Gable, Alexis Smith, Wendell Corey, Audrey Totter, Frank Morgan, Mary Astor, Barry Sullivan, Lewis Stone. 112 minutes.

Key to the City (MGM, 1950). **Producer:** Z. Wayne Griffin. **Director:** George Sidney. **Screenplay:** Robert Riley Crutcher, based on the story by Albert Beich. **Photography:** Harold Rosson. **Film Editor:** James E. Newcom. **Cast:** Clark Gable, Loretta Young, Frank Morgan, James Gleason, Marilyn Maxwell, Raymond Burr. 99 minutes.

To Please a Lady (MGM, 1950). **Producer and director:** Clarence Brown. **Screenplay:** Barre Lyndon and Marge Decker. **Photography:** Harold Rosson. **Film Editor:** Robert Kern. **Cast:** Clark Gable, Barbara Stanwyck, Adolphe Menjou, Will Geer, Roland Winters, William McGray. 91 minutes.

Across the Wide Missouri (MGM, 1951). **Producer:** Robert Sisk. **Director:** William Wellman. **Screenplay:** Talbot Jennings, based on a story by Jennings and Frank Cavett. **Photography:** William Mellor. **Film Editor:** John Dunn. **Cast:** Clark Gable, Ricardo Montalban, John Hodiak, Adolphe Menjou, Maria Elena Marques, Jack Holt. 78 minutes.

Callaway Went Thataway (MGM, 1951). **Producers, directors and screenwriters:** Norman Panama and Melvin Frank. **Photography:** Ray June. **Film Editor:** Cotton Warburton. **Cast:** Fred MacMurray, Dorothy McGuire, Howard Keel. **Guest stars:** Clark Gable, Elizabeth Taylor, Esther Williams. 81 minutes.

Lone Star (MGM, 1952). **Producer:** Z. Wayne Griffin. **Director:** Vincent Sherman. **Screenplay:** Borden Chase and Howard Estabrook, based on Chase's magazine story. **Photography:** Harold Rosson. **Film Editor:** Ferris Webster. **Cast:** Clark Gable, Ava Gardner, Broderick Crawford, Lionel Barrymore, Beulah Bondi. 94 minutes.

Never Let Me Go (MGM, 1953). **Producer:** Clarence Brown. **Director:** Delmer Daves. **Screenplay:** Ronald Millar and George Froeschel, based on the novel *Came the Dawn*, by Roger Bax. **Photography:** Robert Krasker. **Film Editor:** Frank Clarke. **Cast:** Clark Gable, Gene Tierney, Richard Haydn, Belita, Kenneth More. 69 minutes.

Mogambo (MGM, 1953). **Producer:** Sam Zimbalist. **Director:** John Ford. **Screenplay:** John Lee Mahin, based on the play by Wilson Collison. **Photography:** Robert Surtees and F. A. Young. **Film Editor:** Frank Clarke. **Cast:** Clark Gable, Ava Gardner, Grace Kelly, Donald Sinden, Philip Stainton. 115 minutes.

Betrayed (MGM, 1954). **Director:** Gottfried Reinhardt. **Screenplay:** Ronald Millar and George Froeschel. **Photography:** F. A. Young. **Film Editors:** John Dunning and Raymond Poulton. **Cast:** Clark Gable, Lana Turner, Victor Mature, Louis Calhern. 108 minutes.

Soldier of Fortune (Twentieth Century-Fox, 1955). **Producer:** Buddy Adler. **Director:** Edward Dmytryk. **Screenplay:** Ernest K. Gann, based on his novel. **Photography:** Leo Tover. **Film Editor:** Dorothy Spencer. **Cast:** Clark Gable, Susan Hayward, Michael Rennie, Gene Barry, Anna Sten, Tom Tully. 96 minutes.

The Tall Men (Twentieth Century-Fox, 1955). **Producers:** William A. Bacher and William B. Hawks. **Director:** Raoul Walsh. **Screenplay:** Sydney Boehm and Frank Nugent, based on the novel by Clay Fisher. **Photography:** Leo Tover. **Film Editor:** Louis Loeffler. **Cast:** Clark Gable, Jane Russell, Robert Ryan, Cameron Mitchell. 122 minutes.

The King and Four Queens (United Artists, 1956). A Russ–Field–Gabco Production. **Producer:** David Hempstead. **Director:** Raoul Walsh. **Screenplay:** Margaret Fitts and Richard A. Simmons, from an original story by Fitts. **Photography:** Lucien Ballard. **Film Editor:** David Brotherton. **Cast:** Clark Gable, Eleanor Parker, Jo Van Fleet, Barbara Nichols, Sara Shane. 86 minutes.

Band of Angels (Warner Bros., 1957). **Director:** Raoul

Walsh. **Screenplay**: John Twist, Ivan Goff, and Ben Roberts, based on the novel by Robert Penn Warren. **Photography**: Lucien Ballard. **Film Editor**: Folmar Blangsted. **Cast**: Clark Gable, Yvonne De Carlo, Sidney Poitier, Efrem Zimbalist, Jr., Patric Knowles. 127 minutes.

Run Silent, Run Deep (United Artists, 1958). **Producer**: Harold Hecht. **Directors**: Robert Wise and Edward I. Beach. **Screenplay**: John Gay. **Photography**: Russ Harlen. **Cast**: Clark Gable, Burt Lancaster, Jack Warden, Brad Dexter. 93 minutes.

Teacher's Pet (Paramount, 1958). **Producer**: William Perlberg. **Director**: George Seaton. **Screenplay**: Fay and Michael Kanin. **Photography**: Haskell Boggs. **Film Editor**: Alma Macrorie. **Cast**: Clark Gable, Doris Day, Gig Young, Mamie Van Doren, Nick Adams. 120 minutes.

But Not for Me (Paramount, 1959). **Producers**: William Perlberg and George Seaton. **Director**: Walter Lang. **Screenplay**: John Michael Hayes, based on the play *Accent on Youth*, by Samuel Raphaelson. **Photography**: Robert Burks. **Film Editor**: Alma Macrorie. **Cast**: Clark Gable, Carroll Baker, Lilli Palmer, Lee J. Cobb. 105 minutes.

It Started In Naples (Paramount, 1960). **Producer**: Jack Rose. **Director**: Melville Shavelson. **Screenplay**: Melville Shavelson, Jack Rose, and Suso Cecchi d'Amico, based on the story by Michael Pertwee and Jack Davies. **Photography**: Robert Surtees. **Cast**: Clark Gable, Sophia Loren, Vittoria De Sica, Marietto. 100 minutes.

The Misfits (United Artists, 1961). **Producer**: Frank E. Taylor. **Director**: John Huston. **Screenplay**: Arthur Miller. **Photography**: Russell Metty. **Film Editor**: George Tomasini. **Cast**: Clark Gable, Marilyn Monroe, Montgomery Clift, Thelma Ritter, Eli Wallach, Kevin McCarthy. 124 minutes.

SELECTED BIBLIOGRAPHY

Davidson, Bill. *Spencer Tracy: Tragic Idol.* New York: E. P. Dutton, 1987; London: Sphere, 1989.

Edwards, Anne. *Vivien Leigh.* New York: Simon and Schuster, 1977; London: Hodder, 1978.

Essoe, Gabe. *The Films of Clark Gable.* New York: Carol Publishing, 1990.

Flamini, Roland. *Scarlett, Rhett, and a Cast of Thousands.* New York: Macmillan Publishing Co., Inc., 1975.

Garceau, Jean. *The Biography of Clark Gable.* New York: Little, Brown and Co., 1961.

Gardner, Ava. *Ava: My Story.* New York & London: Bantam, 1990.

Graham, Sheilah. *Hollywood Revisited.* New York: St. Martin's Press, 1984.

Guiles, Fred Lawrence. *Norma Jean.* New York: McGraw-Hill, 1969; London: Grafton, r.e., pbk., 1986.

Harris, Warren G. *Gable and Lombard*. New York: Simon and Schuster, 1974.

Hay, Peter. *MGM: When the Lion Roars*. Atlanta: Turner Publishing, 1991.

Kelley, Kitty. *Nancy Reagan: An Unauthorized Biography*. New York: Simon and Schuster, 1991; London: Bantam, 1991.

LaGuardia, Robert. *Monty: A Biography of Montgomery Clift*. New York: Arbor House, 1977.

Lambert, Gavin. *The Making of "Gone With the Wind."* New York: Little, Brown and Co., 1973.

Loos, Anita. *Kiss Hollywood Good-Bye*. New York: The Viking Press, 1974.

Loy, Myrna. *Being and Becoming*. New York: Alfred A. Knopf, 1987; London: Bloomsbury Pub, 1987.

Marx, Samuel. *Mayer and Thalberg*. Hollywood, Cal.: Samuel French Trade, 1975.

Morella, Joe, and Edward Epstein. *Loretta Young*. New York: Delacorte Press, 1986.

Parish, James Robert, and Ronald L. Bowers. *The MGM Stock Company: The Golden Era*. New Rochell, N.Y.: Arlington House, 1974.

Quirk, Lawrence J. *Norma: The Story of Norma Shearer*. New York: St. Martin's Press, 1988.

Fasten Your Seat Belts: The Passionate Life of Bette Davis. New York: William Morrow and Co., 1990; London: Robson Books, 1990.

Rooney, Mickey. *Life Is Too Short*. New York: Villard Books, 1987; London: Hutchinson, 1988.

Russell, Jane. *Jane Russell*. New York: James Watts, Inc., 1985.

St. Johns, Adela Rogers. *The Honeycomb*. New York: Doubleday, 1969.

Shipman, David. *The Great Movie Stars of the Golden Era*. New York: Crown Publishers, 1970; London: Macdonald, r.e., 1989.

Spada, James. *Grace: The Secret Life of a Princess*. New

York: Doubleday and Co., 1987; London: Sidgwick & Jackson, 1987.

Swanson, Gloria. *Swanson on Swanson*. New York: Random House, 1980.

Swindell, Larry. *Screwball: The Life of Carole Lombard*. New York: William Morrow and Co., 1975.

Tierney, Gene. *Self-Portrait*. New York: Wyden Books, 1976.

Tornabene, Lyn. *Long Live the King: A Biography of Clark Gable*. New York: G. P. Putnam's Sons, 1976.

Turner, Lana. *The Lady, the Legend and the Truth: Lana*. New York. E. P. Dutton, Inc., 1982.

Wayne, Jane Ellen. *Gable's Women*. New York: Prentice Hall Press, 1987.

Robert Taylor: The Man With the Perfect Face. New York: St. Martin's Press, 1989; London: Robson Books, 1987.

Wellman, William A. *A Short Time For Insanity*. New York: Hawthorn Books, Inc., 1974.

Winters, Shelley. *Shelley*. New York: William Morrow and Co., 1980.

INDEX

I n d e x